High-Speed Management
and
Organizational Communication
in the 1990s
A Reader

SUNY Series, Human Communication Processes
Donald P. Cushman and Ted J. Smith III, editors

High-Speed Management and Organizational Communication in the 1990s

A READER

Sarah Sanderson King
and
Donald Peter Cushman, editors

State University of New York Press

HD
3 0. 3
·H53 .
1994

Published by
State University of New York Press, Albany

© 1994 State University of New York

For information, address State University of New York Press,
State University Plaza, Albany, N.Y., 12246

Production by Marilyn P. Semerad
Marketing by Theresa A. Swierzowski

Library of Congress Cataloging-in-Publication Data

High speed management and organizational communication in the 1990s:
    a reader / Sarah S. King and Donald P. Cushman, editors
        p.   cm. — (SUNY series, human communication processes)
    Includes bibliographical references and index.
    ISBN 0-7914-1813-8 (acid-free paper). —ISBN 0-7914-1814-6 (pbk.
    : acid-free paper)
    1. Communication in management.   2. Communication in
organizations.   3. Competition, International.   I. King, Sarah
Sanderson, 1932–   .   II. Cushman, Donald P.   III. Series: SUNY
series in human communication processes.
HD30.3.H53 1994
658.4'5—dc20   93-9980
                                                            CIP

10   9   8   7   6   5   4   3   2   1

To the women in our lives . . .

Sarah Laurie Sanderson
Linda Rose LaTrenta
Sarina Mary Patterson
Cynthia Dorothy Cushman
Kimberly Ann Williams

Contents

CHAPTER ONE

High-Speed Management and Organizational Communication: A Road Map

Sarah Sanderson King

Until recently the search for unique communication principles capable of yielding significant cross-organizational generalizations has been rather barren. Instead, textbooks on organizational communication have looked very much like textbooks on management. The reason has been simple. Organizational strategy, the prime candidate for locating such powerful cross-organizational theoretic principles, has had at its core noncommunication activities. For example, if an organization has pursued a strategy of competitive advantage based on product cost, then the control organizational process yielding cross-organizational theoretic principles has been production or manufacturing activities. On the other hand, if an organization has pursued a strategy of obtaining competitive advantage based on product differentiation, then the central organizing activity has been product uniqueness or R&D activities.

While human interaction in communication is involved in both organizational manufacturing and R&D, the primary cross-organizational theoretic principles are unique to the mass and batch production and technological innovation processes, not in

1

human communication processes. Communication functions as a second-level support activity and, given its regularity, is based on the primary organizational processes of production and innovation.

However, when speed of response time becomes the primary source of competitive advantage or organizational strategy, then all this changes. How communication is to function effectively within and between organizational functions and business processes becomes the primary cross-organizational theoretic activity. Other organizational functions such as R&D, manufacturing, sales, and service become secondary activities to the primary process of speed in getting products to market.

Speed in getting products to market became an important organizational activity due to three factors that have created unusually high volatility in the business environment: rapidly changing technology, quick market saturation, and unexpected global competition. These volatile forces, when combined with regional core market recessions and sector economic declines, are placing considerable stress upon organizations participating in the global economy. The fallout in the form of bankruptcies, downsizings, and consolidations have been significant, creating precipitous drops in income, profits, stockholder value, and jobs.

High-speed management is a set of communication and management principles designed to buffer a firm against environmental volatility by allowing for rapid adaptation to changing environmental conditions. High-speed management employs communication principles and information technology in creating a rapid response system that is innovative, adaptive, flexible, and efficient.

The results have been more startling than organizational communication theorists could have hoped. It happens that order of magnitude changes in response time from high-speed management principles have led to the need to simplify management systems in order to create ease and effectiveness in speeding up organizational communication processes. This in turn has led to order of magnitude changes in increased productivity, product quality, and market shares, yielding order of magnitude changes in profits.

Equally exciting is the way in which high-speed management has transformed our understanding and use of traditional organizational principles. Speed of response has created a transformational resolution in our conceptualizations of such key organizational communication processes as leadership, corporate culture, teamwork, R&D, and marketing. In our book, *High-Speed Management: Organizational Communication in the 1990s*, D. P. Cushman, and I explicated at both a theoretic and practical level the transformation of traditional organizational topics by this new theoretic perspective. The result was a new theory of organizational communication. In this reader we want to take the theoretic perspective a step further by helping serious scholars of high-speed management extend and apply these initial insights. The results are illuminating.

Chapter 2 by Donald P. Cushman and Sarah S. King provides a broad overview of the volatile global economic environment, a summary of high-speed management's role in responding to this volatility, and an outline of how continuous improvement programs involving self-managed teams, cross-functional teams, and international benchmarking offer the promise of continuous and dynamic adaptation to change. Case studies of the Danville Bumper Works and General Electric illustrate this analysis.

Chapter 3 by Andrzej K. Kozminski provides a broad overview of high-speed management and global competitiveness. Here some of the tools provided by this theory are applied to constrain the volatility of the global economic environment in such a manner as to create competitive advantage. A case study of Asea Brown Boveri Ltd. illustrates this analysis.

Chapter 4 by Branislav Kovacic provides an analysis of high-speed management, environmental scanning, and coalignment of external resources through strategic alliances. Here a new approach to acquisitions, mergers, joint ventures, and the like is provided, based on a communication analysis of the firms involved. IBM and ABB are employed as case studies to illustrate the analysis.

Chapter 5 by Krzyszt Obloj explores the transformation of the leadership process under high-speed management theory and the rise in importance of leadership in the acquisition, integration, and disposal of organizational resources. A case study of Komatsu is employed to illustrate his analysis.

Chapter 6 by Anne Maydan Nicotera investigates how corporate culture must be modified in a high-speed management firm in order to cope with rapid changes in an organization's

4SARAH SANDERSON KING

internal and external linkages. IBM and GE are utilized as contrasting case studies in the effective use of high-speed management cultures.

Chapter 7 by Yanan Ju deals with organizational teamwork and its conceptualization and application from a high-speed management theoretic perspective. Intensity, permanent dissatisfaction, speedy and effective communication, and consistency are explicated as principles guiding the effective use of teamwork processes. Toyota Motors Corporation then illustrates the author's claims.

Chapter 8 by Nils M. Larsen and Pat Joynt examines time as a basis for competitive advantage. In so doing they explicate the role of contingency value chain analysis in the global marketplace. They then turn to examples from the auto industry to illustrate their analysis.

Chapter 9 by George Tuttle explicates how new product development in the drug industry is governed and guided by high-speed management principles. He explores how AXT, Mevacov, Exosuf, and Nuromax were brought to market under such a system.

Chapter 10 by Rowland G. Baughman explores the influence of high-speed management on small business and strengths and limitations on organizational adaptation. Here we see some of the limits and strengths of high-speed management in the small business context.

Chapter 11 by Janet M. Flynn and Franca Caré explores the use of Workout as a continuous improvement program at General Electric. Once again the strengths and limitations of continuous improvement programs are made manifest.

Chapter 12 by Scott R. Olson examines Toyota and General Electric as two of the best exemplars of high-speed management theory and practice illustrating the strengths and limitations of this approach to organizational communication.

Chapter 13 by Sarah S. King and Donald P. Cushman looks back over this volume and projects their observations forward into the global economy in an attempt to see where high-speed management goes from here.

This, then, is our map, our road signs for visiting the insights offered by high-speed management in the 1990s. Please drive carefully and enjoy the view.

CHAPTER TWO

High-Speed Management: A Revolution in Organizational Communication in the 1990s

Donald P. Cushman and Sarah S. King

A series of revolutions has taken place within the global economy, transforming the theoretic basis for organizational coalignment and thus all information and communication processes. This chapter tracks the principal basis for that transformation. It then explicates a new theory of organizational communication: high-speed management. High-speed management has as its goal the achievement and maintenance of sustainable competitive advantage by the innovative, flexible, adaptive, efficient, and rapid response to environmental change. This chapter then details the transformation high-speed management has made in small group communication processes by exploring organizational continuous improvement programs. Continuous improvement programs aim at establishing and maintaining a sustainable competitive advantage through four communication processes: (1) a linking and negotiation process, (2) a New England town meeting process, (3) a cross-functional teamwork process, and (4) case studies in world-class benchmarking processes.

Regardless of which corporations or nations emerge as leaders in the high-technology race, the world high-technology market has given rise to a new system of management that is revolutionizing the way work gets done. This new high-speed management system is a set of principles, strategies, and tools for coming up with a steady flow of new products, making sure they are what the customer wants, designing and manufacturing them with speed and precision, getting them to the market quickly, and servicing them promptly in order to make large profits and satisfy consumer needs (Pepper, 1989). High-speed management, which began in the high-technology sector, is now diffusing to all public, private, and nonprofit sectors of the world economy with promising results (Stalk, 1988). High-speed management systems have at their core a new conceptualization of the role information and communication must play in organizational functioning, a role that generates a unique form of sustainable competitive advantage and is grounded in a new set of principles, strategies, and techniques of organizational communication (Cushman and King, 1993).

TRENDS LEADING TO THE EMERGENCE OF HIGH-SPEED MANAGEMENT

The convergence of four trends has led to the restructuring of the global economic environment, placing new demands on corporate management and giving rise to high-speed management systems.

First, several breakthroughs have taken place in information and communication technologies which have dramatically changed how organizational manufacturing, marketing, and management work.

Second, this information and communication revolution has helped facilitate a dramatic increase in world trade, the emergence of a global economy, and the development of three large core markets.

Third, these technological breakthroughs and increases in world trade have created a volatile business climate characterized by rapidly changing technology, quick market saturation, and unexpected competition, making succeeding in business difficult.

Fourth, to compete successfully in such an environment requires that executives employ management theories and practices which emphasize innovation, adaptation, flexibility, efficiency, and rapid response.

Let us explore each of these trends briefly and in turn.

Breakthroughs in Information and Communication Technologies

Several technological breakthroughs have taken place that make possible the generation, processing, and instant delivery of information and communication throughout the world, creating a revolution in organizational manufacturing, marketing, and management. At the center of this revolution is a constellation of new management tools based on computers and telecommunication and classified as manufacturing, marketing, and management technologies. Taken collectively, these tools provide a new way of thinking and acting in regard to all the problems that confront management in dealing with a rapidly changing economic environment.

New manufacturing technologies employ computer-aided and telecommunication-linked engineering, manufacturing, and resource planning processes to allow for the rapid development, production, sales, and service of customized new products at low cost, high quality, and easy access throughout the world (Young, 1990). Allen-Bradley, a Milwaukee manufacturer of industrial controls, possesses one of the world's most modern computer-aided and telecommunication-linked engineering, manufacturing, and resource planning facilities. This facility can produce one of a product or one hundred thousand of the same product at the same per unit cost. This plant can receive the specifications for an order one day and deliver the product at its destination the next, cutting the average turnaround time on orders from four weeks to two days. Under such a system, engineering and manufacturing costs decreased 40 percent while profits increased by 32 percent and product quality increased by 200 percent (Port, 1986, pp. 100–108).

New marketing information technologies employ computer-aided and telecommunication-linked environmental scanning, electronic test marketing, and real-time merchandising for speed in providing customers with world-class products when and where they want them in order to increase market shares (Young, 1990). Campbell Soup Company, for example, can scan the environment to determine customer desire for a new soup; computer model its contents; simulate its production; calibrate its cost, price, profit, and sales potential; develop an artificial intelligence system to control its rate and quality of production; pretest its name, taste, shelf placement, and type and content of its advertising; and run its test markets—reducing a management decision process that used to take years to a matter of two or three days. These new marketing technologies cut the cost of this process by 30 percent while increasing product success rates by 80 percent (Russell, Adams, and Boundy, 1986).

New management information technologies employ computer-aided and telecommunication-linked decision support, operational research, artificial intelligence, and group technology systems to integrate, coordinate, and control management processes in order to create competitive advantage. American Express recently implemented an artificial intelligence system that provides decision support for managers making authorization decisions on individual purchases from four hundred thousand shops and restaurants throughout the world. This expert system reduced by 20 percent the turnaround time per transaction, reduced by 50 percent the number of authorizations in trouble ninety days after approval, while providing annual savings of $27 million (Feigenbaum, McCorduck, and Nii, 1988). New manufacturing, marketing, and management information technologies, when appropriately employed, allow for more effective integration, coordination, and control of all organizational processes, creating the potential for competitive advantage (Young, 1990).

These, then, are some of the new information and communication tools which, when taken collectively, are creating a new way of thinking and acting in regard to all management problems. They have in common the technology that allows organizations to track and respond in real-time to the interests of managers, stockholders, workers, customers, and competitors throughout major portions of the globe. Similarly, such a world-class information and communication capability allows organizations to track and respond in real-time to international changes in cost of capital, labor, raw materials, consumer taste, and competitor response.

Breakthroughs in Information and Communication Technologies Are Increasing World Trade

The ability of corporations to track in real-time the needs of customers and changes in the cost of capital, labor, and raw materials throughout the world has led to a rapid increase in world trade, the emergence of a global economy, and strong regional markets. Driven by information and communication technologies and the comparative advantage they create, world trade over the past four decades has grown much faster than the world's gross national product. International exports and imports were about one-fifth the world GNP in 1962, one-fourth in 1972, one-third in 1982, and are projected to approach one-half the world GNP by 1994 (The global giants, 1990).

Over the past decade a single model of economic development has emerged that is influencing economic policies throughout the global economy. The generalization of such a model does not imply all governments or economies are alike; it merely suggests broad central tendencies in the economic policies of most nations as they begin to participate in the global economy. This model includes seven general features: (1) control of inflation through fiscal austerity and monetary restrictions; (2) reduction of labor costs as a percentage of product cost; (3) increased productivity and profitability through the effective use of information and communication technology; (4) restructuring of industrial and service sectors by disinvesting from low-profit areas and investing in high-growth, high-profit areas; (5) privatization and deregulation of some aspects of the economy by withdrawing from state ownership and control in favor of open market forces; (6) relative control over the pricing of raw materials and energy, assuring the stability of pricing systems and exchange flows; and (7) opening up gradually to world markets and increased internationalization of economies. As Castells (1986, p. 300) argues:

> Such a model is not necessarily linked to a particular political party or administration, or even to a country, even though the Reagan or Thatcher governments seem to be the closest examples of the fulfillment of these policies. But very similar policies have developed in most West European countries, in those governed by Socialists, and even in Communist-led regions (Italy) or Communist-participating governments (France, for a certain period). At the same time, in most Third World countries, austerity policies, inspired or dictated by the International Monetary Fund and

world financial institutions, have also developed along the same lines, establishing not without contradictions and conflicts (Walton, 1985) a new economic logic that is not only capitalistic but a very specific kind of capitalism.

With the emerging global economy, comparative advantage is shifting toward those regions of the world with a large core market, a strong scientific and technological workforce, and a private and public economic sector that can attract the capital necessary to provide the infrastructure needed for increased growth and technological changes. The U.S.-Canadian core market, the EEC core market, and the Japanese area of influence in Asia appear to meet these criteria (Baig, 1989).

The Information and Communication Revolution and the Rise in World Trade Has Created a Volatile Business Climate

"Rapidly changing technology, quick market saturation, unexpected global competition—these all make succeeding in business, particularly a high technology business, harder than ever today" (Fraker, 1984:34). The volatile business climate engendered by the information technology and communication revolution and the globalization of economic forces has led to a significant realignment of individual corporate resources. In order to understand this corporate realignment we will explore the unique problem this realignment creates for individual corporations, and outline the new corporate perspective for responding to this problem.

The Unique Problem of the Shrinking Product Life Cycle.   Most of the environment forces precipitating the need for rapid change in corporate operations arise from a single problem—the fact that firms are confronted by shrinking product life cycles. The product life cycle is the period of time available from the inception of an idea for a product until the market for that product is saturated or disappears due to new product development. A product life cycle normally involves several stages—product conceptualization, design, testing, refinement, mass production, marketing, shipping, selling, and servicing.

Dominique Hanssens, a professor in UCLA's Graduate School of Management, has studied the product life cycle in electrical appliances for years. He reports (Fraker, 1984) that years ago the product life cycle for refrigerators took over thirty years to mature, providing considerable time for each phase of the product life cycle to develop. However, all of this has changed. The market for microwave ovens has taken ten years to mature; CB radios, four years; computer games, three years. Perhaps the most dramatic example of shrinking product life cycles as a result of rapidly changing technology, quick market saturation, and unexpected competition, can be found in the computer industry (Berlant, Browning, and Foster, 1990).

The first commercially successful computer, containing an eight-bit memory chip, came to market in 1977; four years later the sixteen-bit memory chip appeared; two years later came the thirty-two-bit memory chip; and one year later came the sixty-four-bit memory chip. By 1987 we witnessed the appearance of the one-megabyte memory chip, by 1989 the four-megabyte memory chip, and by 1990 the development of a sixteen-megabyte memory chip was well underway. The industrial shakedown from such rapid changes has taken its toll. Large U.S. companies, once dominant in their respective markets, such as Hewlett Packard, Macintosh, and DEC, who were unable to respond effectively to the end of one product life cycle and the beginning of a new one, lost their market position, with still other firms going out of the computer business altogether.

How can a company avoid these unpleasantries and prosper? What new techniques and skills must managers master to respond to this challenge? Only recently have executives who have responded successfully to this challenge begun to report a consistent pattern of attack that shows promise of providing a foundation for a new corporate perspective on how to respond to rapid environmental change.

A New Corporate Perspective on Rapid Change. Fraker (1984) argues that a rapidly changing technology, quick market saturation, and unexpected competition have led to the emergence of a new corporate perspective for coping with a volatile business climate.

- First, companies must stay close to both their customers and their competitors. Successful companies always know what the customer needs and attempt to provide it. When products and manufacturing processes change rapidly, it is crucial to keep up with the investment strategies and product costs of rival companies. In order to accomplish this, companies must develop and maintain a rapid and accurate intelligence system capable of preventing surprises.

- Second, companies must think constantly about new products and then back up that thinking with quick investment. A good new product strategy requires a large, active, and focused research and development team with ready access to and the prudent use of large amounts of capital.

- Third, rapid and effective delivery requires close coordination among design, manufacturing, testing, marketing, delivery, and servicing systems. The interdependence of these systems combined with the short lead time in product delivery makes certain that any error within or between systems will delay product delivery, endangering market penetration. Close cooperation among these systems requires strong, quick, and responsive integration, coordination, and control systems.

- Fourth, product quality, user friendliness, ease of service, and competitive pricing are essential for market penetration. In an environment where consumer and investor representatives compare, rate, and effectively communicate product differences, market penetration depends on quality, utility, and readily serviceable products. This in turn requires the active monitoring, testing, and checking the servicing of one's own and one's competitive products.

- Fifth, companies that introduce new products must consider the processes and costs required to cannibalize their own products and to retrench the workers involved. Companies faced with rapidly changing technology, quick market saturation, and unexpected competition must be prepared to change or withdraw their own products rather than let their reputation and market shares be eroded by a competitor. Corporate planning for new products must include contingencies for shifting, retraining, or retrenching large product sectors rapidly.

- Sixth, a corporate vision must be developed that emphasizes change, allows for the assimilation of new units with alternative values, and encourages members to learn from mistakes without reprisal. Corporate cultures that cannot change rapidly will impede market adaptation. Corporations faced with stiff competition will often acquire other corporations with alternative values that will have to be integrated without delay into their corporate culture. Finally, a certain number of new initiatives are doomed to failure for all the reasons previously cited. Talented members of an organization must learn quickly from their failures and press on to new projects.

• Seventh, a corporate strategy must be developed that scans the globe for potential acquisitions, joint ventures, coalitions, value-added partnerships, and tailored trade agreements that can give a corporation a technological edge, market access, market control, and/or rapid response capabilities. Such a pooling of corporate resources is necessary for survival in a rapidly changing, highly competitive, international economic environment.

Each of these seven issues forms the basis for a new set of corporate assumptions and practices (Cushman and King, 1989).

Successful Organizations Are Employing New Management Assumptions

Rapid environmental change creates organizational problems, but it can also create organizational opportunities. An organization's management system, with its integration, coordination, and control processes, must have certain specifiable characteristics in order to respond to the opportunities created by successive, rapid environmental change. A management system that capitalizes on environmental change must be innovative, adaptive, flexible, efficient, and rapid in response.

Innovative management refers not only to product development, but to innovation in corporate structure, manpower utilization, outsourcing, inventory control, manufacturing, marketing, servicing, and competitive positioning.

Adaptive management refers to an organization's appropriate adjustment to change in employee values, customer tastes, investor interests, government regulations, the availability of global economic resources, and the strategic positioning of competitors.

Flexible management refers to the capacity of an organization to expand, contract, and shift direction on products and competitive strategy; to assimilate acquisitions, joint ventures, and coalitions; and to excise unproductive or underproductive units.

Efficient management refers to maintaining the industry lead in world-class products, productivity, investor's equity, return on investment, employee satisfaction, customer support, product quality, and serviceability.

Rapid response management refers to setting and maintaining the industry standard in speed of response to environmental change.

The organizational benefits that flow from a high-speed management system can be very significant.

First, order of magnitude changes occur in response time. General Electric reduced the amount of time required to deliver a custom made circuit breaker from three weeks to three days. Motorola used to turn out electronic pagers three weeks after the factory order arrived; now the process takes two hours (Ruffin, 1990).

Second, order of magnitude changes occur in productivity, product quality, and market shares. A recent survey of fifty major U.S. corporations by Kaiser and Associates, a large consulting firm, found that all listed time-based management strategies at the top of their priority list (Dumaine, 1989, p. 54). Why? Because speed of response tends to provide order of magnitude improvements in productivity, profits, product quality, and market shares.

Third, order of magnitude changes occur in profits. McKinsey & Company management consulting group demonstrates that high-tech products that come to market six months late earn 33 percent less profit over five years than products that come out on time, while 50 percent over budget increase in product development cuts profits only 4 percent when the product is on time (Vesey, 1991, p. 25).

The focus of this new corporate perspective and thus the goal of high-speed management is the use of the new information technologies and human communication process to rapidly develop, test, and produce a steady flow of low-cost, high-quality, easily serviced, high-value products that meet the customers' needs and of quickly getting these products to market before one's competition in an effort to achieve market penetration and large profits.

AN OUTLINE OF THE THEORY OF HIGH-SPEED MANAGEMENT

Competitive advantage in a rapidly changing economic environment will depend upon a corporation's capacity to accurately monitor changes in external economic forces and then to rapidly reorder a firm's internal resources to effectively respond to these external economic forces. In order to accurately monitor changes in external economic forces, an organization must have a world-class information and communication capability. A world-class information and communication capability must allow an organization to track and respond in real-time to international changes in the cost of capital, labor, and raw materials as well as changes in consumer tests and competitor response.

Similarly, sustainable competitive advantage in the 1990s will depend upon a corporation's capacity to rapidly orient and reorient product development, purchasing, manufacturing, distribution, sales, and service systems in response to volatile environmental change. To understand and systematically employ a high-speed management system, we are in need of a theoretic framework to guide the development and maintenance of such a world-class information and communication capability. It is the purpose of this portion of the chapter to explicate such a general theoretic framework. Our explication of this framework will proceed in two stages.

First, we will explore a theory of environmental scanning as an information and communication framework for monitoring and evaluating rapid changes in an organization's external economic forces.

Second, we will explore value chain theory as an information and communication framework for rapidly orienting and reorienting an organization's internal resources in response to changing external environmental forces.

A Theory of Environmental Scanning

Environments create both problems and opportunities for organizations. Organizations must cope with changes in the cost of capital, labor, raw materials, consumer taste, governmental regulations, political stability, and unexpected competition. Similarly, organizations depend upon the environment for scarce and valued resources, for developing strategic alliances such as coalitions, licensing, acquisitions, joint ventures, consortiums, value-added partnerships, and tailored trade agreements aimed at improving a firm's R&D, manufacturing, distribution and service, and sales capabilities. An organization's environment, perhaps more than any other factor, affects organizational strategy, structure, and performance. However, whether changes in organizational strategy, structure, and performance lead to positive or negative consequences rests almost entirely upon the speed, accuracy, and interpretation of the information and communication regarding various environmental changes and the rapid reorientation of an organization's strategy, structure, and resources in order to take advantage of such changes.

An Explication of a Theory of Environmental Scanning. If environmental scanning is an essential information and communication process for reorienting organizational strategy, structure, and resources, then how is this monitoring to be achieved?

Each industry and market in which a firm operates will contain its own unique underlying dynamic based upon what one's competitors are doing to influence sales and the influences to which one's customers are responding in buying products. Thus, environmental scanning of industry and market forces must track the organizational strategies, structures, and resources employed by one's competitors and the tasks, inclinations, products, and potential products that one's customers will want or demand.

Once the competitive dynamics of an industry and market are understood, then top management normally scans the economic, technical, political, and social forces at work in the global economy that might be employed by one's competitors and/or self to influence these competitive dynamics. For example, capital can frequently be borrowed from Japanese banks at 3 to 5 percent less than other sources; skilled labor can be obtained in Singapore, Taiwan, and Korea at 30 to 60 percent less than in the U.S.-Canadian and European Economic Community core market; parts and manufacturing processes can frequently be subcontracted from other firms less expensively than provided in-house. These global forces can significantly influence the competitive dynamics of an industry and market and are central to reorienting one's own firm to achieve competitive advantage.

Environmental Scanning in a High-Performance Organization. Environmental scanning is at once a simple and complex process. It is simple in that the critical information required to analyze the underlying dynamics of an industry and market is frequently readily available to all the competitors. It is complex in that the number of areas monitored to affect this dynamic may be large. Let us explore the elements in this process using a concrete example.

Jack Welsh, CEO of General Electric (a very successful global competitor), describes the two levels of environmental scanning and their effect on corporate alignment in his firm. Once a year at the annual meeting of GE's top one hundred executives, each of the firm's thirteen business leaders is required to present an environmental scanning analysis of his or her respective businesses. Each business leader is asked to present one-page answers to five questions:

1. What are your business' global market dynamics today and where are they going over the next several years?
2. What actions have your competitors taken in the last three years to upset those global dynamics?
3. What have you done in the last three years to affect those dynamics?
4. What are the most dangerous things your competitors could do in the next three years to upset those dynamics?
5. What are the most effective things you could do to bring about your desired impact on those dynamics?

Welsh concludes:

> Five simple charts. After those initial reviews, which we update regularly, we could assume that everyone at the top knew the plays and had the same playbook. It doesn't take a genius. So when Larry Bossidy is with a potential partner in Europe, or I'm with a company in the Far East, we're always there with a competitive understanding based on our playbooks. We know exactly what makes sense; we don't need a big staff to do endless analysis. That means we should be able to act with speed.
>
> Probably the most important thing we promise our business leaders is fast action. Their job is to create and grow new global businesses. Our job in the executive office is to

facilitate, to go out and negotiate a deal, to make the acquisition, or get our businesses the partners they need. When
our business leaders call, they don't expect studies, they
expect answers.

Take the deal with Thomson, where we swapped our
consumer electronics business for their medical equipment
business. We were presented with an opportunity, a great
solution to a serious strategic problem and we were able to
act quickly. We didn't need to go back to headquarters for a
strategic analysis and a bunch of reports. Conceptually, it
took us about 30 minutes to decide that the deal made
sense and then maybe two hours with the Thomson people
to work out the basic terms. (Tichy and Charzon, 1989,
p. 115)

Environmental scanning allows firms to focus on external
forces that significantly influence internal relationships. Value
chain theory allows us the opportunity to reorient an organization's internal relationships in an effort to influence that
organization's response to external forces.

An Explication of Value Chain Theory

We are in need of a theoretic framework for analyzing the kinds
of international markets, the types of competitive advantage, and
the issues involved in configuring and linking a firm's activities
relative to one's competitors so as to obtain a sustainable competitive advantage. Particularly useful in this regard is value chain
theory.

The basic unit of analysis in understanding international competition is the industry, because it is in the industry that market
shares are won or lost. In order to analyze how international competition functions, we must explore various market strategies, types
of competitive advantage, and how value chain theory can serve as
a theoretic approach for developing the sources of competitive
advantage within an organization's functioning.

The forms of international competition within an industry
range from multidomestic to global. A multidomestic approach
to markets treats each country or core market as a unique arena
and adjusts a firm's strategy for obtaining a competitive advantage to the specific issue in that market. When a firm takes this

market-by-market approach, its international strategy is multidomestic. A multidomestic firm views its industry as a collection of individual markets. In such an instance, a firm normally operates relatively autonomous subsidiaries in each market.

A global approach to markets is one in which a firm's competitive position in one country or core market is significantly affected by that firm's competitive position in other countries or core markets. International competition in a global industry is more than a collection of independent subsidiaries located in individual markets with unique strategies for obtaining competitive advantage in each market. A global approach rests on a series of interdependent activities that are integrated, coordinated, and controlled so that competitive advantage in one part of the world can be leveraged to obtain competitive advantage throughout the linkage system.

Competitive advantage can be viewed conceptually as emanating from four sources.

First, a firm's product or service may provide customers with comparable value at lower cost than those of competitors, creating low cost competitive advantage. Japanese automakers have consistently produced cars at $750 to $950 per unit lower cost than comparable American manufacturers, leading to low cost competitive advantage (Treece and Howr, 1989, p. 75).

Second, a firm's product or service may be comparable in cost but contain some unique quality, styling, service, or functional features relative to those of competitors, creating differentiation competitive advantage. Toyota and Honda automobiles require less repairs, are easier to service, and have more standard features included in the product price such as air conditioning, power brakes and steering, and AM-FM radios, and thus create higher customer satisfaction than similar U.S. and European cars.

Third, a firm may provide a broader range of products or services than competitors, thus creating scope competitive advantage. The Ford Motor Corporation provides its customers with small, medium, large, luxury, sport, and station wagon cars to select from as well as a broad range of trucks and minivans, creating competitive advantage relative to the Chrysler Corporation based on product scope.

Fourth, due to the high demand for certain products or services the first producer into the market with a quality product can dominate the market, and obtain high-end pricing and maximized profits based on speed of response, creating a time competitive advantage. The Chrysler Corporation's development, production, and marketing of minivans beat its competitors to market by one year, allowing Chrysler to capture all of the market for minivans for one year and get high-end pricing for maximum profits, and to hold a majority of the market (51 percent) for the next two years due to its time competitive advantage.

Most top international firms seek to exploit competitive advantage from all four sources. To diagnose where the sources of a firm's competitive advantage are and how each organization's functional units and business processes add value or fail to add value to products, we are in need of a theoretic framework for disaggregating a firm's discrete activities and evaluating their value-added contribution to an organization's products. Particularly useful in this regard is value chain theory. Managers term the discrete activities involved in producing a product or service the "value chain" and arrange them into functional unit activities and business processes (see Figure 2.1).

In an organization's functional unit level of the value chain, the two circles that denote suppliers and customers are normally found outside the organizational structure while the square boxes denote functional activities performed *within* an organization's structure. In an organization's business process level, each process includes some activities unique to each business process and some activities that overlap with other business processes.

Functional units and business processes may be located anywhere on the globe where they can gain competitive advantage from their location. Product development processes are normally located in regions where firms have access to a steady supply of state-of-the-art engineers, such as the United States, Japan, and Germany, where competitive advantage can be obtained from product differentiation. Product delivery processes are normally located near sources of inexpensive and skilled labor and automated production facilities such as Korea, Singapore, and Taiwan, where competitive advantage can be obtained from low-cost production. Customer service and management teams are normally located in the core markets a firm services in order to

Figure 2.1
An Organization's Value Chain

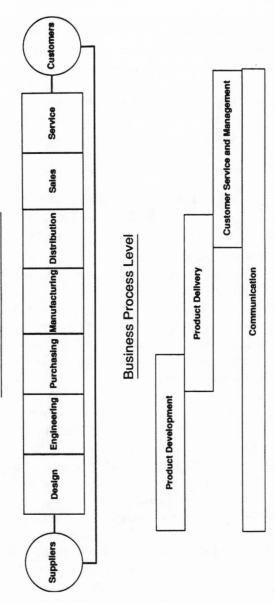

Functional Business Unit Level

Suppliers — Design | Engineering | Purchasing | Manufacturing | Distribution | Sales | Service — **Customers**

Business Process Level

Product Development

Product Delivery

Customer Service and Management

Communication

(*Source:* Revised from J. Rockart and J. Short, "IT in the 1990s," *Sloan Management Review* 30 (1989):12.)

obtain competitive advantage from rapid response time. A firm may obtain competitive advantage and/or value-added contributions from one or more of these sources. However, competitive advantage and value-added activities gained in one functional unit or business process can be added to or cancelled out by an organization's performance in other functional units or business processes. This is what is meant by value-added or value-diminishing chains of activities. If a functional unit or business activity fails to provide a source of competitive advantage or add value to an organization's products, then it needs to be improved or replaced. A primary function of management is to employ information and communication to monitor, evaluate, and improve the value chain in order to gain competitive advantage.

An Application of Value Chain Theory to the Global Auto Industry

The international auto market is a multibillion-dollar industry. Ten firms account for approximately 78 percent of world sales. Table 2.1 provides a profile of their September 1988 to September 1989 global performance.

The top three firms—General Motors, Ford, and Toyota—account for over 40 percent of the world auto market. We shall, for reasons of space, limit our analysis to the international competition among the top three firms in the U.S. core market. The central competitive dynamics operating in the global automobile industry, according to Harold Poling, CEO of Ford Motor Corporation, are "vehicle attributes, customer satisfaction and value for money" (Poling, 1989: E8). Vehicle attributes refer to styling, power train performance, and road handling. Customer satisfaction refers to vehicle comfort, safety, quality, and ease of maintenance. Value for money refers to cost, standard features, gas mileage, and insurance costs.

Table 2.2 provides the relevant high-speed management data upon which our analysis for the U.S. market is based.

The General Motors Corporation is the world's largest producer of automobiles. Its U.S. market shares fell from 45 percent in 1980 to 35 percent in 1989. A one percentage point drop amounts to 114,526 cars. GM's market shares at the lower-end auto price range have been eroded by Ford Escort and Toyota Tercel; at the middle price range by Ford Taurus and Tempo and

Table 2.1
World Auto Market, September 1988–September 1989

	World % of Market Shares	Auto Revenues (U.S. $ Billions)	Net Earnings (U.S. $ Thousands)	Vehicles (Thousands)	Worldwide Productions Autos (%)	Worldwide Productions Trucks (%)
1. GM	17.7	99.7	$3,831	7,946	74	26
2. Ford	14.6	76.8	4,259	6,336	70	30
3. Toyota	9.4	53.8	2,836	4,115	76	24
4. Volkswagon	6.6	34.4	921	2,948	93	7
5. Nissan	6.4	36.4	945	2,930	77	23
6. Chrysler	5.4	30.8	629	2,382	48	52
7. FIAT	5.4	26.4	2,453	2,436	90	10
8. Peugeot	4.6	22.8	1,518	2,216	88	12
9. Renault	4.2	26.4	1,451	2,053	80	20
10. Honda	4.0	25.2	945	1,960	86	14

(*Source:* Adapted from A. Borrus, "Japanese Streak Ahead in Asia," *Business Week* 31 (May 7, 1990):54–55.

Table 2.2
High-Speed Management Data for U.S. Market

	GM	Ford	Toyota
% Market Shares 1980	45	20	6
% Market Shares 1989	35	22	7
% Market Shares 1990	35	21	9
Productivity 1990 (Worker Hours per Car)	20	17	12
Av Replacement Time 1990 (Years per Model)	5	5	2
Factory Utilization (% 1990 Capacity)	70	78	110
Productivity Increase 1990 (%)	4.8	6.2	10.2

(*Source:* Compiled from *Automotive News*, 1989–1900.)

the Toyota Corolla; and at the upper price range by Ford Lincoln and Toyota Camry. GM has invested $46 billion in plant modernization (a sum equal to the amount needed to purchase Toyota Motors in 1990) and is still the high-cost producer. GM in the past three years cut $15 billion from its operating budget, closed several plants, and laid off workers, but still ran its remaining plant at 70 percent compared to 78 and 110 percent for Ford and Toyota. As the high-speed management data in Table 2.2 show, GM requires more worker hours per car and more model replacement time, and has a lower productivity increase than its two competitors. In addition, GM's Cadillac, Oldsmobile, and Buick cars ranked 7, 8, and 9 in quality ratings, while Toyota's Corolla and Camry ranked 2 and 3, with no Ford cars appearing in the top ten (Taylor, 1990).

The Ford Motor Corporation was one of America's most successful global competitors in the 1980s. Ford's market shares increased from 20 percent in 1980 to 22 percent by 1989. Ford produces vehicles at $200 less per unit than GM but trails Toyota by $650 per unit in cost. Over the past five years Ford has invested $21 billion in plant modernization and has significantly improved its production capabilities. It is evident from high-speed management data that Ford outperformed GM in productivity, replacement time, factory utilization, and productivity increases in 1989. However, Ford still trailed Toyota in all categories (Taylor, 1990).

Toyota Motors has established itself as the low-cost, high-quality, and best value automobile producer among the top three. Toyota's cars cost $675 to $950 less to produce than Ford and GM vehicles (Treece and Howr, 1989). In addition, Toyota leads Ford and GM in all high-speed management measures. It costs less, takes less worker hours per car, and takes less time to replace a car; on average, Toyota workers are also more productive than Ford and GM workers. That may be why Toyota went from 6 percent of the U.S. market in 1980 to 9 percent in 1990. In 1989 Toyota's market shares increased 3 percent in the United States, 3 percent in the European Economic Community, and 4 percent in Japan, yielding a 10 percent increase worldwide—an increase in sales of over one million cars. A one percentage point gain amounts to 114,526 cars. While Ford and GM have lost market shares in the last ten years, Toyota has gained. Toyota's innovative, adaptive, efficient, and rapid response systems according to Taylor (1990) accounted for the firm's competitive advantage in product cost, differentiation, scope, and timing.

Implications for High-Speed Management

While environmental scanning and value chain theory appear to be useful as analytic tools for exploring the types and sources of competitive advantage employed in the auto industry, two questions arise regarding the framework's generalizability.

First, can the appropriate use of environmental scanning and value chain theory to analyze change in the environment and quickly adjust an organization's value chain to meet these changes separate successful from unsuccessful international competitors based on configuration and linking processes, irrespective of industry?

Second, can environmental scanning and value chain theory demonstrate that firms with a competitive advantage based on time also have improved performance ratings on all forms of competitive advantage?

Cvar (1986) attempted to answer the first question when he undertook a study at twelve international corporations in 1984.

For his research, Cvar selected eight successful and four unsuccessful firms for study. Four of the successful firms were American, while one each was Swiss, British, Italian, and French. Three of the four unsuccessful firms were American and one was Swiss. These twelve firms each competed in separate industries. Successful firms were distinguished from unsuccessful firms by their high investment in information and communication technology and by the effective use of information and communication to analyze and evaluate quickly changes in the external organizational environment and then to reorient rapidly internal resources in response to those changes.

Smith et al. (1989) attempted to answer our second question in their study of twenty-two top-level managers from high-technology electronics firms. They explained major portions of the variance in organizational performance or increases in profits and sales from decreases in response time to environmental change. They found that an external orientation by a firm, a rapid response to competitor threat, and the radicalness of the change initiated in the organization were all positively related to increased profits and sales and the general performance of an organization. Decreases in response time to external change were highly correlated with communication systems improvements in an organization's R&D, manufacturing, and marketing.

Value chain theory does appear to be capable of separating successful from unsuccessful international firms, and revealing how competitive advantage based on integration, coordination, and control improves overall organizational performance. We are now in a position to explore the transformations the general theory of high-speed management has brought about in the traditional conceptualization of organizational communication processes.

HIGH-SPEED MANAGEMENT TRANSFORMATIONS OF TRADITIONAL ORGANIZATIONAL COMMUNICATION PROCESSES

Within every organization there are tacit assumptions about how individuals and groups must share information and interact through communication in order to perform organizational tasks.

These tacit assumptions create an organization's mind-set and define how members of that organization perceive and interact with an organization's stakeholders. These tacit assumptions that govern and guide perception and interaction create an organization's information and communication climate. What has our analysis thus far taught us about the broad outline of such a set of necessary assumptions in successful high-speed management organizations?

The first section of this chapter argued that a series of breakthroughs have taken place in information and communication technology that have dramatically altered how organizations do work. This information and communication revolution in organizational processes has led to a dramatic increase in world trade, the emergence of a global economy, and the development of three large core markets anchored by the United States, Germany, and Japan. This dramatic increase in world trade has created a volatile business climate characterized by rapidly changing technology, quick market saturation, and unexpected competition, making succeeding in business very difficult. To compete successfully in such an environment requires that organizations employ management assumptions that emphasize innovative, adaptive, flexible, efficient, and rapid response to change—high-speed management assumptions.

The second section of this chapter argued that obtaining competitive advantage in a volatile business environment will depend upon an organization's capacity to rapidly and accurately monitor changes in the external environment and then to quickly reorient its internal and external resources in order to effectively respond to that change. Rapidly and accurately monitoring an organization's external environment requires the real-time tracking of changes in consumer taste, competitor strategies, global economic forces, and core market demand. Quickly reorienting an organization's external and internal resources requires scanning the globe for acquisitions, joint ventures, and strategic alliances, and exploiting the value-added potential of one's own organizational activities. Finally, a world-class information and communication capability or high-speed management system is required in order to successfully employ such an environmental scanning and value chain alignment capability.

It is the purpose of this final section of our chapter to explore the philosophical rationale, theoretic principles, and practical basis for such a world-class information and communication capability and to indicate how high-speed management has transformed the traditional conceptualizations of organizational communication.

Philosophical Rationale for the Transformation of Organizational Communication Processes

While it is clear from our previous analysis that a successful global competitor carefully monitors changes in global economic forces and then quickly reorients an organization's value chain to meet those changes in ways that create value-added activities and thus competitive advantage, it is far from clear what the philosophical rationale is for guiding the communication activities involved in these organizational adaptation processes. Fortunately, several well-developed studies have explored this problem in detail with convergent results (Rockart and Short, 1989; Venkatraman and Prescott, 1990; Cvar, 1986; Smith, et al., 1989).

The Center for Information Systems Research at the MIT Sloan School of Management in 1989 summarized these convergent studies when it stated that an organization's ability to continuously improve its effectiveness in managing organizational interdependencies was the critical element in successfully responding to the competitive forces of the 1990s (Rockart and Short, 1989). Effectiveness in managing organizational interdependencies refers to an organization's ability to achieve coalignment among its internal and external resources in a manner that is equal to or greater than existing world-class benchmarks for responding to environmental change.

Coalignment is a unique form of organizational interdependence in which each of a firm's subunits clearly articulates its needs, concerns, and potential contributions to the organization's functioning in such a manner that management can forge an appropriate value-added configuration and linkage between units. An appropriate value-added configuration and linkage between units is one that integrates, coordinates, and controls each unit's needs, concerns, and contributions so that the outcome is mutually satisfying to the units involved and optimizing in value-added activities to the organizational functioning as a whole.

World-class benchmarking refers to the standards one holds in setting goals for improvement. These benchmarks or goals to be met in improving an organization's innovation, adaptation, flexibility, efficiency, and rapid response to environmental change must be set at world-class levels. They must reflect the highest standards of the best companies in the world. Only then will improvement in an organization's coalignment process provide for the value-added gains necessary for sustainable competitive advantage.

Our analysis of the philosophical rationale for the primary function of communication within its organizational context suggests that communication serves to continuously improve organizational effectiveness in managing a firm's coalignments between its internal and external resources benchmarked against world-class standards in responding to environmental change. Coalignment is a unique communication relationship in which each of a firm's stakeholders clearly articulates its needs, concerns, and contributions in such a manner that management can forge an appropriate value-added configuration and linkage between stakeholders that is mutually satisfying and optimizing to the value-added activities of the organization when benchmarked against world-class standards, thus creating a sustainable competitive advantage.

While such a philosophical rationale seems clear and responsive to a volatile economic environment, what theoretic principles are available to guide this continuously improving communication process of organizational coalignment and world-class benchmarking?

The Theoretic Bases for the Transformation of Organizational Communication Processes

Four dynamic communication processes, each with its own theoretic rationale, currently form the basis for the continuous improvement of organizational coalignment processes based on world-class benchmarking. These are: (1) negotiation linking, (2) a New England town meeting, (3) a cross-functional teamwork, and (3) a best practices case study program.

A Negotiated Linking Program.   A unit or function is created within an organization whose purpose is to continuously scan the globe in order to locate resources in the form of customers, partners, technologies, or consultants that are capable of enhancing an organization's competitiveness. Such resources may include land, labor, capital, market entry, distribution channels, technology, and training. This unit then

- interacts with the unit holding the potential resource in order to locate its interests, concerns, and contributions to coalignment
- develops the form of coalignment preferred by both units, such as acquisition, joint venture, alliance, partnership coalition, collaboration, licensing technology leasing, transfer or training
- determines the world-class benchmarking targets in market shares, productivity, quality, flexibility, rapid response time to be met before coalignment can take place

The organizational negotiated-linking program then formulates the negotiated coalignment agreement aimed at mobilizing external resources for organizational usage.

A New England Town Meeting. A unit or function is created within the organization to implement a worker continuous improvement program within a New England town meeting format. Its goal is to improve an organization's productivity, quality, flexibility, adaptability, and response time. It is an attempt to eliminate nonessential, nonproductive, or "bad work" and replace it with "good work." These New England style town meetings last from one to three days. They begin with the division head calling together twenty to one hundred workers, suppliers, and customers.

The meeting then proceeds in the following manner.

- The division head opens the meeting with a presentation of key market issues, the organization's vision in responding to these issues, how the organization and its competitors are responding to this vision, and specific organizational needs for increased productivity, quality, flexibility, adaptability, and rapid response time. The division head leaves at this point in the meeting.
- Teamwork facilitators take over and generate a list of bad work to be eliminated and good work to be undertaken in

responding to the various areas of concern.

- The group is then divided into teams of five to ten members to analyze, discuss, and debate potential areas for improvement.
- Each team then provides a cost/benefit analysis and action plan for the solutions recommended.
- The division head then returns and listens to a cost/benefit analysis and action plan from each group.

The division head acts on all high-yield ideas by selecting a team champion, training the team champion in project management, empowering a team to implement the change, and setting performance targets, measurement criteria, time frame, and feedback procedures. The worker improvement team then implements the action plan.

A Cross-Functional Teamwork Program. A unit or function is created to set up cross-functional teams whose goals are to map and then improve cross-functional organizational processes. Many of the most significant improvements in organizational performance have come from mapping important cross-functional organizational processes and then asking those involved in the process to simplify and/or improve the functioning of that process. This approach has been very profitable for organizations since many of these processes have developed and expanded over time without anyone examining the entire process and exploring its improvement.

Here cross-functional teams are set up and assigned the task of mapping the decision, implementation, and review levels of important organizational processes. The cross-functional team is then asked to evaluate and make improvements in the process mappings. This is accomplished in four steps:

- developing a clear understanding of the process goal
- identifying the necessary and sufficient critical success factors for achieving that goal
- mapping and improving the essential subprocesses to meet these critical success factors
- rank ordering each subprocess and evaluating its productivity, quality, flexibility, adaptability, and how to make improvements

The unit and/or function then implements the change process and fine tunes its subprocesses.

A Best Practice Case Study Program.   A unit or function is created to scan the globe for world-class competitors and to study how various parts of these organizations succeeded in setting world-class benchmarking standards in regard to productivity, quality, flexibility, adaptability, and response time. This unit usually

- locates such organizations and makes a site visit
- develops a case study of the processes involved
- trains its personnel in ways to adapt these innovations to its organization

This unit then sets up monitoring and feedback procedures for and implements the change.

These then are our four dynamic communication processes, each with its own theoretic rationale for developing an organizational continuous improvement program employing environmental scanning and value chain theory aimed at achieving coalignment between an organization's external and internal resources.

PRACTICAL BASES FOR A WORLD-CLASS INFORMATION AND COMMUNICATION CAPABILITY

Continuous improvement programs aimed at improving organizational coalignment through negotiated linking, cross-functional teamwork, New England town meetings, and case studies in world-class benchmarking are necessary elements in establishing a world-class organizational information and communication capability. Continuous improvement programs are essential information and communication processes in high-speed management that have rapidly defused to small and large organizations in the private and public sectors of the world economy. Let us therefore examine the practical bases of continuous improvement programs by exploring the four dynamic communication processes functioning in a small local organization, the Danville, Illinois Bumper Works, and in a large multinational organization, the General Electric Corporation.

The Danville, Illinois Bumper Works

In 1978 Shahid Khan, a naturalized U.S. citizen from Pakistan, borrowed $50,000 from the Small Business Loan Corporation and took $16,000 of his own savings to establish the one hundred-person Bumper Works in Danville, Illinois. This company designed and manufactured truck bumpers. Between 1980 and 1985 Khan approached the Toyota Motors Corporation on several occasions, attempting to become a supplier of bumpers for their trucks but without much luck.

In 1987 the Toyota Motors Company called together a group of one hundred potential suppliers and released their design, quality, quantity, and price range specifications for the product. The officials at Toyota Motors also indicated that they expected increased quality and a reduction in price each year from the supplier. By late 1988 only Khan's Bumper Works company could produce a product that met Toyota Motors' exacting requirements. In 1989 Toyota Motors sent a manufacturing team to Danville, Illinois, to negotiate the contract and coalignment agreement between the two firms. The negotiations failed because the Bumper Works could not produce twenty different sized bumpers and ship them in a single day. If they could not do this, it would slow down the production of all Toyota trucks, increasing their price dramatically (White, 1991, p. A7).

Khan called a New England town meeting of workers from his own and Toyota Motors Japanese factories to explore how this problem might be solved in terms of Toyota's design, quality, quantity, and price requirements. It was decided that the Bumper Works would have to switch the factory from a mass production to a batch production line and that a massive stamping machine that took ninety minutes to change each cutting die would have to be modified to make such changes in twenty minutes (White, 1991, p. A7).

Next, the workers at both the Bumper Works and Toyota Motors set up cross-functional teams to make a process map of current production procedures. They studied, simplified, and restructured the process so as to allow for batch production. The large stamping machine was studied for modifications that would speed up die changes. All this was done with considerable help from Toyota Motors who had solved these same problems, but in a different way, back in Japan (White, 1991, p. A7).

Then, the Bumper Works' remodeled assembly line was ready to begin production. For six months employees with stop watches and cost sheets observed the restructured process and benchmarked its operations against the world-class standards of the Toyota plant in Japan—but still could not meet Toyota's quality, quantity, and speed of delivery specifications. They videotaped the process, studied it, modified it, and sent it to Japan for review. In July 1990 Toyota Motors sent a team over to help retrain the workers. They returned again in December 1990 to fine tune the process, meeting Toyota Motor's contract requirements.

The new production line increased productivity 60 percent over the previous year, decreased defects 80 percent, cut delivery time by 850 percent, and cut waste materials cost by 50 percent. A manual and videotape of the manufacturing process were prepared for training, the first of their kind at Bumper Works, and continuous improvement teams were formed in order to meet contract requirements for Toyota Motors of increased quality and decreased costs for each subsequent year.

Now that representatives of each unit involved in the value chain linking the Bumper Works and Toyota Motors had communicated their interests, concerns, and contributions to the coalignment process, each firm's management was able to forge a linking process that was satisfactory to the units involved and optimizing to the value-added activities of each organization in order to create a sustainable competitive advantage. Khan has profited from this experience and is building a new plant that will employ two hundred workers in Indiana and will supply truck bumpers for a new Isuzu Motors plant located there (White, 1991, p. A7).

The General Electric Corporation

In 1990 General Electric had $58.4 billion in sales, $4.3 billion in profits, and 298,000 employees worldwide. As Stewart (1991, p. 41) indicates:

> Few corporations are bigger; none more complex. GE makes 65 cent light bulbs, 400,000 pound locomotives, and billion dollar power plants. It manages more credit cards than American Express and owns more commercial aircraft than American Airlines. Of the seven billion pounds of hamburger Americans tote home each year, 36 percent keep fresh in GE refrigerators, and after dinner, one out of every five couch potatoes tunes in GE's network NBC.

This is the organization CEO Jack Welch, Jr. wants to be lean, agile, and aggressive, to run like a small business. His corporate goal is to make GE the most competitive corporation in the world by having each of its thirteen businesses ranked number one or two in world market shares, while increasing sales 15 percent, profits 10 percent, and productivity 5 percent per year, and decreasing costs by 5 percent per year. It goes without saying that Welch is a strong advocate of continuous improvement programs.

Since 1981 GE has divested itself of $5.9 billion in low-growth businesses and acquired $11.1 billion in high-growth businesses in order to maintain its number one or two world market shares in each of its thirteen businesses. It is a difficult task for an environmental scanning unit to locate such a large number of potential acquisitions capable of performing at the level required by GE and then to negotiate the linking agreement so that the acquisition is quickly brought up to speed. For example, Philips Corporation of Holland purchased Westinghouse's lighting business, Electrolux of Sweden purchased White Consolidated's major appliance division, and Brown and Bovevi of Switzerland and ASEA of Sweden merged their power systems divisions. Each of these acquisitions and mergers threatened GE's number one and two market shares ranking in the lighting, major appliances, and power systems industries. In each case GE scanned the globe for potential linking arrangements that could restore their market dominance and meet their world-class growth, productivity, product quality, and rapid response targets. Acquisitions were located, linking arrangements negotiated, and coalignment processes put in place so that market shares and performance targets could be met. Over ten years, such acquisitions amounted to $11.1 billion.

In order to make GE the most competitive corporation in the world, Welch realized that his business leaders had to find a better fit between their organization's needs and their employees' capabilities. To reorient this fit, GE in 1987 established a New England town meeting program called "Workout." The purpose of Workout town meetings, according to Welch, were:

> To see a team work together to face its problems and candidly discuss issues which negatively affect their work by giving each employee the power to define and shape his job, to give it meaning so he can feel responsible for it, get

value from it, and have it be an enriching experience instead of a draining, numbing nuisance. In the end, each employee will have worked to create move customers, more job security, and more job satisfaction. That's our ultimate goal for the 1990's at GE. (Workout, 1989, p. 1).

By the end of 1991 over fifty thousand GE employees had participated in three-day Workout town meetings with remarkable results. In GE's plastics division alone, over thirty Workout teams have been empowered to make changes. One team saved GE plastics $2 million by modifying one production process, another enhanced productivity fourfold, while a third reduced product delivery time 400 percent (Workout, 1991, pp. 1, 2). Another business, NBC, used Workout to halt the use of report forms that totaled more than two million pieces of paper a year (Stewart, 1991, p. 44). GE Credit Services used Workout to tie its cash registers directly to the mainframe, cutting the time for opening a new account from thirty minutes to ninety seconds. Similar results have been reported from Workout projects in GE's other businesses, demonstrating a remarkable companywide reorientation of coalignment processes between worker capabilities and organizational needs.

While this internal transformation of GE's value chain was taking place, Welch also realized that some other global organizations were achieving greater productivity, quality control, flexibility, adaptability, and rapid response time than GE, even with the Workout program in place. In the summer of 1988 GE began its "Best Practices" program, aimed at locating those organizations that had outperformed GE in a given area, developing a case study of how they did it, and then employing these case studies as world-class benchmarks for improving GE's performance.

GE scanned the globe and located twenty-four corporations that had in some area outperformed GE. They then screened out direct competitors, and companies that would not be credible to GE employees. Welch then invited each corporation to come to GE to learn about its best practices and in return to allow GE people to come to their companies and study their best practices. About one-half of the companies agreed. They included AMP, Chapparral Steel, Ford, Hewlett Packard, Xerox, and three

Japanese companies. GE sent out observers to develop case studies and ask questions. These best practices case studies have been turned into a course at Crotonville, GE's leadership training center, and is offered to a new class of managers from each of GE's thirteen businesses each month (Stewart, 1991, pp. 44–45).

Finally, as GE's top management team reviewed the projects that had been successful from both their Workout and Best Practices program, they noticed a difference in the types of project that saved up to $1 million and those that saved $100 million. The latter always involved changes in organizational processes that spanned the entire value chain. They cut across departments and involved linking with supplies and customers. All emphasized managing processes, not functions. This led GE to establish its cross-functional teamwork program aimed at mapping and then improving key organizational processes. Such process maps frequently allowed employees for the first time to see and understand organizational processes from beginning to end. They also demonstrated the need for a new type of manager, a process manager who could coalign an organization's total assets. It allowed employees to spot bottlenecks, time binds, inventory shortages, and overflows.

Since implementing a cross-functional teamwork program, GE appliances has cut its sixteen-week manufacturing cycle in half, while increasing product availability 6 percent and decreasing inventory costs 20 percent. The program has cost less than $3 million to implement and has already returned profits 100 times that (Stewart, 1991, p. 48). Product-mapping programs have also provided an empirical basis for changing how GE measures its management and workers' performance. GE now employs world-class cross-functional process benchmarking standards to evaluate its various business performances and to award its bonuses and merit awards for process improvements.

Continuous improvement programs like those at the Bumper Works and General Electric are using negotiated linking, New England town meetings, cross-functional teamwork, and case studies of world-class benchmarking to revolutionize how the practical basis for communication affects the coalignment of organizational processes in order to obtain a sustainable competitive advantage.

SUMMARY

Our rather long journey into the theory of high-speed management is over. In summary, we began this chapter by noting how the convergence of four trends has created a volatile business environment. Next we explored how the general theory of high-speed management attempts to give managers some control over rapid change through the use of environmental scanning theory and value chain theory. Finally, we explored how organizational coalignment was affected by four theoretic and practical communication processes: (1) negotiated linking, (2) New England town meetings, (3) cross-functional teamwork, and (4) case studies of world-class benchmarking.

Our goal throughout this chapter has been to explicate a macrotheory of organizational communication processes (environmental scanning and value chain theory) and demonstrate how that macrotheory can guide the development of microtheories and research on continuous improvement programs and their communication processes. This macrotheory can be employed to reorient micro-organizational communication theories of leadership, corporate climate teamwork, and the like (Cushman and King, 1993). High-speed management thus shows promise of providing a new approach to all organizational communication issues, strategies, and techniques, through an information and communication approach to organizational processes.

NOTE

This chapter, which is a reprint from the Proceedings of the Fifth Conference on Corporate Communication held at Fairleigh Dickinson University, May 1992, is largely drawn from the book *High-Speed Management: Organizational Communication in the 1990s* (Cushman and King, 1994). This book elaborates on all the coordination relationships within an organization and the issues and content used to resolve the appropriate coalignment or coordination, integration, and control of these processes. Chapters on the forms of leadership, corporate climate, and teamwork present new conceptions of each of these processes from a high-speed management perspective. The chapters in this reader draw heavily from that book.

REFERENCES

Automotive News. 1989–90. All issues.

Baig, E. 1989. Where global growth is going. *Fortune* 120 (July):71–88.

Berlant, D., R. Browning, and G. Foster. 1990. How Hewlett-Packard gets numbers it can trust. *Harvard Business Review* 68 (Jan.–Feb.):178–82.

Borrus, A. 1990. Japanese streak ahead in Asia. *Business Week* 31 (May 7):54–55.

Castells, M. 1986. High-technology, world development and the structured transformation: The trends and debate. *Alternatives* 11:297–342.

Cushman, D. P., and S. S. King. 1989. The role of communication in high technology organizations: The emergence of high-speed management. In S. S. King, ed., *Human Communication as a Field of Study.* Albany, N.Y.: SUNY Press.

————. 1994. *High-Speed Management: Organizational Communication in the 1990s.* Albany, N.Y.: SUNY Press.

Cvar, M. 1986. Case studies in global competition patterns of success and failure. In M. Porter, ed., *Competition in Global Industry.* Boston, Mass.: Harvard Business School Press.

Dumaine, B. 1989. How managers can succeed through speed. *Fortune* 119 (Feb. 13):54–59.

Feigenbaum, E., P. McCorduck, and P. Nii. 1988. *The Rise of the Expert Company.* New York: Times Books.

Fraker, S. 1984. High-speed management for the high tech age. *Fortune* 119 (Feb. 13):34–60.

The global giants. 1990. *Wall Street Journal,* Sept. 21, p. R27.

Pepper, C. B. 1989. Fast forward. *Business Month* (Feb.):25–30.

Poling, H. 1989. An interview with the CEO designate of Ford Motor Company. *Automotive News,* Nov. 7, p. E8.

Port, O. 1986. High tech to the rescue. *Business Week* (June 16):100–108.

Rockart, J., and J. Short. 1989. IT in the 1990's: Managing organizational interdependencies. *Sloan Management Review* 30 (Winter):7–17.

Ruffin, W. 1990. Wired for speed. *Business Month* (Jan.):56–58.

Russell, E., A. Adams, and B. Boundy. 1986. High-technology test marketing Campbell Soup Company. *Journal of Consumer Marketing* 3(1) (Winter):71–80.

Smith, K. G., et al. 1989. Predictors of response time to competitive strategic action: Preliminary theory and evidence. *Journal of Business Research* 19:245–58.

Stalk, G., Jr. 1988. Time—the next source of competitive advantage. *Harvard Business Review* 66 (July–Aug.):41–51.

Stewart, T. 1991. GE keeps those ideas coming. *Fortune* (Aug. 12):41–49.

Taylor, A. 1990. Can American cars come back? *Fortune* 121 (Feb. 26):62–65.

Taylor A., III. 1990. Why Toyota keeps getting better. *Fortune* 122 (Nov. 19):66–79.

Tichy, N., and R. Charzon. 1989. Speed, simplicity, self-confidence: An interview with Jack Welch. *Harvard Business Review* 67:112–20.

Treece, J., and J. Howr. 1989. Shaking up. *Business Week* (Aug. 14):24–80.

Venkatraman, N., and J. Prescott. 1990. Environment-strategy coalignment: An empirical test of its performance implications. *Strategic Management Journal* 11:1–23.

Vesey, J. 1991. The new competitors: They think in terms of speed-to-market. *Academy of Management Executive* 5:22–33.

Walton, J. 1985. *The IMF Riot.* Paper delivered at the ISA Conference on the Urban Impact of the New International Division of Labor, Hong Kong.

White, J. 1991. Japanese auto makers help U.S. suppliers become more efficient. *Wall Street Journal,* Sept. 9, pp. A1, A7.

Workout. 1989, 1991. Special edition of *GE Silicones News.*

Young, J. 1990. An American giant rethinks globalization. *Information Strategy* (Spring):5–10.

CHAPTER THREE

High-Speed Management and Global Competition

Andrzej K. Kozminski

GLOBAL MANAGEMENT AND GLOBAL COMPETITION

Kenichi Ohmae, in his persuasive vision of contemporary industrial (or rather postindustrial) economy, presents the Triad as a place where all the important things happen, where 90 percent of the world's high value-added and high-technology products are manufactured, sold, used, and consumed. The "Triad" includes North America, Western Europe, and the developed Far East (Ohmae, 1985, 1987). The Triad is a home for the enterprises practicing a new type of management called "global management" and a platform for global competition. Let us discuss briefly some of the most important features of a business environment within the Triad that sustain global competition and management practices.

Global competition and global management can be explained primarily by the growing number of industries becoming global. According to Porter's concept, which is widely accepted, a global industry is one in which a firm's competitive position in one country is considerably influenced by its competitive position in a number of other countries (Porter, 1986). Such a globalization trend means that in more and more industries,

41

more and more competitive advantage is gained by integrating activities on a worldwide basis with a clear focus on the Triad, its markets, and its resources.

The following self-reinforcing factors underlie globalization trends and shape global competition:

- falling direct labor cost as a percentage of total cost
- increasing global markets for raw materials, components, and other inputs
- a world market for technology and unification of technological standards
- an international currency system enhancing global capital and securities market and global banking
- new supranational economic systems (such as the EEC or North American free trade zone) promoting integration and standardization within them and taking down tariff barriers
- increased productivity and profitability through use of information and communication technology
- homogenization of consumers' and buyers' needs and behavioral patterns enhancing standardization of promotion, advertising, and retailing
- worldwide standardization of transportation networks, logistics, packing, and storage
- emergence of a new standard of compatible (facilitating cooperation) government economic policies including control of inflation through fiscal austerity and monetary restrictions, restructuring of industrial and service sectors (promoting development of high value-added industries and elimination of low value-added ones), privatization and deregulation of the economy (with relative control over the pricing of raw materials and energy and selective protection of some industries still maintained), active promotion of education, scientific research, and information technology
- increasingly intensive capital flows, mergers, acquisitions and partnerships between strong players within the Triad (Porter, 1986; Ohmae, 1985; Cushman and King, 1987).

Global management is understood here as a process of optimization and integration of business activities on a worldwide basis. Its main objective is to achieve a competitive advantage of global dimension by capturing linkages among local, international, and global activities, resources, and markets. Global management can be characterized by four elements: global cooperation for global competition, high-speed management, global structures, and parallel political games (Kozminski, 1993).

The most recent lesson to be learned from the Western world's corporate leaders is that success depends upon the ability to develop and enhance company-to-company relationships across national, political, and cultural boundaries.

Perlmutter and Heenan (1986) call such alliances "global strategic partnerships" and characterize them as follows:

1. two or more companies develop a common long-term strategy aimed at world leadership as low-cost suppliers, providers of a unique product or service (differentiated marketeers), or both in an international arena.
2. partners share their specific strengths.
3. the reach of the alliance is global, not limited to a specific group of countries.
4. the partnership is organized along horizontal lines and takes such forms as technology exchange, resource pooling, joint research and development, and joint marketing.
5. the participating companies can still compete in the markets excluded from partnership.

Most of value-added technology products are being developed, produced, distributed, and serviced worldwide by global strategic partnerships, which seem to have an incredibly powerful impact on the worldwide process of resource allocation. Because of the nature and changing patterns of such partnerships their power seems to be partially hidden from nonspecialists. It especially applies to politicians and managers in postcommunist countries, where the world economy is still perceived in terms of nation-states, "national economies," and companies with clear-cut national identities.

High-speed management is a modern management philosophy and a set of management tools and techniques enabling companies and global strategic partners to cope successfully with shortening life cycles on the global (Triad) market.

Cushman and King (1989) indicate that high-speed management enables a new product to be quickly designed for the world market, manufactured in large volumes, and successfully sold simultaneously in all Triad markets. High speed of the whole operation is necessary to assure the advantage over competitors before they develop similar products and to accumulate huge profits over a short period of time. These profits should be immediately reinvested into the development of new generations of products to be marketed again on an increasingly integrated Triad market.

Such a new management philosophy initially began in the high-technology sector but is being quickly imitated by other global industries and becomes a standard requirement for success in the global arena.

Three main types of high-speed management tools can be identified (Cushman and King, 1989):

1. *Product portfolio modeling*: highly sophisticated marketing skill of developing alternative product life cycle scenarios (based upon the assessment of users' needs, technology, and competition). A set of such scenarios, slightly different for different parts of the globe and different cultures, enables a company to generate a global strategy of product innovation.

2. *World-class manufacturing* (Schonberger, 1987): highly capital-intensive computerized manufacturing techniques (CAD, CIM, etc.) enabling economies of scale combined with speed and flexibility (in the case of some mass production systems, such as automobile manufacturing, providing for custom design by a client of each unit). The use of the most advanced and sophisticated technology in design, development, production, transportation, and storage has become a standard requirement for global competition, blocking the entry of firms unable to mobilize huge resources and cooperate with global leaders.

3. *Structured innovation*: research and development capacity enabling a constant ability to generate new products. Structured innovation systems cannot be separated from strategic planning, marketing, production, and entrepreneurial dimensions of the firm. They have to be built into the organizational environment to the point that the whole firm or the whole global network of firms becomes innovation-driven.

Companies practicing global management and participating in the partnerships of a global reach develop specific organizational structures and organizational cultures. A new type of global business structure is emerging. It is based upon an exchange between partners (mainly exchange of technology and skills). It involves integrated logistics, common databases, decision-making rules and procedures, shared perspectives, and converging managerial culture (Barlett and Ghosal, 1987).

In terms of strategy it means orientation toward the global market (as opposed to a country, subsidiary, or regional perspective). It has meaningful consequences in terms of control and power structures. "The new global model is more flexible about ownership and managerial control. It encourages joint decision making, vertical and horizontal planning, and fusion of competent allies around the world, despite cultural differences" (Perlmutter and Heenan, 1986, p. 152).

Collaboration between global competitors is probably the most striking fact about new structures. Hamel, Doz, and Prahalad (1989) have studied the inner workings of fifteen such alliances and were able to formulate a set of simple but powerful principles to which successful alliances adhere.

1. Collaboration is competition in a different form. Successful companies do not forget that their new partners might be willing to disarm them by appropriating their unique skills, technologies, accesses to markets, and other resources. They clearly formulate their objectives and are fully aware of objectives of their partners and competitors.
2. Harmony is not the most important measure of success. Confrontation or even occasional conflict often benefits common undertakings.
3. Cooperation must have clearly defined limits. Companies entering a partnership must know precisely what information and what resources are traded for what and what is off-limits to the partners.
4. Learning from a partner is a benefit of a partnership that goes beyond the scope of a formal agreement. Winners are able to learn more and faster (Hamel, Doz, and Prahalad, 1989, p. 134).

Such a new international structures can be formed only by more or less equal partners on similar levels of technological, managerial, and marketing sophistication.

Parallel political games inevitably coupled with the global management process explain both the stakes and political logic of the game (Kozminski, 1992). The stakes are market share, global control over resources, and global influence. Profit is considered to be an instrumental value.

Global companies are willing and able to use their political leverage to protect and expand some of their resources and interrelated markets. Both national governments and supranational structures (such as the EEC) are approached. Politics-business relationships also work the other way around: governments use international companies in return for support and favors. Arms deals, technology transfer agreements, concessions, and negotiations offer abundant examples of such a mixture of politics and business.

Global management contributes greatly to the economization of global politics and politicization of the global economy. Such an interface between economy and politics in the international arena has been known for centuries. Global management, however, has added a completely new dimension to this relationship. It has become an organizing force of the new world economy

> not as an international system (including a colonial system) but as a world capitalist system. Indeed, there are now, actually in operation in the world-system, two fundamentally different principles of organization. The one is essentially political and organizes the world population as a subject of formally distinct 'sovereign states'. The other is, essentially, economic (capitalist) and organizes the world population as participants in a single and organized, world production system. (Hopkins, et al., 1982, p. 87)

These two simultaneously applied principles of organization are translated into an increasingly complex network of partnerships, agreements, negotiations, and contracts that create economic, political, and military interdependence overpowering even superpowers such as the United States, Japan, and Germany.

The Soviet Union and its communist satellites failed miserably to transform the world system and to dominate it. This failure was caused by evident economic inefficiency and inconsistency with the value systems developed in Western civilization. Now these countries are in the process of deep transformation themselves, striving to become part of the world system dominated by the Triad. In order to do so they have to become compatible with economic mechanisms and institutions of the Triad countries. This can be achieved only through compatibility of postcommunist enterprises with their Triadic counterparts.

High-speed management is a core element of global management. It indicates its objectives and key instruments; it shapes the alliances, structures, and political actions of the global players; it dictates internal logic and the specific culture of global management.

Global competition and global management promote the self-reinforcing trend of homogenization of management culture and practices worldwide.

Managers' educational backgrounds are becoming similar. The same body of knowledge and expertise is used by all of the participants of the global management game and others are trying to imitate and follow. Standardized accounting systems, communication systems combining written communication with electronic mail, teleconferencing, computer networks, and personal contact are becoming standard. Conferences and negotiations are held and reports written in a standardized way. Disputes are solved through standardized procedures of negotiations and arbitration. Managers' promotions are based on similar performance evaluation criteria. Postcommunist managers do not fit these standards and that is why management education, training, and development are rightly considered to be key factors conditioning the transformation to market economy.

Contemporary global management originated in the Western corporate culture is strongly influenced by the American perspective. It is based on individualistic values of freedom, opportunity, and self-realization with social welfare values (justice, order, civilization, etc.) (Bernthal, 1962).

The proliferation of global management seems to promote individualistic values even in the countries where not long ago such values were considered morally doubtful if not totally evil. Such an individualistic attitude is more likely to be adopted by a younger generation of managers. Studies of the recent changes in the Japanese management culture strongly support this hypothesis (Seethi, Namiki, and Swanson, 1984). In some cultures, however, strong ties of solidarity, togetherness, and conformity serve to moderate this individualistic attitude (Forss, Hawk, and Hedlund, 1984; Kostera, 1990).

Cultural flexibility and adaptability to the new environments and the ability to develop cultural empathy are becoming standard requirements for today's managers (Harris and Moran, 1987). Mechanical transplants of Western management to some third world countries (such as Iran under the Shah) clearly indicate that danger.

Successful managers and rich entrepreneurs have become folk heroes within the Triad: millions of copies of biographies of Iacocca, Geneene, and Tapie are sold all over the world. Similar phenomena can be observed in the former Soviet Republics and Eastern Europe undergoing transition to the market economy. Russia has its Tarasov and Kadiroff, Poland its Gawronik, and Hungary its Szeles and Rubik.

The English language (or rather its simplified version, which might be called "global English") has been universally adopted as a global management communication vehicle (Kuffner, 1988). Working knowledge of business English by managers preconditions cooperation between enterprises across the borders and entering into partnerships. In this key dimension postcommunist managers in Eastern and Central Europe have a long way to go but they know it and make an effort especially visible in contact with the younger generation.

GLOBAL COMPETITORS

Global competition and high-speed management require new enterprises capable of meeting the new challenges of the global arena. The new global competitive environment has altered considerably both behavioral patterns and internal characteristics of traditional multinational companies dominant in the 1960s, 1970s, and early 1980s.

1. Today's global winners seek global leadership in a relatively wide range of somewhat related products. Global leadership means one of the handful of dominating positions on the Triad markets with strong inroads into other markets (South

American, third world, Eastern European). The notion of "somewhat related products" is certainly not precise but adequate to the complex reality. These products can be related on different grounds, such as common core technologies and research base (ABB); common distribution channels and marketing skills (Philip Morris); common sets of management skills required to develop, manufacture, and sell the products (3M); or common characteristics of the client base (airlines, global hotel and restaurant chains). Such criteria are not mutually exclusive and often coexist within one global company.

2. Global winners spend much more than average in the industry on research and development of new products and environmental scanning.

3. Successful global players are extremely active in international acquisitions, mergers, partnerships, alliances, joint ventures, and sellouts. The logic behind such frenetic activity is to consolidate and reinforce the firm's position on the fastest growing markets where global leadership is possible and to get rid of declining products and markets or those where global leadership is out of the firm's reach.

4. Global competitors are also active in acquiring and developing the most valuable human resources: managerial, engineering, marketing, and scientific talents.

5. Enterprises practicing global management and success in global competition have a visibly powerful strategic thrust and constantly develop and update long-range strategic plans.

6. The emerging group of global players is characterized by the giant size of individual firms. These firms employ hundreds of thousands of people in dozens of countries all over the world with a strong concentration within the Triad. Such firms can easily mobilize enormous human, material, and financial resources required by high-speed management. They usually have their own internal capital-generating financial institutions, such as GE Financial Services.

7. The new global competitors combine strong leadership both in functional and product matters with a high degree of autonomy of SBUs (strategic business units), encouraging entrepreneurship, innovation, and initiative. Decentralization does not inhibit tight financial controls and close monitoring of the financial performance of all the organizational units.

8. Global enterprises are extremely communication-intensive. Vertical and horizontal communication links imposed by high-speed management require both high technology and high interpersonal communication skills. Spontaneous, across the border communication flows enable better coordination and dissemination of the best practices within the organization as well as rapid restructuring of newly acquired companies.

9. Leading global companies have distinctive organizational cultures highly internalized by the core personnel. These companies are headed by charismatic leaders such as GE's Jack Welch or ABB's Percy Barnevik, who have a clear vision of what their companies should become in the next century.

10. Global winners operate at the minimum employment level and constantly increase value-added per employee. Their staffs are "lean and mean," unstructured and highly mobile.

In spite of all the similarities among the emerging global players two distinctively different types of such enterprises can be identified: integrated diversity companies and multidomestic companies. The expression "integrated diversity" comes from GE's Jack Welch (Quickel, 1990, p. 66) and GE is the best example of such a company. The expression "multidomestic company" comes from ABB's Percy Barnevik (Taylor, 1991) and Asea Brown Boveri Ltd. exemplifies the characteristic features of such a company.

Integrated diversity companies are visibly dominated by one strong management culture (such as American, German, or Japanese) with an attitude of superiority. Nearly all top management positions are held by representatives of one nationality. The same applies to the subsidiaries located outside the home base country. Key management positions are given to the representatives of the dominant nationality or at best to the perfectly acculturated veteran company insiders usually foreign to the countries where they operate. In other words, in integrated diversity companies, foreign subsidiaries are run by expatriates.

Integrated diversity companies keep their "brains" concentrated in the home base country, where they work on research and development, strategic planning, training, and management development. Such an arrangement somewhat centralizes global integration and coordination processes. The organizational structure of integrated diversity companies facilitates this centralization.

Strategic business units of integrated diversity companies are not local but global; they cover the whole world market of a given group of products. These SBUs are huge global organizations themselves.

Multidomestic companies, in contrast, are "melting pots" of many different national management cultures. None of them dominates the others. Top management is composed of representatives of many different nationalities and local subsidiaries are managed entirely by local managers. This enables them to pass for local companies and to be accepted as such by local communities.

Research and development, strategy formulation, training and development, coordination of complex product groups, and other "brain-intensive" activities are dispersed in different and often changing locations. Coordination in multidomestic companies is clearly focused on the key issues common to all the subunits of the company: mastering core technologies and building platforms for synergy effect.

Multidomestic companies are composed of large numbers (in some cases thousands) of relatively small local companies—distinctive profit centers. These locally managed and autonomous companies are "double-coordinated" within the framework of a matrix structure: on the national subsidiary level (such as ABB Germany or ABB Poland) and on the worldwide business segments level (such as industry systems or power distribution). Sometimes these large business segments are broken down into smaller business areas such as power transformers or electric metering (using ABB's example again). Such an extremely complicated structure requires informal and unstructured communication and perfect knowledge of common goals and strategies brought down to the operational level.

Since integrated diversity companies such as GE, Siemens, and Matsushita are relatively well known and often described in the literature, ABB will be presented as an example of multidomestic company.

ASEA BROWN BOVERI LTD.

Asea Brown Boveri Ltd., known as ABB, is the world's largest electrotechnical corporation, with revenues approaching $27 billion and with nearly 215,000 employees in over 1,100 companies and 4,500 profit centers operating in 140 countries. Its Swedish CEO, Percy Barnevik, is certainly one of the most outspoken European managers. Thirty-one percent of ABB's sales come from the EEC countries; 26 percent from European Free Trade Association (EFTA); 21 percent from North America; 15 percent from Asia and Australasia; 7 percent from Africa, Eastern Europe, and Latin America combined. Thirty-three percent of the group's employees work in the EEC countries; 32 percent in EFTA countries; 16 percent in North America; 9 percent in Asia and Australasia; and 10 percent in Africa, Eastern Europe, and Latin America (ABB, 1991, pp. 2–3).

ABB is much less diversified than GE: its business remains concentrated around electrical engineering. ABB is the world leader in the generation, transmission, and distribution of electrical power. This is the traditional core of its business, which is still responsible for almost half of the sales. Other businesses, however, are also electrical energy related. The most prominent among them are transportation (mainly electrical trains), environmental control technologies, and industrial automation and control. ABB is the world's largest manufacturer of industrial robots (ABB, 1991, pp. 2–3).

Worldwide business operations of ABB are organized into eight business segments: power plants, power distribution, industry systems, transportation systems, environmental control technologies, financial services, and various activities. Each business segment oversees several business areas. For example, the various activities business segment includes such areas as motors, robotics, superchargers, telecommunication, communication and information systems, service, integrated circuits, installation materials, power lines, and general contracting, district heating, and energy ventures (ABB, 1991).

In 1990 the ABB group invested over $1.4 billion in research and development and employed 11,000 highly qualified scientists and engineers. Research activities are carried out by a network of corporate research centers in Finland, Germany, Italy, Norway, Sweden, Switzerland, and the United States. Corporate research centers focus on basic research in such areas as high-power semiconductors, fuel cells, high-voltage insulations, high-temperature superconductors, combustion and energy, and software and computer science. Basic research involves frequent collaboration with leading universities and research institutes. Corporate research centers also serve more practical purposes. They help to ensure development of resources of broad interest to business areas.

Ninety percent of the total R&D budget goes directly to the business areas for development of their next-generation products. Corporate research centers assist in this process but business areas closest to the marketplace play a decisive role in assuring technological vitality and leadership of the group. Results are impressive. ABB has developed the world's most advanced high-voltage direct current (HVDC) submarine cable now linking Sweden to Denmark, which has set new records in voltage and power ratings. Studies in combustion process resulted in a breakthrough gas turbine burner concept. The power transmission segment is benefiting from advances in transformers, high-voltage equipment, relays, and introduction of fiber-optic technology (ABB, 1991, pp. 4–5).

ABB's income before taxes was $536 million in 1988 and $589 million in 1990. It has 17 percent return on working capital. Because of its huge liquid reserves estimated at $3.5 billion in 1988 and at $3.9 billion in 1990, ABB is constantly expanding its business through a series of mergers and acquisitions rather than alliances. Barnevik believes that ABB is setting a new pattern for European industrial restructuring but he is not satisfied with the pace and depth of change: "I worry that many European alliances are poor substitutes for doing what we try to do—complete mergers and cross-border rationalization" (Taylor, 1991, p. 100).

ABB resulted from the merger of two famous European companies (Swedish ASEA created in 1890 and Swiss Brown Boveri created in 1891). ABB, which is headquartered in Zurich, Switzerland, functions as an operating company combining all assets and holding responsibility for its Swiss and Swedish parents who have become holding companies while maintaining their previous status of stock companies listed on national stock exchanges (Arbose, 1988, pp. 25–26).

Barnevik took over ASEA as a centralized traditional electrical equipment manufacturer whose profits and sales hardly kept up with inflation. Explains Barnevik:

Revenues in 1987 were 4 times greater than in 1980, profits were 10 times greater and our market value was 20 times greater. But the handwriting was on the wall. The European electrical industry was crowded with 20 national competitors. There was up to 50% overcapacity, high costs, little cross-border trade. Half the companies were losing money. The creation of ABB started the painful but long overdue-process of restructuring. (Taylor, 1991, p. 100)

Between 1987 and 1991 ABB acquired a minority position in sixty companies representing investments worth $3.6 billion. Among them are two major acquisitions in the United States. In 1989 ABB acquired Westinghouse's transmission and distribution operations. The deal involved twenty-five businesses generating yearly revenues of $1 billion. The same year ABB invested $1.6 billion in the acquisition of Combustion Engineering, well known for its technological leadership in manufacturing power generation and process automation equipment (Taylor, 1991, p. 91). Other major acquisitions included 40 percent participation in the British railway manufacturing group BREL; takeover and reconstruction of the CCC group, Spain's largest electrotechnical manufacturer; acquisition of the German automation company MTA GmbH; and acquisition of Emerson Electric's Industrial Service Division.

In some cases ABB enters alliances and cooperation agreements. Agreement with Matsushita Electric Industrial Co. Ltd. serves as an example. It stipulates that MEI will sell and distribute ABB robotic products on the Japanese market as well as buy ABB robots for internal use (ABB, 1989, p. 4).

ABB's unprecedented global expansion and success can be explained by the uniqueness of its strategy, leadership, and management culture. Let us examine them briefly.

A good example of ABB's strategy is its approach to newly acquired U.S. boiler manufacturer Combustion Engineering, which represents eighty years of excellence in this technology. The company fell into financial trouble during the 1980s because of the severe downturn in the industry. Explains Barnevik:

> Today, however, the business is coming back and we have a game plan for the United States. We plan to beef up the Windsor research centre to three or four times its current size. We want to tie Windsor's work in new materials, emission reduction and pollution control technology with new

technologies from our European labs. That will let us respond more effectively to the environmental concerns here. Then we want to combine Combustion's strength in boilers with ABB's strength in turbines and generators and Westinghouse's strength in transmission and distribution to become a broad and unique supplier to the U.S. utility industry. We also have an ambition for Combustion to become much more active in world markets, not with sales agents but through the ABB multi-domestic network. (Taylor, 1991, p. 105)

Mastering core technologies and assuming technological leadership in all the business areas where ABB competes worldwide enables it to be a unique supplier. ABB carefully combines and pools the unique R&D capabilities and accomplishments existing in its growing worldwide network. Cross-fertilizing and international cooperation in R&D are not only encouraged but planned and organized.

Because of technological leadership, ASEA was able to beat GE on a big Amtrak order for locomotives on the Metroliner between New York and Washington. Over ten years of research on high-speed trains paid off: ASEA was the only one able to run the trains at 125 miles per hour safely in spite of the poor condition of the track. For the first time in history American railroads bought locomotives from abroad. Since 1987 this experience has been merged with Brown Boveri's pioneering in AC technology. That is why ABB is a major player in development of the high-speed rail network in Europe.

ABB's operations enable them to push cross-border economies of scale. ABB has all over the world factories highly specialized in components and doing ten times the volume of competitors. To explain this strategy Barnevik once again points to the locomotive business: one of the newly acquired plants builds power electronics for all the locomotives they sell in Europe (Taylor, 1991, pp. 92–93). That specialization creates enormous cost and quality advantages over fragmented European competition. (There are still in Western Europe twenty-four companies building locomotives, some of them only ten or twenty a year, while the United States has only two such companies and Japan three.) Business segments and business areas along with corporate research are responsible for pushing that specialization as much as possible in all ABB's lines of business.

When it comes to orders from clients with distinct nationality, ABB is following the "think global, act local" principle. Local national companies are headed and staffed by local nationals; employed local engineers and workers are registered on local stock exchanges and work closely with clients during the design, manufacture, delivery, installation, and service of the product. Because of that stress on being local, ABB is able to win huge government contracts such as the $420 million "order of the century" from the Swiss Federal Railways to build locomotives that will move freight through the Alps and eliminate polluting trucks or Norwegian government contracts for supplying the country's landmark oil industry. It is also able to adjust to local conditions and conduct in many countries such "super local" businesses as electrical installation and service completely determined by local regulations, technical infrastructure, and the like (Taylor, 1991).

ABB's strategy is somewhat paradoxical: they want to be global and local, big and small, centralized and decentralized.

The contradiction between global and local is resolved through the "multidomestic enterprise" (another of the company's buzz expressions). Barnevik describes it somewhat poetically as follows: "We are a federation of national companies with a global coordination centre. We are not homeless, we have many homes" (Taylor, 1991, p. 91). The multidomestic character of the company is reflected in its matrix structure (Agthe, 1990).

Business segments and business areas are the global side of the matrix. Managers responsible for them craft strategy, decide product mixes, allocate markets to different factories, decide how factories should pool their expertise and research funds, and track engineering and managerial talents. They work with multinational teams of managers, experts, and engineers and have a totally global perspective.

Country managers are the local side of the matrix. They stay close to the local markets, cultivate client and government relations, negotiate with local trade unions, guarantee compliance with local laws and regulations, and assure that companies are perceived as local by local customers, local authorities, and the local community. At the same time, however, they have to know and respect the company's global strategies and policies.

The global scope of ABB's activities and its constant dealings with many local governments make some observers think that companies like ABB symbolize a power shift from national governments to supranational companies. Comments Barnevik: "Are we above governments? No. We answer to governments. We obey the laws in every country in which we operate and we don't make the laws. However we do change relations between countries. We function as a lubricant for worldwide economic integration" (Taylor, 1991, p. 105). Multinational companies negotiate with the host governments on specific issues such as incentives and performance requirements. These negotiations are closely related to a given business segment (Prahalad and Doz, 1987, p. 99) and at ABB are mainly conducted by country management. Country management, however, is bounded by overall (global company) policy and is backed by global resources and global influence. ABB is conscious of the fact that it can play one government against others in trying to improve the business climate for its operations. "Today I can tell Swedish authorities that they must create a more competitive environment for R&D or our research there will decline" (Taylor, 1991, p. 105).

Global and local perspectives meet at the level of over 1,200 individual local companies with an average of only two hundred employees, some of them broken down into a couple of different profit centers (with an average of fifty employees). Local companies' managers are expected to be excellent profit center managers and to cope successfully with the ambiguity inevitably resulting from having two bosses: a country manager and a business area manager. They have to balance local and global perspectives. But first of all they have full responsibility for the profitability of their operations; they have real shareholders; they have to pay real dividends and solve cash flow problems on their own. In short, they are intended to come as close to individual small entrepreneurs as possible. In such a way internal contradiction between being small and being big is solved. ABB is clearly following the "small within big" pattern (Agthe, 1990).

The contradiction between centralization and decentralization is solved through a centralized, highly sophisticated reporting system combined with considerable freedom of action at the lowest levels of the hierarchy.

A reporting system called Abacus collects monthly performance data on all 4,500 profit centers and compares actual performance with planned objectives, budgets, and forecasts. Data collected in local currencies are all translated into U.S. dollars to enable comparisons. The system can aggregate and desegregate results by business segments, business areas, regions, and companies within countries as well as profit centers within companies.

Access to Abacus enables thirteen members of the executive committee responsible for each business segment to monitor constantly all the major developments within the company. When something strikes their attention, they do not start automatically giving orders but rather try to get more information and to dialogue with the managers about the issue. Members of the executive committee meet every three weeks in different parts of the world for the whole day and discuss key issues (Agthe, 1990).

A monitoring system is not meant to lead to interference with decision making by ABB's operatives in the field. Middle and lower-level managers are encouraged to react as quickly as possible to take advantage of opportunities and to avoid threats. Speed even at the expense of precision is Barnevik's religion. As he explains: "Finally you have to accept a fair share of mistakes. I tell my people that if we make 100 decisions and 70 turn out to be right, that's good enough. I'd rather be roughly right and fast than exactly right and slow" (Taylor, 1991, p. 101).

Breaking ABB down into small quasi-independent, autonomous units leaves higher levels of the hierarchy with support and coordination functions. The monitoring system makes informed intervention from above still possible in exceptional situations, especially during restructuring. Top management remains a chief architect of the system, designing it, overseeing construction, and selecting builders and operators. Such a system intended to harmonize centralization and decentralization makes ABB ever thirsty for management talent.

Immediately after ABB was created Barnevik, deputy CEO Thomas Gasser, and the personnel directors of both merging companies spent literally days and nights interviewing and cross-interviewing hundreds of managers. Recalls Barnevik: "It was a tremendous people exercise with Gasser and I personally interviewing at least 100 managers each. Before I began, I warned our personnel directors: Say goodbye to your families. You are going to do more work in three months than most personnel directors do in 30 years" (Arbose, 1988, p. 27). In such a careful selection process emphasis was placed on identifying flexible individuals who could operate in a complex and turbulent multicultural environment, had strong leadership potential, and felt at ease taking risks. Once again explains Barnevik: "We sought people capable of becoming superstars, tough-skinned individuals who were strong on their feet, had good technical and commercial background and had demonstrated the ability to lead others" (Arbose, 1988, p. 27). ABB needs literally thousands of such managers to resolve its internal contradictions between global and local, big and small, centralized and decentralized.

The issue of management talent leads us to the next group of factors conditioning ABB's success: leadership, management style, and management culture.

Barnevik himself is a unique business leader to whom ABB owes a great deal of its expansion and success. This turned-around artist and MBA graduate of the Gotheborg School of Economics in Sweden is a truly cosmopolitan manager. He has ten years' experience in the United States, where he attended Stanford University for two years before working for Swedish Axel Johnson Group and Sandvik AB. He also lived and worked in France, Italy, and Germany. Not long after his thirty-ninth birthday Barnevik was nominated CEO of ASEA, and after turning it around he engineered a merger with Swiss BBC leading to the creation of ABB. Barnevik gained a buccaneer's reputation for adventurism, speed, and ruthlessness.

In a 1988 internal GE publication, Paolo Fresco, then senior vice president of international operations, described Barnevik in the following way:

> The lights are going out all over Europe, and the buccaneers have been turned loose. Among them is Percy Barnevik—this Swede with the beard who swings from country to country like the actor Errol Flynn, cutting deals and forming alliances. In six weeks he put together the Asea-Brown Boveri deal and formed a $15 billion power systems company. This product of socialist Sweden is calling for a reduction of 50,000 jobs in Europe, for delayering, down-

sizing and rationalizing—all alien terms in socialist lexicon. A self-described enemy of incrementalism, his announced intention is to strengthen his U.S. position. A convalescing GE Power Systems may find him the most formidable adversary it has ever faced. (Arbose, 1988, p. 25)

In the years that followed, Fresco was proven to be 100 percent right.

In spite of the fact that only 30 percent of ABB's managers are native English speakers, Barnevik insisted on making English the official language of the company, enabling communication between different nationalities. ABB's thirteen-member executive committee is a mixture of Swedes, Swiss, Germans, and Americans. Barnevik's deputy Thomas Gasser is German. What is more important is that all national companies are headed by locals and staffed predominantly by locals. This enables them to keep a national character. Top management is completely multinational and so is the management of business segments and business areas. In spite of the fact that ABB is headquartered in Zurich, Switzerland, most of the members of the executive committee are not stationed there. Eberhard von Koerber, the member of the executive committee located in Manheim, Germany, is responsible for Germany, Austria, Italy, and Eastern Europe as well as worldwide business area installation materials and some staff functions. Gerhard Schulmeyer, stationed in Stamford, Connecticut, is responsible for the North American region and the industry systems business segment. The business area leader for power transformers, who coordinates twenty-five factories in sixteen countries, is Swede Sune Karlsson, vice president of ABB who works out of Mannheim, Germany. The business area leader for instrumentation is British and the business area leader for electric metering is an American based in North Carolina. Meetings of the executive committee are held all over the world, and Barnevik himself travels two hundred days a year. Zurich headquarters mainly plays a role as a post box.

Barnevik is known for practicing a very direct and informal management style but shows a lot of sensitivity to cultural differences. He believes in understanding and showing tolerance for cultural differences without being paralyzed by them. According to him, global managers should understand both the very formal style of German managers and the forcefully informal American style, and they should feel comfortable enough with both styles to concentrate on issues. Global managers should "sort through the debris of cultural excuses and find opportunities to innovate" (Taylor, 1991, p. 94). They have to separate communication style from the content and concentrate on the meaning of a message. People form such qualities by living in various places in the world, taking longer assignments in foreign countries, and constantly participating in mixed nationality teams.

A global company like ABB needs only a relatively restricted core group of truly global managers, 500 out of 15,000 managers. Others should be locals, fully adjusted to their respective environments and capable of top performance in their native setting. Global managers, however, should set up a stage, enabling smooth cooperation between different individuals and groups within the company. This does not necessarily mean too much softness and oversensitivity. Barnevik believes in quick, decisive moves and rapid, radical restructuring, dealing with confrontation when necessary (Arbose, 1988). He explains it in the following way: "Restructuring operations creates a lot of pain and heartache, so many companies choose not to begin the process, to avoid the pain" (Taylor, 1991, p. 101). He believes in speed: "You must avoid the 'investigation trap'—you can't postpone tough decisions by studying them to death. You can't permit a 'honeymoon' of small changes over a year or two. A long series of small changes just prolongs the pain" (Taylor, 1991, p. 101). Barnevik resists everything that slows him down, legal procedures included. That is why his "deal of the century" between ASEA and Brown Boveri was finalized in just six weeks. "There were no lawyers, no auditors, no environmental investigations and no due diligence" (Taylor, 1991, p. 101). He was able to avoid political obstacles that could potentially block the deal, such as the powerful Swedish trade unions resisting the fact that the headquarters of a century-old Swedish industrial jewel (ASEA) was moved to Switzerland—a country where unions do not have the same political leverage as in Sweden.

ABB's history is full of examples of radical restructuring processes. Layingoff workers is only a minor part of ABB's recipe. For example, immediately after the merger between ASEA and BBC, BBC's disproportionably large German operation was reduced by four thousand workers (10 percent of the workforce) (Arbose, 1988). Similar cuts took place in all factories acquired by ABB. Much more radical cuts, however, are reserved for management ranks. Barnevik believes in a "lean and mean" staff and management personnel reduced to the bare minimum. He explains:

> We operate as lean as humanly possible. It's no accident that there are only 100 people at ABB headquarters in Zurich. The closer we get to top management the tougher we have to be with head count. I believe you can go into any traditionally centralized corporation and cut its headquarters staff by 90% in one year. You spin-off 30% of the staff into free standing service centres that perform real work— treasury functions, legal services—and charge for it. You decentralize 30% of the staff—human resources for example—by pushing them into the line organization. Then 30% disappears through head count reductions. (Taylor, 1991, p. 99)

This philosophy has been applied many times. For example, when ASEA acquired Stromberg in Finland there were 880 people in headquarters; in 1991 only 25 left. In the Mannheim headquarters of the BBC's German operation, there were 1,600 people; in 1991, 100. Respective figures for Stamford, Connecticut, headquarters of Combustion Engineering are 600 and 100. Instead of avoiding the issue of reforming management and rationalizing operations, ABB confronts it openly and immediately after closing the deal and does it quickly and without hesitation. Because of that approach when smoke and dust fade away those who stay (workers, unions management), realize that they have a much better and more stable company to work for and forget about protests and grievances. This was the case of restructuring of oversized ABB Germany, where Eberhard von Koerber who led the effort had to confront violent demonstrations and strikes organized by the unions as well as silent resistance from the managers (Arbose, 1988).

A small staff and less management result from a strong belief in informal "horizontal" management style closely linked to the decentralization principle. As Agthe puts it, such a management style "substitutes collegiality and teamwork for hierarchical structure and it places the highest premium on entrepreneurial spirit" (Agthe, 1990, p. 41). Such management philosophy reduces the number of layers in management structures, increases the span of control, and relies on personal competence, integrity, and superior leadership rather than elaborated formal regulations. ABB's managers are supposed to provide strong leadership without being dictatorial. Their power and influence should be based on vision, competence, entrepreneurial spirit, and ability to mobilize and motivate people by releasing their own creativity and channeling it toward common goals.

Formalization is largely postponed and replaced by a "play it by ear" principle applied to competent, well-informed, and highly self-motivated managers, who behave like entrepreneurs looking for opportunities to seize the initiative and assume responsibility for success and failure. Entrepreneurial managers go beyond assigned tasks to pursue their personal goals. As Agthe puts it: "the organization does not move the entrepreneur, rather the entrepreneur moves the organization" (Agthe, 1990, p. 42).

Horizontal management philosophy puts faith in the people making decisions rather than in the formalization of the corporate structure. Such an approach serves well in contemporary global business environments marked by constant change, considerably shortening reaction times required to get ahead of the competition and making mistakes deadlier than before, when the global economy was not yet integrated in the form of the Triad. In such an environment speed becomes more important than coordination through bureaucratic procedures. "Above all, the entrepreneurial approach enables the competent manager to translate the worldwide business segment plan into effective action at the country or local level" (Agthe, 1990, p. 43).

The horizontal approach to management as practiced by ABB requires an enormous amount of unstructured information to be exchanged between corporate levels and units along with structured information such as Abacus. Says Barnevik: "you don't inform, you over-inform" (Taylor, 1991, p. 104). This means that a tendency to be selective about sharing information has to be overcome. Barnevik himself meets with five thousand people a year in big and small groups. Working sessions include managers from all over the world, discussing such practical topics as cutting cycle times, raising quality, or squeezing accounts receivable.

Such sessions take usually two or three days. Managers from different parts of the globe live in close quarters, where they communicate, discuss, work out solutions, and meet with several members of the executive committee for an open, honest dialogue. In such a communication-intensive environment cultural diversity becomes a prized asset, offering multifocal perspective as a key to success for multidomestic enterprises.

Intensive communication processes involving many well-established informal or loosely structured communication channels and platforms help the negotiation process within the company by facilitating informal coordination of different spontaneous activities resulting from the entrepreneurial spirit of hundreds of managers. It also helps demonstrate the benefits of being part of the federation of companies called ABB.

CONCLUSION: THE COMING SHAPE OF GLOBAL COMPETITION

It is difficult to judge to what extent multidomestic company types will inspire the new breed of global competitors. As of now, the integrated diversity company model is dominating but some elements of multidomestic enterprises such as locally managed, highly autonomous foreign subsidiaries or holding companies are becoming increasingly popular. It is also hard to determine which of the two types of global competitors will dominate in the future. It can be taken for granted, however, that both of them will dramatically change the shape of global competition. Some of the most important of these changes are inevitable.

The number of industries becoming global is rapidly increasing and this trend will continue due to the spread of high technology to previously less advanced industries such as services, retailing, and garment and textile and to globalization processes (homogenization of consumer tastes and needs, standardization of technical and safety requirements and legal systems, globalization of logistic and financial networks). These processes will contribute to the consolidation of industries worldwide, to the elimination of smaller, less innovative, and less aggressive competitors, and to the emergence of a few major players in most of the industries. The European "white goods" industry (appliances) is undergoing such a process right now.

In such a business environment, successful implementation of high-speed management principles and mastering of its techniques are becoming keys to global competition. As a consequence, the club of global players is becoming increasingly exclusive. High-speed management requires huge financial material and human resources combined with technological leadership, management sophistication, effective communication marketing of the global reach, and a distinctive organizational culture. Very few companies can accumulate all this "under one roof."

New pools of economic development and social progress will emerge in the countries or regions that create the most hospitable and friendly environment for global companies. Different forms of cooperation with global competitors (subcontracting, supplying, selling, servicing, etc.) will also offer some opportunities for future growth. Countries and regions "forgotten" by global companies for various reasons (such as political instability, social unrest, hostile attitude of the government, or lack of coherent and stable economic and industrial policy) will almost certainly find themselves unable to overcome economic underdevelopment. As a result the global economy is likely to be represented by four concentric circles, with the core Triad markets in the center followed by "close periphery" markets intensively cooperating with the global companies (and aspiring to join the Triad), distant periphery markets marginally cooperating, and "forgotten orphans" living on scarce and shrinking internal resources and humanitarian aid from the Triad.

Global companies will gradually become more and more international and closer to a multidomestic model. The ones that now have it will gradually lose their clearly national character. They will not be able to afford to serve "national interests" of any kind.

Consolidation of enterprises and industries will continue in parallel with consolidation of markets. National markets merging into free trade zones will gradually evolve toward supranational organizations and eventually supranational governments conducting supranational economic and industrial policies and regulating global competition. Growing interdependence between economies and supranational economic regions will increasingly keep national governments from shaping independently economic policies without consulting major partners. The economic environment of global competition will become more and more "negotiable" between major partners (economic superpowers, supranational economic organizations, and major global corporations). "Minor" partners will have to follow in order to promote their growth and eventually join the club.

Global competition dominated by giant companies will enable small and medium-size businesses to exploit remaining local markets or very specific, narrow niches in the global markets (mainly high-tech and luxury goods). Most of these small companies, however, will be somehow linked to the global players.

REFERENCES

ABB. 1989. *Six Months Report.* Zurich: ABB.

―――. 1991. *The Art of Being Local Worldwide.* Zurich: ABB Marketing Services.

Agthe, K. E. 1990. Managing the mixed marriage. *Business Horizons* (Jan.–Feb.):37–43.

Arbose, J. 1988. ABB—the new energy powerhouse. *International Management* (June):24–30.

Barlett, C. A., and S. Ghosal. 1987. Managing across borders: New strategic requirements. *Sloan Management Review* (Summer):7–16.

Bernthal, W. F. 1962. Value perspectives in management decisions. *Academy of Management Journal* 5:150–96.

Cushman, D., and S. King. 1987. The impact of high technology on international management. In R. Shuter and S. Chatarjea, eds., *International Management and Comparative Management Systems.* Wawatosa, Wis.: Cultural Press.

―――. 1989. The role of communication in high-technology organizations: The emergence of high-speed management. In S. S. King (ed.), *Human Communication as a Field of Study: Selected Contemporary Views.* Albany, N.Y.: SUNY Press.

Forss, K., D. Hawk, and G. Hedlund. 1984. *Cultural Differences— Swedishness in Legislation, Multinational Corporations and Aid Administration.* Stockholm: Institute of International Business, Stockholm Handelshogskola.

Hamel, G., Y. Doz, and C. K. Prahalad. 1989. Collaborate with your competitors and win. *Harvard Business Review* (Jan.–Feb.):133–39.

Harris, P. R., and R. T. Moran. 1987. *Managing Cultural Differences: High Performance Strategies for Today's Global Manager.* Houston: Gulf.

Hopkins, T. H., et al. 1982. *World System Analysis: Theory and Methodology.* Beverly Hills: Sage.

Kostera, M. 1990. Szwedzki Styl Zarzadzania (Swedish Management Style). Unpublished doctoral dissertation, University of Warsaw.

Kozminski, A. K. 1993. Global management: A new road to social progress. In A. K. Kozminski and D. Cushman, eds., *Organizational Communication and Management: A Global Perspective,* Albany, N.Y.: SUNY Press.

Kuffner, K. 1988. English: The common language of Europeans. *International Management* 4(42):24–29.

Ohmae, K. 1985. *Triad Power: The Coming Shape of Global Competition.* New York: Free Press.

———. 1987. The Triad world view. *Journal of Business Strategy* (Spring):8–19.

Perlmutter, H. V., and D. A. Heenan. 1986. Cooperate to compete globally. *Harvard Business Review* (Mar.–Apr.):132–52.

Porter, M. E. 1986. Changing patterns of international competition. *California Management Review* 2(28):9–40.

Prahalad, C. K., and Y. Doz. 1987. *The Multinational Mission: Balancing Local Demands and Global Vision.* New York: Free Press.

Quickel, S. W. 1990. Welch on Welch. *Financial World* (Apr. 3):62–70.

Schonberger, R. 1987. *World Class Manufacturing.* New York: Free Press.

Seethi, S. P., N. Namiki, and C. L. Swanson. 1984. The decline of the Japanese system of management. *California Management Review* 4(24):35–45.

Taylor, W. 1991. The logic of global business: An interview with ABB's Percy Barnevik. *Harvard Business Review* (Mar.–Apr.):91–105.

CHAPTER FOUR

High-Speed Management, Environmental Scanning, and Coalignment of External Resources: Strategic Alliances

Branislav Kovacic

Organizational communication guided by high-speed management principles is a web of three interrelated mechanisms, processes, and activities: (1) scanning of environmental (external) organizational interdependencies, (2) tracking of internal organizational interdependencies, and (3) continuous improvement programs aimed at achieving coalignment of external and internal interdependencies.

However, high-speed management is also a way of intertwining continuous improvement programs—what some call a "deepening" model of organizational development (Clegg, 1990; Ergas, 1987; Ewer, Higgins, and Stevens, 1987, chap. 4)—and a discontinuous organizational improvement/change or "shifting" model of organizational development (Clegg, 1990; Kenney and Florida, 1988).

Global corporations must achieve coalignment in the form of flexible linkages between internal (organizational) and external (environmental) resources. This requires the strategic use of frequently conflicting interests, concerns, and contributions of an organization's "internal" stakeholders (managers and workers) and "external" stakeholders (stockholders, customers, competitors, suppliers, government, and social movements) in order to achieve a value-added competitive advantage. The role of high-speed organizational communication is to provide mechanisms for an exchange of information concerning interests, concerns, and contributions of different stakeholders/audiences in such a manner that management can forge a sustained value-added competitive advantage. Interests are defined as reasons for and expectations from linkages, concerns as justified and/or unjustified worries about partners' real motives and competencies, and contributions as value-adding, unique competencies that partners are willing to share.

This chapter argues that environmental scanning helps achieve a sustained, value-added competitive advantage only if it satisfies a certain number of necessary conditions. By continually tracking external organizational interdependencies, environmental scanning provides information necessary for coalignment—in the form of strategic alliances—between an organization and its relevant environment.

TYPES OF UNCERTAINTY

Global corporations need three general types of information about interdependence: (1) information regarding the economic, political, and cultural trends in the global political economy; (2) information regarding industry-market unique dynamics; and (3) information on internal organizational processes and activities. In general, interdependence can be defined as a link between elements in any system. Interdependence can be pooled (a common set of resources); sequential (a linear, input-output chain); or reciprocal (mutual causality).

The global system is characterized by the interpenetration of three types of practices and institutions on the global level: economic (transnational corporations as globally coordinated business systems); political (international managerial class that identifies with the capitalist global economy); and cultural (a global "business culture," converging life-styles and consumption patterns, and values of consumerism) (Sklair, 1991; Gill and Law, 1988). This global political economy rests on hierarchically ranked channels of interdependence or social integration between countries such as political and military (security) alliances; international money and financial institutions and practices; global production and transfer of knowledge and technology; and global trade (Gill and Law, 1988).

Value Chains and Value Systems

Each industry can be described in terms of its unique interdependencies operationalized as a "value system" composed of a certain number of "value chains" that summarize each company's distinct technological and economic activities (Porter, 1985; Porter and Millar, 1985). From the focal firm's point of view, this entails linkages between its own value chain and the value chains of its suppliers, distributors, and buyers. These linkages (interdependencies)—whether they dovetail or contradict each other—may be in the form of competitive, free-market transactions or interorganizational (sub)contracting.

Within the firm itself the value chain consists of adjacent, interdependent, discrete activities such as product design, engineering, purchasing, manufacturing, distribution, sales, and service (Rockart and Short, 1989). Traditionally, links between these functional activities were optimized (strategic trade-offs) and coordinated (Porter and Millar, 1985), independent of a firm's suppliers and customers. This multistage value-added chain can be collapsed into three macro-organizational activities or business processes: (1) product development (design, engineering, and purchasing); (2) product delivery (purchasing, manufacturing, and distribution); and (3) customer service and management (distribution, sales, and service) (Rockart and Short, 1991).

From the focal firm's point of view, the global political economy is operationalized as a set of external value chains. Its industries-markets are operationalized as subsets of external value chains. An organization's internal interdependencies are operationalized as its internal value chain. These operationalizations of interdependencies incorporate, in an ascendant manner, role-based interactions and face-to-face communication (for conceptual distinctions, see Boudon and Bourricaud, 1989).

Different combinations of role-based interactions and face-to-face communication have serious implications for environmental scanning.

Environmental Scanning

To achieve a continual improvement of coalignment between external and internal organizational interdependencies (value chains), global corporations must possess a fast and accurate intelligence system that scans (monitors and evaluates) rapid changes in an organization's external environment, and enables reorientation of organizational strategy, structure, resources, and performance. A successful environmental scanning requires the creation of a full-time scanning unit (Keegan, 1980).

Environmental scanning is a highly systematic process of information acquisition (collection) and evaluation (Keegan, 1980). This global information system is organized around three necessary axes. The *scope axis* distinguishes between extensive scanning of only a few dimensions of a large number of heteregeneous external value chains, and intensive scanning of a large number of dimensions of "homogeneous" external value chains (Geertz, 1978). The *mode axis* separates passive (surveillance) scanning of messages regarding external value chains that simply cross the scanning attention field from active (search) scanning of information on external value chains needed for specific purpose (Keegan, 1980). The *topics axis* divides scanning of the global political economy operationalized as a set of external value chains from scanning of industry-market unique dynamics operationalized as subsets of external value chains. The former focuses on political and military (security) alliances, international money and financial institutions and practices, global production and transfer of knowledge and technology, and global trade (Gill and Law, 1988). The latter concentrates on the value process–product-market life cycle intersection (Collins and Doorley, 1991; Macdonald, 1991; Rockart and Short, 1991; Vernon, 1966, 1979).

Research findings suggest that role-based interactions and face-to-face communication determine to a large extent the completeness, timeliness, relevance, and usefulness of information executives acquire and use for making strategic decisions. Consequently, information regarding internal organizational value chains is the best, information concerning specific industry-market dynamics is of a poorer quality, and the most incomplete is information on the global political economy (Davidson, 1991; Keegan, 1980). Information that sketches future developments or evaluates current happenings is mostly exchanged through interpersonal, face-to-face communication (Keegan, 1980). The interpersonal, face-to-face bias accounts for the finding that the headquarters executives ignored information from lower-level employees, and more attractive opportunities outside existing areas of operation (Davidson, 1991; Keegan, 1980).

For example, the sample of the headquarters executives of major U.S. multinational firms reported that they had collected 73 percent of external information through passive (surveillance) scanning, and 27 percent through active (search) scanning. In addition, 67 percent of this international information came from human sources, of which 75 percent were the face-to-face encounters mainly during business trips by jet aircraft. The headquarters executives acquired 60 percent of all information about the world environment from "external sources"—the same functional area company executives based abroad in subsidiaries, affiliates, and branches. Of these sources, 80 percent were personal (a friend or acquaintance) and 20 percent impersonal (a stranger) (Keegan, 1980).

To avoid these shortcomings of environmental scanning, the best global corporations rely on benchmarking or tracking noncompetitors with the world-class business standards. Benchmarking, introduced by the Xerox company a decade ago, is a process of detecting, learning, and innovatively implementing the best business processes in the world (Altany, 1991; Linsenmeyer, 1991; Waasdorp, 1991). Consequently, the world-class product development, product delivery, and customer service and management business processes are used to evaluate an organization's internal value chains, competitors' internal value chains, and opportunities for strategic alliances.

Benchmarking sharply focuses environmental scanning by tracking the best business processes in the global political economy (the entire set of external value chains), in specific industries-markets (particular subsets of external value chains), and by adjusting an organization's internal value chain to these world-class standards. In a word: benchmarking is a high-speed management way of evaluating organizational effectiveness relative to the best competitors' performance (Etzioni, 1960).

Environmental scanners must simultaneously rely on the following information sources for detecting companies with best-in-class business processes: more than two thousand business information databases (only in the United States), trade and professional associations, industry analysts, corporate customers and suppliers, business books and their authors, magazines and newsletters and their authors, company specialists and experts, company executives, interpersonal contacts in large companies, university reports and professors, consultants, and Baldridge Award winners (Altany, 1991).

The best global corporations use high-speed environmental scanning to provide mechanisms for exchange of information concerning internal and external contributing units' interests, concerns, and contributions. Benchmarking—the world-class standards—allows managers of internal and external business processes to accurately assess and seize an opportunity to forge mutually satisfying and productive strategic alliances.

Strategic alliances are meaningful only if they improve a sustained value-added competitive advantage without enlarging internal capacity (Kanter, 1989). Roughly 70 percent of strategic alliances are unsuccessful because partners do not use environmental scanning for benchmarking. Consequently, partners cannot assess whether their relationship is important (mutually satisfying and beneficial), whether long-term investment is justified, whether their business processes are interdependent in the sense of value-added competitive advantage, whether their business processes are integrated, coordinated, and controlled, whether each is informed about the plans of the other, and whether their alliance is appropriately institutionalized (Kanter, 1989). Without benchmarking, partners in strategic alliances cannot assess whether they are learning from each other.

Types of Uncertainty and Information Regarding General Globalization Trends

Global, transnational corporations coordinate successive stages of activities of their suppliers, manufacturing units, intermediaries such as distribution channels, sellers, and customers or buyers (Sklair, 1991; Coves, 1982; Dunning, 1983). Through global strategies, transnational corporations ensure capital accumulation (preserving and expanding the value of capital) and continued growth. In their activities global corporations simultaneously rely on and use all organizational forms available. These are: (1) free-market, competitive business transactions (Johnston and Lawrence, 1988); (2) different types of interorganizational (sub)contracting (Dore, 1983) labeled as the "value-adding partnerships (Johnston and Lawrence, 1988), quasi-firms (Eccles, 1981; Bradach and Eccles, 1989), a "virtual" organization (Morton, 1991), global strategic linkages (Nohria and Garcia-Pont, 1991), and strategic alliances (Collins and Doorley, 1991); and (3) hierarchies of common ownership (Johnston and Lawrence, 1988).

When scanning the global political economy (the entire set of external value chains), global corporations must assess types of uncertainty induced by general trends of globalization.

Political Uncertainty. The world is still divided into separate nation-states that vie for power within the capitalist world economy (Gill and Law, 1988). After the collapse of communist political institutions in Eastern Europe and the breakup of the Soviet Union, the international political regime (order) seems to have shifted from the bipolar structure of the world—a balance of military and political power between the United States and the Soviet Union—to a global empire with the hegemony of the United States as a single superpower. In today's world class conflicts seem to have given way to conflicts based on race, religion, and nationalism (Sklair, 1991). Ironically, this implies that global military and political trends are quite uncertain—more complicated and less predictable than at any time in modern history.

Financial Uncertainty. The global "financial revolution" has been linked to modern computer and telecommunication technology. In the open world economy an internationally interdependent financial system is increasingly frustrating national governments (Spencer, 1990), because foreign interest rates and domestic interest and exchange rates are necessarily interdependent (Arestis, 1990). Financial innovations such as credit or cash cards, electronic money transfers, financial futures, options or swap markets, new interest-bearing bank accounts, note insurance, convertible bonds, multiple option facilities, and off-balance sheet activities very often circumvent traditional government restrictions (Padolski, 1990). The globalization of financial markets is characterized by (1) mergers (conglomeration) between diverse financial institutions; (2) banks as highly complex multiproduct, multimarket organizations that achieve scope competitive advantage; (3) the inability of governments to control the creation of money since banks are not privileged "creators of money" but rather intermediaries in financial transactions; and (4) governments that coordinate floating exchange rates as the main lever to harness interest rates and inflation.

Rising international capital mobility suggests that the financial sector is a perfectly competitive market (Shaw, 1990). Expectations about the prices of financial assets—on auction (flexprice) markets that clear (Shaw, 1990)—are short-term (Arestis, 1991). Uncertainty on the financial markets is created by the difficulty in extracting information from all financial and monetary indicators. However, capital markets in the global economy vary by region. In the United States they are dominated by stock markets that encourage quick returns to stockholders and function as the "market for corporate control" (Sawyer, 1985). In the United States banks are "weaker" partners (Scott, 1991; Chandler, 1984). In continental Western Europe and Japan the banks directly intervene in industrial decision making and encourage long-term investment and returns (Scott, 1991; Chandler, 1984).

Uncertainty in Labor and Product Markets. Consumer-oriented and highly differentiated global markets favor flexible organizations revolving around flexible manufacturing—automated technology, generalist skills, and overlapping teams. These post-Fordist, "postmodern" organizations (Clegg, 1990; Piore and Sabel, 1984; Cross, 1985; Lever-Tracy, 1988) invest in company-specific skills of the core (mostly male) workers, but not in skills of part-time (mostly female) employees. To deal with the rapid obsolescence of products, global corporations "disaggregate" methods of factory production. They replace vertically integrated coordination with relational (sub)contracting or recurring contractual economic exchanges between firms, and with market coordination between a large number of small, fragmented firms (Swedberg, 1991; Dore, 1983). The global economy is characterized by the relative mobility of capital and the relative immobility of labor (Reich, 1991; Gill and Law, 1988). In the era of knowledge-based, high-technology economic development, the international production of transnationals is growing more rapidly than both international trade and world output.

Like markets for many goods, labor markets—especially in the most advanced countries—are imperfectly competitive. These fixprice markets do not clear; they are characterized by price and wage rigidity (Arestis, 1990; Shaw, 1990). Labor markets are still regulated by long-term contracts. Internal labor markets (promoting within) are based on "implicit contracts" (Granovetter, 1988; Bluedorn, 1982; Gartrell, 1982; Gordon, Edwards, and Reich, 1982; Price, 1977); "efficiency wages" (Shaw, 1990; Yellen, 1984); and "social capital" in the form of a stable network of employee relationships within and outside a firm (Granovetter, 1988). Because corporations invest in firm-specific human capital with firm-specific skills acquired through on-the-job training, they pay higher wages to experienced "insiders" even if the unemployed are willing to work for less. Consequently, labor markets are "distorted" by wage stickiness. Since both product and labor markets are based on long-term expectations of systematic downward price rigidity (Arestis, 1990), uncertainty is relatively lower than in the financial markets. Adaptive expectations (agents rely predominantly on the past knowledge and experience) seem to be more important than rational (agents ignore the past and use only new information) expectations (Peel, 1990).

Uncertainty in Global Trade. Global trade takes place within and between clusters of trading partners. Three global "hierarchies" constitute the "Triad"—the three core markets of the global economy (Green and Lutz, 1978; Drucker, 1989; Ohmae, 1987). The leading economies of the Triad—the United States, Japan, and the European Community—have large markets, a strong scientific and technological workforce, and sufficent capital investments (Baig, 1989). For example, the United States has 250 million potential consumers, generates 26 percent of the world GNP, and accounts for 18 percent of the world trade. Japan counts on 120 million potential consumers, adds 11 percent to the world GNP, and accounts for 12 percent of the world trade. The European Community (EC) has 320 million potential consumers, makes 22 percent of the world GNP, and accounts for 40 percent of the world trade (Silva and Sjogren, 1990). Worldwide trade is annually worth $4.3 trillion. Figures suggest that 90 percent of the world trade takes place within the three core markets. In 1988 trade between the United States and Japan was $187 billion, between Japan and the European Community (EC) $43 billion, and between the United States and the European Community (EC) $164 billion (Silva and Sjogren, 1990). Uncertainty in global trade is created by the general slowdown in the world economy, and difficulties in successfully concluding a new world trade pact.

The global economy's growth rate fell from 4.3 percent in 1988 to 3 percent in 1989 to 1 percent in 1990 to zero in 1991. The developed market economies grew 1.4 percent in 1991, the third world 3.5 percent. China had the highest rate, 5.5 percent in 1991, after rising 4.8 percent in 1990. However, in Eastern Europe and the former Soviet Union output plunged 9.5 percent in 1991 after dropping 6.3 percent the year before. In Eastern Europe more than 16 million people are unemployed (at least 12 million in the former Soviet Union), and this number is expected to double. In addition, it is highly uncertain whether the five-year-old talks known as the Uruguay Round, involving 108 countries, will generate a new version of the General Agreement on Tariffs and Trade (GATT) (Golden, 1992; Samuelson, 1992; Silk, 1992).

In summary, a high level of uncertainty in the global economic environment has been created by a volatile business climate in which the emergence of unexpected competition is commonplace, and by the rapid shrinking of product life cycle.

THE VALUE PROCESS—
PRODUCT-MARKET LIFE CYCLE TEMPLATE

In order to understand how global corporations scan unique industry-market dynamics, it is necessary to introduce a conceptual framework that can guide and trace these complex activities.

Successful global corporations include the activities of their suppliers and customers into a single value chain (Rockart and Short, 1991), thus creating a "virtual" organization with the permeable organization boundary (Morton, 1991), or a global network of "lean" enterprises (Womack, Jones, and Roos, 1990).

Transnational corporations use this template—the interdependent macro-organizational activities (business processes)—to scan the globe and acquire a specific type of information. Product development requires information on state-of-the-art technologies, engineers, and R&D activities of main partners and competitors. Product delivery needs information on costs of labor given the level of skill and availability of automated and flexible production facilities. Customer service and management require information on retail networks and practices, consumer preferences and purchasing power, and efficient ways of managing customer relationships. The template—the interdependent macro-organizational activities—is a tool that enables global corporations to optimize the entire set of their activities. Ideally, competitive advantage gained in one functional unit or business process should add to competitive advantage derived from other units or processes. In addition, global corporations must achieve value-added chains of activities at the global level.

Although value chains and value systems focus on costs of the "internal" operations of an organization, the available information seldom reveals what activities actually take place and how much they really cost (Macdonald, 1991). To remedy this shortcoming, global corporations could use a "value process model" that represents actual activities within an industry's "value system": their own, their partners', and their competitors' (Macdonald, 1991). The "value process model" allows global organizations to manage: (1) alternative sequences of concrete activities and their costs as a basis for cost competitive advantage, (2) time necessary for accomplishing alternative sequences of concrete activities as a basis for time competitive advantage, (3) unique and unreproducible (by competitors) sets of alternative sequences of concrete activities as a basis for differentiation competitive advantage, and (4) linkages between alternative sequences of concrete activities as a basis for scope competitive advantage.

To get a conceptual framework of even higher granularity, it is useful to cross-tabulate the five stages of the product-market life cycle (Collins and Doorley, 1991; Vernon, 1966) with the three macro-organizational activities (business processes). This provides a grid with fifteen cells that indicate what type of information should be used at a particular time to exploit, ideally, competitive advantage from all four sources simultaneously (see Table 4.1).

A. The development stage of product-market life cycle.

1. Product development (design, engineering, purchasing) business process. Corporations are tracking state-of-the-art technology, engineering talent, and R&D activities of the main partners and/or competitors. Competitive advantage at this stage of the product-market life cycle derives from product differentiation (unique features of a product keeping cost constant). Corporations at this stage of the product-market life cycle usually form two types of strategic alliances: (1) precompetitive collaborative R&D partnerships that avoid antitrust problems associated with downstream collaboration; and (2) corporate venturing with a minority equity in unlisted, growth prospect companies that provide options on the future (Collins and Doorley, 1991).

2. Product delivery (purchasing, manufacturing, and distribution) business process. Small specialist companies, operating at the leading edge of technologies, possess technological competitive advantage in the form of innovative product design and efficient production methods. In other words, they are at the cutting edge of product development (design, engineering, and purchasing) and only part of product delivery (purchasing and manufacturing) business process. To compensate for this disadvantage, small companies forge vertical supply alliances and strategic investments (Collins and Doorley, 1991). The most frequent

Table 4.1
Market-Product Life Cycle Template

Business Process	A Develop	B Grow	C Shakeout	D Mature	E Decline
Product Development	1	4	7	10	13
Product Delivery	2	5	8	11	14
Customer Service & Development	3	6	9	12	15

example of vertical supply alliance is the OEM (original equipment manufacturer customer) relationship. OEM customers, very often large and established organizations, provide the missing link within the product delivery business process-distribution. OEM customers act as intermediaries, brokers who either rebrand a small firm's products and distribute them directly, or add some components to rebranded products and then distribute them (Collins and Doorley, 1991).

3. Product service and management (distribution, sales, and service) business process. OEM customers also sell and service rebranded products of small firms.

It is important to note that coordination of activities within and between each business process can be achieved by (1) free-market, competitive transactions, (2) strategic interorganizational linkages (partnerships), and (3) transfer pricing within a horizontally and/or vertically integrated firm. A product development business process provides a differentiation competitive advantage (innovative product design and production methods). Product delivery and customer service and management business processes—through efficient manufacturing and market access (share), respectively—provide cost competitive advantage. Scope competitive advantage can be achieved by either simultaneously or sequentially introducing a broad range of products and/or services, and then "pushing" them through the three business processes. Time competitive advantage is gained by the speed of linking of activities within and between business processes.

B. The growth stage of product-market life cycle.

4. Product development (design, engineering, and purchasing) business process. There is continuous improvement of a new product that is in its money-making phase. The goal is to establish a leading commercial position. At this stage there are many market entrants (competitors). This stage approximates a "perfect" market competition. Firms in a perfect competition system often do not get what they want. High productivity attracts numerous competitors who must slash prices and thus reduce profits (Pareto, 1935).

5. Product delivery (purchasing, manufacturing, and distribution) business process. The key in this phase is building market shares, which in turn may establish industry standards (Collins

and Doorley, 1991). Although competitive advantage still rests primarily on product differentiation (product design business process), it must be linked to product delivery (purchasing, manufacturing, and distribution) business processes, consequently, at this stage companies frequently form joint ventures and supply alliances (Collins and Doorley, 1991).

6. Customer service and management (distribution, sales, and service) business process. Companies frequently forge joint ventures and supply alliances (Collins and Doorley, 1991).

C. The shakeout stage of market-product life cycle.

7. Product development (design, engineering, and purchasing) business process. There is a continuous improvement of product design and manufacturing methods that has become standardized. Price cutting and falling profitability at this stage lead to overcapacity. Since a product becomes a standardized commodity, it is difficult to derive competitive advantage from product differentiation and specialization.

8. Product delivery (purchasing, manufacturing, and distribution) business process. Size of a corporation is a critical asset. Large corporations can afford continuous R&D despite lower prices and falling profits. Main competitive advantage is based on low cost. Product delivery (purchasing, manufacturing, and distribution) and customer service and management (distribution, sales, and service) are more important than product development (design, engineering, and purchasing). Acquisitions, partial mergers, and mergers—all increasing the size of a corporation—are very common at this stage.

9. Customer service and management (distribution, sales, and service) business process. Supply alliances, acquisitions, partial mergers, and mergers are frequent.

D. The maturity stage of product-market life cycle.

10. Product development (design, engineering, and purchasing) business process. At this stage entry costs incurred by new competitors are very high. It is more expensive to continuously improve standardized products or commodities. Cost (price) is the main source of competitive advantage.

11. Product delivery (purchasing, manufacturing, and distribution) business process. Size of a firm is a crucial advantage. Since economies of scale in manufacturing are important, more efficient production methods must be developed. Progressive con-

centration in an industry takes place. Acquisitions, partial mergers, and consortia are frequent.

12. Customer service and management (distribution, sales, and service) business process. At this stage, costs of establishing distribution channels are very high. The maturity phase of product-market life cycle is characterized by the oligopolistic market structure. Oligopolistic firms very often achieve their objectives: rising productivity coupled with higher prices yields higher profits (Pareto, 1935). Acquisitions, partial mergers, and consortia are frequent.

E. The decline phase of the product-market life cycle.

Cost (price) is the only source of competitive advantage at this stage. Consequently, all three business processes—product development (13), product delivery (14), and customer service and management (15)—are involved in phasing down operations. Withdrawal and partial mergers take place. The latter are usually guided by the multimarket product life cycle strategy (Cundiff and Hilger, 1984). To prolong the life cycle of a particular product, corporations sequentially introduce the product to different local, national, and regional markets. As a result, the product is at different stages of the life cycle on different markets. The rapidly shrinking product life cycle, however, renders this strategy less and less useful.

IBM AND ABB: STRATEGIC ALLIANCES AS A FORM OF COALIGNMENT OF EXTERNAL RESOURCES

Two multinational giants—IBM and ABB—each in its own way use environmental scanning to coalign internal and external resources in the form of strategic alliances. These examples show how, why, and at what point in time the two giants used external resources—specific strategic alliances with other companies—to achieve and sustain competitive advantage.

IBM

This giant reduced its employment by 65,000 between 1986 and 1991, and it will eliminate an additional 20,000 jobs at a cost of some $3 billion. Currently IBM boasts some 350,000 employees (Markoff, 1991; Schwartz and Shenitz, 1991). Software design accounted for more than 30 percent, and integration of computer systems for 20 percent of IBM's profits in 1990. The rest is "sales and support" or customer service and management business process. Less than 5 percent of IBM's employees in 1990 were classified as production workers engaged in traditional manufacturing. That same year 40 percent of IBM's world employees were foreign. IBM Japan, with more than 18,000 Japanese employees and annual sales of more than $6 billion, is one of Japan's major exporters of computers (Reich, 1991).

Roughly 75 percent of IBM's $100 billion annual revenue comes from non-U.S. markets (Silva and Sjogren, 1990). One-third of all commercial research and development (R&D) in information technology in the core markets is funded by IBM (Collins and Doorley, 1991).

Although IBM dominates 60 to 70 percent of the world informatics market (Fadul and Straubhaar, 1991), the Big Blue has recently announced that it would break up into a loose federation of more competitive businesses (Schwartz and Shenitz, 1991). Since mainframes, its core business, are at the maturity life cycle stage, IBM believes that software and services are at the growth stage of the life cycle. Restructuring is expected to produce, above all, time competitive advantage.[1]

In the recent past IBM has forged a variety of strategic alliances in order to achieve and sustain competitive advantage. For example, IBM joined a collaborative (precompetitive) R&D with Joint European Submicron Semiconductor Initiative (JESSI), a $5 billion project launched to develop 64MB DRAMs and logic chips (cell 1). JESSI is part of the EUREKA pan-European collaborative R&D program. Initially, JESSI was formed by Philips, Siemens, and SGS Thomson. IBM became a member later (Collins and Doorley, 1991).

IBM also formed a vertical supply alliance (cell 3) with Stratus Computer Inc., a Boston-based manufacturer of fault-tolerant computers for on-line transactions processing (OLTP). In 1984, Stratus proposed an OEM alliance to IBM, and an agreement was signed in January 1985. Since IBM's own R&D team had failed to develop a satisfactory product for the OLTP market, IBM decided to use OEM as a means of market entry. With sales of $184 million and net income of $19 million, by 1987 Stratus was the world's second-largest fault-tolerant superminicomputer company.

IBM sells the Stratus machines as rebranded System 88, and accounts for some 25 percent of Stratus sales (Collins and Doorley, 1991).

IBM also formed a joint venture with the X/OPEN Group (cell 4). Hardware manufacturers have been forming shifting alliances in the quest for open network architectures. As an example, in early 1985 the leading European computer manufacturers—Bull, ICL, Nixdorf, Olivetti, Phillips, and Siemens—formed the X/OPEN Group. Their goal was to provide an alternative standard to the dominant proprietary IBM operating standard. They tried to establish open standards around the UNIX operating system over which AT&T has some proprietary rights. However, AT&T announced that it would team up with Sun Microsystems to develop a standard version of UNIX. As a reaction, the X/OPEN Group has decided to form a new alliance with IBM (the Open Software Foundation) to develop their own version of open environment for software (Rotemberg and Saloner, 1991).

ABB

ABB, the largest electrotechnical company in Europe, headquartered in Zurich, was formed on August 10, 1987, through the largest cross-border merger in the world (Silva and Sjogren, 1990). Sweden's ASEA and Switzerland's Brown-Boveri were combined to form ABB. By January 1990 more than 1,000 companies in over 100 nations comprised ABB. In no country has ABB more than 15 percent of its 220,000 employees. ABB is a consortium, a new type of global competitor, in which a parent company without national loyalty coordinates business activities and assets in multiple countries. ABB is managed like a federation of companies (Silva and Sjogren, 1990).

ABB has invested $3.6 billion in 60 companies around the world. Its annual revenues are more than $25 billion (Taylor, 1991).[2]

In May 1990 ABB formed a joint venture (cell 11) with Zamech, Poland's large manufacturer of steam turbines, transmission gears, marine equipment, and metal castings (Taylor, 1991). All of these products are at the mature life cycle stage. ABB had an interest in Zamech's product delivery (purchasing, manufacturing, and distribution) business process. Zamech's size

(4,300 employees) is a crucial advantage as well as its skilled but cheap labor force. From ABB's point of view, Zamech should provide cost and scope competitive advantage.

CONCLUSION

Necessary conditions of successful environmental scanning are met when environmental scanning is simultaneously organized around the scope axis (extensive and intensive scanning); the mode axis (passive and active scanning); the topics axis (scanning of the entire set of external value chains and particular subsets of external value chains); and is sharply focused by benchmarking. Only then can we track, evaluate, and implement the best business processes in the global political economy (the entire set of external value chains); in specific industries-markets (particular subsets of external value chains); and an organization's internal value chain adjusted to these world-class standards.

Environmental scanning is a highly systematic process. High-speed management allows global corporations to extract from the external environment two general types of information: (1) information regarding the economic, political, and cultural trends in the global economy (the entire set of external value chains); and (2) information regarding industry-market unique dynamics (specific subsets of external value chains).

In addition, the chapter has provided a conceptual grid for the scanning of industry-market unique dynamics (specific subsets of external value chains)—the value process–product-market life cycle template. The main advantage of the template is that it isolates the set of necessary conditions that must be met before any particular strategic alliance can be considered—what type of information should be used at what particular time to exploit, ideally, all types of competitive advantage simultaneously that any particular strategic alliance can provide.

Finally, this chapter has illustrated how two multinational giants—IBM and ABB—each in its own way used environmental scanning to coalign internal and external resources. These examples showed how, why, and at what point in time the two giants used external resources—specific strategic alliances with other companies—in order to achieve and sustain competitive advantage.

NOTES

1. Why was IBM—the sixth largest global corporation (out of 500) in 1991, and the fourth largest corporation (out of 500) in the United States in 1992—the second largest money loser (out of 500 global industrial corporations) in 1991 when it lost $2,827 million, and the third largest money loser (out of 500 American industrial corporations) in 1992 when it lost $4,965 million (*Fortune* 1992; 1993)? Why was Big Blue, out of fifteen corporations in the global computer and office equipment industry, the first in sales and the last in profits in 1991 (*Fortune*, 1992)? Why was IBM, out of twenty five companies in the "American" computer and office equipment industry, the first in sales and the last in profits in 1992 (*Fortune*, 1993)?

Why did IBM's revenues drop from $70 billion in 1990 to $65 billion in 1992? Why did Big Blue's $6 billion in profits in 1984 evaporate in a $5 billion loss in 1992? Why did IBM's market value (market capitalization, net worth) drop $77 billion, from $106 billion in 1987 to less than $30 billion in 1992? Why did Big Blue's worldwide computer market share shrink from more than 30% in 1983 to less than 20% in 1992? Why did IBM's stock plummet from $176 a share in 1987 to $50 a share in 1992? Why was its dividend cut by more than half in 1992? Why was Big Blue's debt of $30 billion downgraded in 1992? Why does IBM—the sixth largest corporate employer in the world in 1991, and the fourth biggest corporate employer in the United States in 1992 which cut its labor force from 406,000 in 1986 to 300,000 in 1992—still have to terminate between 50,000 and 100,000 employees at the estimated cost of $9 billion? Why did Big Blue trim a quarter of its manufacturing capacity since the mid-1980s (*Fortune* 1992, 1993; Kirkpatrick, 1992; Loomis and Kirkpatrick, 1993; Sellers and Kirkpatrick, 1993)?

A unique combination of internal, organizational, and external, industry-specific and global-market, processes may account for a pattern of decline at Big Blue. The breakup of the old computer industry coupled with IBM's vast size, centralized hierarchy, organizational complexity (nine manufacturing and development businesses, and four geographically organized marketing and service companies), and monopolistic, inward-looking organizational culture, resulted in an inability to get quickly to market with the new machines. For years Big Blue was protecting established lines of business (mainframe computers) instead of quickly embracing new technologies (networks of desktop units, and computer-related services). It is not surprising, then, that IBM spent $42 billion on mainframe-related plants and equipment in the 1980s (Schlender, 1993; Stewart, 1993; Behr and Fromson, 1993; Lohr, 1993; Levinson, 1993; Loomis and Kirkpatrick, 1993). Although the share of services in IBM's revenues jumped from only 9% in 1991 to 18.6% in 1992, mainframes and minicomputers still accounted for 21.55% of the total revenues in 1992 (Kirkpatrick, 1992; Lohr, 1993).

Despite the fact that it spends $10 billion a year on capital expenditures and R&D, IBM was 11 years late with minicomputer, 5 years late with engineering workstation, 5 years late with PC-compatible laptop, 4 years late with personal computer, and 3 years late with RISC workstation (Kirkpatrick, 1992; Loomis and Kirkpatrick, 1993).

When the old, vertically aligned, computer industry was supplanted by a new horizontal model, competition based on proprietary and completely integrated products gave way to time-to-markets competition for market share within each horizontal specialty or product line (Sherman, 1993). Since systems integration is now based on international standards for compatibility of hardware and software, competing products from different companies must be fairly interchangeable. Consequently, the new computer industry/market rewards companies best able to form alliances, rather than the ones trying—like the old IBM—to be self-sufficient giants (Schlender, 1993). In addition to forming subsidiaries and joint ventures worldwide to sell services such as benefits processing, hiring, and maintenance to itself and others, a few years ago Big Blue started linking up with competitors to offer better products and services to customers. For example, IBM North America, one of the four geographically organized marketing and services companies, has alone over 4,000 partners. Big Blue did try to share risks and gain expertise through partnerships even with its main competitors such as Borland, Siemens, Wang, Novell, Toshiba, Lotus, Sears, Mitsubishi, Intel, Apple Computer Inc., and Motorola Inc. (Kirkpatrick, 1992). However, IBM did not use strategic alliances to co-align internal and external resources in a coherent and focused fashion. Its current troubles are due partly to an inability to use external alliances as a core strategic tool rather than an auxiliary one.

2. Unlike IBM, ABB (Asea Brown Bovery) was rather successful in 1991. It was the thirty third largest global industrial corporation (out of 500) in terms of sales. Its sales in 1991, $28,883 million, were 4.3% higher than in 1990. ABB was the seventy eighth largest global corporation in terms of profits ($587 million). A 109.6% increase in profits from 1990 made ABB the twenty third most successful corporation. With 214,399 employees, ABB was the fifteenth largest global corporate employer. Out of 27 corporations in its global industry (industrial and farm equipment), ABB was the first in sales, and the second in profits. Unlike the global computer industry which lost $2,126 million in 1991, and the "American" computer industry which lost $6,051 million in 1992, the global industrial and farm equipment industry scooped $1,368

million in profits in 1991 (*Fortune,* 1992; 1993). Part of the ABB's success is partly due to its use of external alliances as a core strategic tool rather than an auxiliary one.

REFERENCES

Aldrich, H. E. 1979. *Organizations and Environments.* Englewood Cliffs, N.J.: Prentice Hall.

Aldrich, H. E. and D. Whetten. 1981. Organization-sets, action-sets, and networks: Making the most of simplicity. In P. C. Nystrom and W. H. Starbuck, eds., *Handbook of Organizational Design,* vol. 1. New York: Oxford University Press.

Altany, D. 1991. Share and share. Benchmarkers are proving the wisdom of mothers' reproach. *Industry Week* (July 15).

Arestis, P. 1990. Post-Keynesian economics: Recent developments and future prospects. In J. R. Shackleton, ed., *New Thinking in Economics.* Aldershot: Edward Elgar.

Baig, E. 1989. Where global growth is going. *Fortune,* vol. 120, no. 3 120:71–88.

Behr, P. & B. D. Fromson. 1993. Taking IBM Past Its Era: For Big Blue's Chief, a Future of Pain and Reinvention. *Boston Globe,* March 28, p. 78.

Bluedorn, A. 1982. The theories of turnover: Causes, effects, and meaning. In S. Bacharach, ed., *Research in the Sociology of Organizations,* vol. 1. Greenwich, Conn. JAI Press.

Boudon, R., and F. Bourricaud. 1989. *A Critical Dictionary of Sociology.* Chicago: University of Chicago Press.

Bradach, J. L. and R. G. Eccles. 1989. Price, authority, and trust: From ideal types to plural forms. *Annual Review of Sociology.* 97–118.

Chandler, A. D., Jr. 1984. The emergence of managerial capitalism. *Business History Review.* 473–503.

Clegg, S. R. 1990. *Modern Organizations: Organization Studies in the Postmodern World.* London: Sage.

Collins, T. M. and T. L. Doorley. 1991. *Teaming Up for the '90s: A Guide to International Joint Ventures and Strategic Alliances.* Homewood, Ill.: Business One Irwin.

Coves, R. E. 1982. *Multinational Enterprise and Economic Analysis.* Cambridge: Cambridge University Press.

Cross, M. 1985. *Toward the Flexible Craftsman.* London: Technical Change Centre.

Cundiff, E. W., and M. T. Hilger. 1984. *Marketing in the International Environment.* Englewood Cliffs, N.J.: Prentice Hall.

Davidson, W. H. 1991. The role of global scanning in business planning. *Organizational Dynamics,* 5–16.

Dore, R. 1983. Goodwill and the spirit of market capitalism. *British Journal of Sociology:* 459–82.

Drucker, P. 1989. *The New Realities.* New York: Harper and Row.

Dunning, J. 1983. *International Production and the Multinational Enterprise.* London: Macmillan.

Eccles, R. G. 1981. The quasifirm in the construction industry. *Journal of Economic Behavior and Organization:* 235–57.

Ergas, H. 1987. Does technology policy matter? In B. Guile and H. Brooks, eds., *Technology and Global Industry.* Washington, D.C.: National Academy Press.

Etzioni, A. 1960. Two approaches to organizational analysis. *Administrative Science Quarterly:* 257–78.

Ewer, P., W. Higgins, and A. Stevens. 1987. *Unions and the future of Australian Manufacturing.* Sydney: Allen and Unwin.

Fadul, A., and J. Straubhaar. 1991. Communications, culture, and informatics in Brazil: The current challenges. In G. Sussman and J. A. Lent, eds., *Transnational Communications: Wiring the Third World.* Newbury Park: Sage.

Fortune. 1992. The Global 5000. *Fortune,* Vol. 126, No. 2, July 27, p. 176–232.

Fortune. 1993. The Fortune 500. *Fortune,* Vol. 127, No. 8, April 19, p. 174–288.

Gartrell, D. C. 1982. On the visibility of wage referents. *Canadian Journal of Sociology:* 117–43.

Geertz, C. 1978. The bazaar economy: Information and search in peasant marketing. *Supplement to the American Economic Review.* 28–32.

Gill, D., and D. Law. 1988. *The Global Political Economy: Perspectives, Problems and Policies.* Baltimore: Johns Hopkins University Press.

Golden, T. 1992. Democracy isn't always enough to repel attempted coups. *New York Times,* Feb. 9, p. E3.

Gordon, D., R. Edwards, and M. Reich. 1982. *Segmented Work, Divided Workers.* New York: Cambridge University Press.

Granovetter, M. 1988. The sociological and economic approaches to labor market analysis: A social structural view. In G. Farkas and P. England, eds., *Industries, Firms, and Jobs: Sociological and Economic Approaches.* New York: Plenum Press.

Green, R., and J. Lutz. 1978. *The United States and World Trade: Changing Patterns and Dimensions.* New York: Praeger.

Hirsch, P. M. 1972. Processing fads and fashions: An organization-set analysis of cultural industry systems. *American Journal of Sociology*: 639–59.

Johnston, R., and P. R. Lawrence. 1988. Beyond vertical integration—The rise of the value-adding partnerships. *Harvard Business Review* (July–Aug.). 94–101

Kanter, R. M. 1989. Becoming PALs: Pooling, allying, and linking across companies. *Academy of Management Executive*: 183–93.

Keegan, W. J. 1980. *Multinational Marketing Management.* 2d ed. Englewood Cliffs, N.J.: Prentice Hall.

Kenney, M., and R. Florida. 1988. Beyond mass production: Production and the labor process in Japan. *Politics and Society*: 121–58.

Kirkpatrick, D. 1992. Breaking Up IBM. *Fortune*, Vol. 126, No. 2, July 27, p. 44–58.

Lever-Tracy, C. 1988. The flexibility debate: Part time work. *Labor and Industry*: 210–41.

Levinson, M. 1993. Can He Make an Elephant Dance. *Newsweek*, April 5, p. 46–7.

Linsenmeyer, A. 1991. Fad or fundamental? A chat with Bob Camp of Xerox, the man who wrote the book on benchmarking. *Financial World* (Sept. 17):34–35.

Lohr, S. 1993. For I.B.M., a Template for Change in a Spinoff. *New York Times*, March 29, pp. D1, D3.

Loomis, C. J. & D. Kirkpatrick. 1993. The Hunt for Mr. X: Who Can Run IBM? *Fortune*, Vol. 127, No. 4, February 22, p. 68–72.

Macdonald, H. K. 1991. The value process model. In M. S. Scott, ed., *The Corporation of the 1990s: Information Technology and Organizational Transformation.* New York: Oxford University Press.

Markoff, J. 1991. The first draft of I.B.M.'s future. *New York Times*, Dec. 6, pp. D1, D4.

Morton, M. S. 1991. Introduction: In M. S. Scott, ed., *The Corporation of the 1990s: Information Technology and Organizational Transformation.* New York: Oxford University Press.

Nohria, N., and C. Garcia-Pont. 1991. Global strategic linkages and industry structure. *Strategic Management Journal*: 105–24.

Ohmae, K. 1985. *Triad Power: The Coming Shape of Global Competition.* New York: Free Press.

Padolski, T. 1990. Financial change and macroeconomic control. In J. R. Shackleton, ed., *New Thinking in Economics.* Aldershot: Edward Elgar.

Pareto, V. 1935. *The Mind and Society.* New York: Harcourt, Brace, Jovanovich.

Peel, D. 1990. Rational expectations and the new macroeconomics. In J. R. Shackleton, ed., *New Thinking in Economics.* Aldershot: Edward Elgar.

Piore, M. J., and C. F. Sabel. 1984. *The Second Industrial Divide: Possibilities for Prosperity.* New York: Basic Books.

Porter, M. E. 1985. *Competitive Advantage.* New York: Free Press.

Porter, M. E., and V. E. Millar. 1985. How information gives you competitive advantage. *Harvard Business Review* (July–Aug.):149–160.

Powel, W. 1990. Neither market nor hierarchy: Network forms of organization. *Research in Organizational Behavior:* 295–336.

Price, J. 1977. *The Study of Turnover.* Ames: University of Iowa Press.

Reich, R. B. 1991. *The Work of Nations: Preparing Ourselves for 21st Century Capitalism.* New York: Alfred A. Knopf.

Rockart, J., and J. Short. 1989. IT in the 1990s: Managing organizational interdependencies. *Sloan Management Review:* 7–17.

————. 1991. The networked organization and the management of interdependence. In M. S. S. Morton, ed., *The Corporation of the 1990s: Information Technology and Organizational Transformation.* New York: Oxford University Press.

Rotemberg, J. J., and G. Saloner. 1991. Interfirm competition and collaboration. In M. S. S. Morton, ed., *The Corporation of the 1990s: Information Technology and Organizational Transformation.* New York: Oxford University Press.

Samuelson, R. J. 1992. The boom has come and gone. *Newsweek,* Feb. 17, p. 45.

Sawyer, M. C. 1985. *The Economics of Industries and Firms.* 2d ed. London: Croom Helm.

Schlender, B. R. 1993. Japan: Hard Times for High Tech. *Fortune,* vol. 127, No. 6, March 22, p. 92–104.

Schwartz, J., and K. Shenitz. 1991. Tighter times at Big Blue. *Newsweek,* Dec. 9, p. 50.

Scott, J. 1991. Networks of corporate power: A comparative assessment. *Annual Review of Sociology*: 181–203.

Sellers, P. & D. Kirkpatrick. 1993. Can Lou Gerstner Save IBM? *Fortune*, Vol. 127, No. 4, February 22, p. 63–67.

Shaw, G. K. 1990. Neo-Keynesian theories of unemployment. In J. R. Shackleton, ed., *New Thinking in Economics*. Aldershot: Edward Elgar.

Sherman, S. 1993. Andy Grove: How Intel Makes Spending Pay Off? *Fortune*, Vol. 127, No. 4, February 22, p. 56–61.

Silk, L. 1992. Potential tragedy of a global slump. *New York Times*, Jan. 10, P. D2.

Silva, M., and B. Sjogren. 1990. *Europe 1992 and the New World Power Game*. New York: John Wiley and Sons.

Sklair, L. 1991. Sociology of the Global System: *Social Change in Global Perspective*. Baltimore: Johns Hopkins University Press.

Spencer, P. 1990. Open-economy macroeconomics. In J. R. Shackleton, ed., *New Thinking in Economics*. Aldershot: Edward Elgar.

Stewart, J. B. 1993. Whales and Sharks: The Unexpected Fates of I.B.M. and A.T.&T. May Offer a Lesson to the Clinton Justice Department. *New Yorker*, February 15, p. 37–43.

Swedberg, R. 1991. Major traditions of economic sociology. *Annual Review of Sociology*: 251–76.

Taylor, W. 1991. The logic of global business: An interview with ABB's Percy Barnevik. *Harvard Business Review* (Mar.–Apr.).

Vernon, R. 1966. International trade investment and international trade in the product cycle. *Quarterly Journal of Economics*: 190–207.

———. 1979. The product cycle hypothesis in a new international environment. *Oxford Bulletin of Economics and Statistics*.

Waasdorp, P. L. 1991. Benchmarking for customer satisfaction. *Maintaining the Total Quality Advantage* (Report #979, Nov. 8, pp. 17–18).

Womak, J. P., D. T. Jones, and D. Roos. 1990. *The Machine That Changed the World*. New York: Rawson Associates.

Yellen, J. 1984. Efficiency wage models of unemployment. *American Economic Review*: 202–5.

CHAPTER FIVE

Leadership—
Creating High-Speed Synergy
in the Organization

Krzysztof Obloj

High-speed management is a system of principles, strategies, and tools that organizations must apply in order to generate sustainable competitive advantage in the turbulent environment. It will be the purpose of this chapter to develop a broad perspective on organizational leadership, particularly its role and significance under the new conditions and demands of high-speed management. It will: (1) discuss briefly the major traditional perspectives that emerged from the research, which constitute a paradigm of transactional leadership, and show their limitations from the high-speed management perspective; (2) outline the theory of transformational leadership, more suitable but still limited in terms of high-speed management; and (3) discuss high-speed management leadership. While the high-speed management leader concept has much in common with that of the transformational leader, it differs in how it deals with the paradoxes, tensions, and demands created by high-speed management in an organization.

TRADITIONAL CONCEPTIONS OF LEADERSHIP

Power and Leadership

One of the earliest approaches to leadership was developed by French and Raven (1959). They suggested five major kinds of managerial power enhancing leadership positions: legitimate, reward, coercive, referent, and expert.

Legitimate power refers to the manager's right (authority) to define tasks subordinates must perform because they have an obligation to comply with legitimate orders. Reward power depends upon the manager's control over valued rewards, such as money, promotion, and recognition. Coercive power reflects the flip-side of rewards. While compliance and good performance are rewarded, lack of discipline and poor performance can be punished, which enhances the influence and control managers have over subordinates' behavior. Referent power is based upon leader reputation and charisma, personal characteristics that create admiration, loyalty, identification, and desire in followers. Expert power refers to superior experience, knowledge, and skills of a leader as a base of power.

The major insight gained from the research of power theories resides in understanding different sources of managerial influence and the powerful results of their combined use. Its weakness is the circular explanation of leadership it offers: a good leader draws on expert, referent, and legitimation powers but in order to acquire them has to prove leadership abilities existed in the first place.

The Traits Perspective

Underlying the traits approach are powerful assumptions that leaders are born, not made, that leadership is a rare skill based upon personality traits, and that leaders are charismatic (Bennis and Naums, 1985). With these assumptions in mind, scholars focused on three major questions: What traits are related to leadership effectiveness? What skills are related to leader effectiveness? How do traits interact to influence leader effectiveness? (Yukl, 1989). The major methodological problem of the traits perspective is its limited generality. Different researchers analyzing individual cases of leaders came up with different and quite extensive sets of characteristics and skills that effective leaders should possess. While such lists of leader traits are useful, stressing the most effective abilities and skills that leaders usually have, they are dangerous. They differ considerably and are not consistent. They are not very helpful in understanding what skills are more important than others and under what circumstances. Finally, they assume that if you do not have all or some of these characteristics, you cannot become a leader.

The Behavioral Perspective

The behavioral perspective concentrates on building effective behavior profiles, trying to establish relationships between leadership styles and their effects on organizational performance. Two major styles of leadership were identified: technically and socially oriented. This distinction was picked up and extended by Blake and Mouton (1964) in their well-known concept of a managerial grid developed upon the distinctions between production-oriented and people-oriented styles. In Blake and Mouton's opinion, the most effective is a team style of leadership. Such leaders have high concern for both people and production, attempting to build commitment, cohesive group works, and relationships of trust, security, and respect.

The behavioral perspective on leadership is still popular because it is simple and persuasive. It tries to balance and blend social and technical aspects of management into leadership. However, its main weakness was quickly noticed by promoters of the situational (contingency) approach: it does not capture the diversity of leaders' behaviors dictated by the situation and circumstances.

The Contingency Perspective

The contingency approach, which dominated organizational and management theories in the 1970s, starts with one major assumption: it all depends. In the case of leadership it translates into a belief that there are not ultimate leadership traits, sources of power, or behaviors. Effective leaders vary their approach and behaviors from situation to situation, searching for an optimal fit between the requirements at hand and management style. The general approach is well reflected in Fiedler's (1967), Vroom and Yetton's (1973), and Yukl's (1989) theories.

Fiedler's theory tries to match two factors: (1) the personal style of the leader (task-oriented and relationship-oriented styles are identified) and (2) situational variables (leader-member relations, task structure, and position power of the leader). The model specifies that task-oriented managers are good leaders in both very favorable and least favorable situations. In favorable situations leader-member relations are good, tasks are well-structured, and the leader has a high level of legitimate, coercive, and reward power. In unfavorable situations, the reverse is true. Relationship-oriented leaders are most effective in intermediate situations, when the leaders are liked but tasks are ill-structured, or they are not liked but tasks are well structured.

Vroom and Yetton's contingency model (1973) is also based on the idea that effective leadership depends upon such conditions as the nature of the problem to be dealt with, the amount of available information for high-quality decisions, and the level of participant's participation and acceptance of organizational goals. Depending upon the type of problem, available information, and the willingness of subordinates to participate in the decision-making process, Vroom and Yetton define five leadership styles within a continuum of authoritarian-democratic leadership. In the pure authoritarian mode, effective leadership solves the problem in a rational fashion, using information available at that time. In the pure democratic mode, leadership shares a problem with subordinates and acts as a moderator of the problem-solving process. Other styles are a mix of these approaches and their effectiveness depends upon the situation.

The multiple linkage model developed by Yukl (1989) begins with the assumption that work unit performance depends upon six intervening variables: member effort, member ability, organization of work, teamwork and cooperation, resources, and coordination with other parts of the organization. Situational variables influence and determine the importance of the intervening variables. The effectiveness of a leader depends upon his or her ability to influence either intervening variables (in the short term) or situational and intervening variables (in the long term).

The major strength of the contingency approach is a recognition that leadership is not a simple phenomenon, and there is not a single cause of effective leadership. In the search for a match among performance, leadership style, and contingencies, researchers uncovered complex and dynamic relations and offered the most comprehensive concept of leadership. However, a contingency perspective also has limitations. Measurement of variables applied in the contingency perspective is rather subjective and general. The general idea that good leaders adapt their styles of management to the requirements of a situation implies a chameleonlike flexibility of leadership styles. So in a relatively stable environment, the contingency models offer a powerful indication that leadership style should fit the situation. In a turbulent environment such a suggestion has little value.

In summary, four decades of research and conceptualizations have offered some important suggestions about effective leadership. First, a leader should have versatile sources of power. Second, leaders should have special personality traits energizing followers and enabling them to build and maintain their personal charismas. Third, leaders should skillfully balance their task and people orientations, integrating two major elements of behavior. The first is structuring tasks and allocating them across the organization. The second is supporting people, taking into account their expectations and preferences. Fourth, effective leaders must adjust their styles to the contingencies and demands of a given situation.

These developments and conceptualizations created a paradigm of a transactional leader (Burns, 1978). A transactional leader flexibly relies on power, rewards, and contingencies to maintain or marginally improve the quality of performance and assure subordinates' compliance and motivation. In order to be effective she or he fulfills the expectations of followers and meets the demands of situation. Bass (1985, pp. 12–13) comments:

> transactional leaders serve to recognize and clarify the role and task requirements for the subordinates' reaching the desired outcomes. This gives the subordinates sufficient confidence to exert the necessary effort. Transactional leaders also recognize what the subordinates need and want and clarify how these needs and wants will be satisfied if the necessary effort is expended by the subordinate. Such effort to perform or motivation to work implies a sense of direction in the subordinate as well as some degree of energization.

Transactional leaders are instrumental in their approach since they focus on structure and reward/punishments procedures to maintain and improve conditions that motivate desired behaviors (Nadler and Tushman, 1990). In a way a transactional leader is mundane: he or she structures, manipulates, matches structure and procedures together, ensures compliance and discipline in order to get things done efficiently, and introduces incremental changes if necessary.

From a high-speed management perspective, the concept of transactional leader is obsolete and has three fundamental deficiencies. First, high-speed management proposes that the key to survival and effectiveness in the global marketplace lies in the fundamental functions of environmental scanning and benchmarking. Only the contingency approach to leadership has taken the environment into account, but even then in a limited sense of passive adaptation. Generally, the transactional leader perspective is internally oriented and does not pay attention to environmental forces and adaptation. Second, the transactional leader concept totally misses the importance of the value chain, both in terms of functions and processes, and in seeing it as fundamental for the high-speed management concept of coalignment, being generally oriented either toward tasks or people. Third, the transactional leader perspective does not allow for transformations and changes that are the driving force in the high-speed adaptation. Tichy and Devanna summarize (1986, p. 27): "Transactional leaders were fine for an era of expanding markets and nonexistent competition. In return for compliance they issued rewards. These managers changed little: they managed what they found and left things pretty much as they found them when they moved out." The flaws of the transactional leadership theory created a fertile ground for the development of the more advanced concept of transformational leadership.

TRANSFORMATIONAL LEADERSHIP

The modern concept of transformational leadership aims at the development of a framework of a charismatic leader oriented toward envisioning, enabling, and energizing members of an organization. The transformational leadership concept restores the

Figure 5.1
The Critical Functions of Transformational Leadership

Envisioning

- scanning the environment
- articulating long-term vision

Coalignment	**Empowering**
• integrating the organization with an environment • integrating functional and business subsystems in the organization	• creating momentum, dreams, and confidence • building sustainable culture

---

role of organizational leader to a dominant position in two re-spects. First, the transformational leader frame of reference is a congruent set of avidly followed core values or standards, such as success, integrity, respect, trust, and fairness (Kuhnert and Lewis, 1987). Second, the transformational leader recognizes the need for change. The test of transformational leadership is successful management of organizational transformations in order to cope with rapid environmental changes and to stay ahead of competitors' responses. In short, transformational leadership breaks existing frames and energetically rebuilds organization.

There are three closely related, major functions of transformational leadership (see Figure 5.1; Tushman, Newman, and Romanelli, 1986; Peters, 1987; Nadler and Tushman, 1990; Kotter, 1990; Cushman and King, 1994):

- envisioning: development of a compelling vision of the organizational future and translating it into a mission anchored in core values and standards
- empowering: inspiring and energizing members of the organization in a credible way to ensure their participation in the process of organizational change
- coalignment: maintaining a tight fit between market opportunities/challenges and the internal, integrative system of the organization

Envisioning

Transformational leaders supply their organizations with bold, exciting, almost unattainable (by common standards) visions of mission, built upon the core values and standards. Transformational leaders of Komatsu (Yashinari and Ryoichi Kawai), Chrysler (Lee Iaccoca), GE (Jack Welch), Apple (Steve Jobs and later John Sculley), Asea Brown Boveri (Percy Barnevik), SAS (Jan Carlzon), and Zanussi (Carlo Verri) had the courage to think the unthinkable, dream about the unattainable, and develop a new, bold vision of their organizations in the future. A visionary, transformational mission stabilizes a dynamic organization, introduces some certainty in the turmoil of transition, creates motivation to overcome the status quo, and thinks and acts in a new way.

Empowering

Transformational leaders are successful in energizing and inspiring organizational members to share and follow the new mission. Aligning mission, strategies, structures, and procedures is helpful but is not enough. Kotter (1990, p. 107) observes:

> Leadership is different. Achieving grand visions always requires an occasional burst of energy. Motivation and inspiration energize people, not by pushing them in the right direction as control mechanisms do but by satisfying basic human needs for achievement, a sense of belonging, recognition, self-esteem, a feeling of control over one's life, and the ability to live up to one's idea. Such feelings touch us deeply and elicit a powerful response.

A transformational mission gives organizational members a dream, which can boost morale, energize people, and hold an organization together during lasting periods of dynamic transitions. Transformational leaders empower and encourage people, helping them build teams, share information, and unleash their energy, initiative, and creativity.

Coalignment

Transformational leaders are skillful in matching the organization to the type of environment in which it must operate, increasing flexibility in a turbulent environment while introducing stability in a placid one. The same applies to the ability to maintain an internal fit among different functional (primary and supporting) subsystems and business processes.

In summary, transactional leadership is based upon three pillars: organizational structure, procedures, and enviromental stability. Allocation of tasks and power, distribution of information, routinization of work, and reward/punishment procedures are frames of reference for transactions between leader and followers. As we also noted, the transactional leadership concept presupposes a relatively stable business environment.

Transformational leadership is based upon three very different foundations: environmental scanning and vision development, empowering people to make things happen, and matching the organization with the environment. In short, transformational leaders manage an organization as a complex system.

HIGH-SPEED MANAGEMENT AND LEADERSHIP: FUSING THE LEADER AND MANAGER ROLE

As its foundation, high-speed management requires stable coalignment between environment and organization. However, due to fundamental new trends in the global economic environment effective management requires constant environmental scanning and adaptation at a growing speed. The constant process of change and adaptation destroys coalignment, creating four fundamental paradoxes a high-speed leader must deal with: (1) the struggle between the needs of stability and change; (2) the struggle between centralization and empowerment; (3) the tension between a growing complexity of system and the need for simple, transparent management; and (4) the necessity to develop internal core capabilities and external linkages at the same time. We will discuss these paradoxes and illustrate them later using the example of Komatsu's long history of high-speed transformation.

The Stability-Change Paradox

The essence of environmental scanning and benchmarking lies in the avid search for new ideas and solutions and their implementation before competitors. Therefore, high-speed leaders differ from other leaders in that they destroy organizational strategies and solutions while they are still successful and effective. Their constant destruction of organizational stability in search of forward-looking adaptation can easily produce misfit and disintegration of values. The high-speed leader's answer to the constant tension between the need for stability and the need for change is twofold. First, leaders are building commitment around compelling, shared missions and general strategies that can provide organizational members with the sense of stability of direction in the flux. Pharmaceutical giant Bristol-Meyers Squibb's mission: "Number 1 by 2001"; IBM's famous mission statement: "IBM Means Service"; toy producer Lego A/S's motto: "Only the best is good enough"; Federal Express' idea: "Absolutely, Positively, Overnight" introduce certainty of direction in the turbulent, risky environment. Second, every action is oriented toward positioning the organization for the distant future while increasing its short-term effectiveness.

The Centralization-Empowerment Paradox

High-speed management demands control over the organizational value chain in order to ensure quick execution of changes and minimum time lag between the adaptive action and results. At the same time, the concept of empowerment demands sufficient decentralization in order to enable organizational subsystems and members to react flexibly. Organizational members can anchor their need for stability in a vision only if it is shared, and this factor also requires decentralization to enhance innovation, participation, and motivation. The high-speed leadership answer to the simultaneous need for centralization and decentralization lies in a system of strict performance targets and clear responsibilities. High-speed leaders establish strict performance targets for each of the organizational units. While tactical errors and mistakes are accepted, failures to meet targets are not. In this way leaders centralize the execution of targets and goals while empowering units to decide on all other issues. This approach is especially visible in harsh targets imposed by Jack Welch at GE where his lack of tolerance for failure gained him the nickname "Neutron Jack." At the same time Welch is pushing to the limits the central theme of empowerment: ownership of the business. This means that people further down have power to make and carry out decisions.

The Complexity-Simplicity Paradox

The major feature of a modern organization adapting to the turbulent environment is its complexity. It has technological, structural, personal, and strategic dimensions. Technological improvements and occasional breakthroughs increase the complexity of organizational technology. The need to manage functions and processes of the value chain increases structural complexity. The pressures of change and tight performance targets drain the psychological resources of an organization. Adaptive changes of strategy force subsequent changes through the organization in order to ensure new levels of coalignment. The high speed of all these processes increases the complexity of an organization and makes it difficult to understand, while the typical stakeholders—competitors, customers, managers, employees, owners, and regulators—demand simplicity of structures and processes.

The answer of high-speed leaders is in the synergistic fusion of management and leadership processes. High-speed management does not differentiate between management and leadership, and reduces the complexity, merging environmental scanning and value chain analysis with the process of development of vision and empowerment. The main tool of such fusion is open, high-speed communication, sharing information, and decision making. In Next, a new computer company established by Steve Jobs, simplicity of high-speed management is assured by a totally open, internal communication system. Computer networks used by all employees constantly hum with opinions, arguments, memos, and mail. Even top strategic decisions, like Canon's offer to buy an equity interest in the company, are put as a matter for debate on the open network. Meetings and retreats are used to share the information, and to put forward complaints and suggestions. Rothman (1990, p. 32) observes: "By letting the process permeate every level of organization, from hiring to strategic planning, Jobs is not merely building a company, he's moulding a team. He's winning a degree of participation and commitment other chief executives would envy."

The Core Capabilities and External Linkages

The leader guards the inherently paradoxical process of achieving and maintaining organizational competitive advantage. The paradoxical nature of the process is the result of two contradictory sources of competitive advantage. One source is in the organization, in the development of the competitive combination of resources and their employment. The process is costly in terms of money and time as it represents long-term collective learning in the organization (Prahalad and Hamel, 1990). Its advantage is that as a result of a unique sequence of actions, it ensures the unique nature of developed skills and capabilities.

Another important source of competitive advantage exists in the extension of external linkages through mergers and acquisitions, joint ventures, cross-equity ownership and minority equity, and agreements over cooperation in the areas of R&D, component sourcing, or distribution. External linkages provide an organization quickly with an alternative: either it can leverage its capabilities by pooling resources with firms with similar skills or it can gain access to new capabilities by linking with firms that have complementary capabilities (Nohria and Garcia-Pont, 1991). For example, Ford's links with Jaguar gave it access to the specific market niche while linkages with Mazda enables it to analyze low-cost production techniques. The limitation of this way of competitive advantage development is imitability of the capabilities acquired in this way and easy access of other linked organizations to the firm's strategic capability base. The high-speed leader must recognize and manage this paradox in a way that enables the firm concurrently to tap experiences and made their applications difficult for others to imitate.

THE TRANSFORMATION OF KOMATSU

The synergistic integration and management of these paradoxes by high-speed leaders are well illustrated in the successful transition of Komatsu from an obscure Japanese earth-moving equipment (EME) producer to a global corporation (Komatsu Limited, 1988; Prahalad and Hamel, 1990).

In the late 1960s Komatsu sales were around $300 million as compared to Caterpillar's (the industry leader) over $2.4 billion. The company dominated the small home market in Japan, offered a narrow range of low-quality products, and had a "cheap and nasty" image. It did not have a strong distribution network and lacked cost benefits of large-scale manufacturing. To make matters even worse, the Japanese Ministry of International Trade and Industry did not believe that Japan possessed any competitive advantage in this industry. Therefore, in 1963 MITI decided to open the earth-moving equipment industry to foreign capital investments in 1965 and Komatsu faced the imminent threat of intense competition in its domestic market. It seemed that the company had no future at all and bankruptcy was only a matter of time.

With the survival of the company at stake Yashinari Kawai, chairman of Komatsu Limited, and his son Ryoichi Kawai developed a bold vision of Komatsu as a future global leader replacing Caterpillar's domination of the EME industry. The mission offered by Kawai to his followers was simple and powerful: "Maru-Cat" (Encircle Caterpillar). Komatsu's vision seemed at this time equally challenging and unattainable. What made it feasible was the skillful leadership of Kawai and other top managers in translating mission into long-term strategies of action and building commitment, inspiration, and energy among Komatsu employees.

Komatsu has proceeded with this mission in mind for the past thirty years, breaking it into subsequent strategies of action, clear targets, and systemic review mechanisms to track progress. The mission was broken down into four long-term strategies: to surpass Caterpillar in terms of technology development, quality, cost reduction, and diversification of products and markets. These strategies were the only stable components in the sea of changes that swept Komatsu during those thirty years.

In the 1960s company leaders decided to license state-of-the-art technologies from International Harvester, Cummings Engine, and Bucyrus-Erie. The major reason was an immediate need for technological upgrading, which company R&D could not provide on time. The licenses were implemented and R&D was given the task of upgrading them in the future. Total quality control procedures were introduced and spread over all activities, from procurement to distribution. All personnel—from top managers to every worker on the assembly line—participated in the quality circles.

Project A, aimed at upgrading the quality of the small and medium-sized bulldozers, was implemented. The costs were ignored—Komatsu aimed at developing world-class standards quality in earth-moving equipment. When the goal of total quality was achieved, the program to cut costs (without impairing quality) was implemented through standardization and unification of parts.

In 1972 Komatsu launched its export program, penetrating the fast-growing markets of Asia, Latin America, and Eastern Bloc countries. It was successfully combined in the late 1970s with a total product development program, which resulted in a number of improvements and technical innovations (like the Radio Controlled Underwater Bulldozer or Amphibious Bulldozer). In the meantime Komatsu shifted its structural design along the value chain. Having well-managed product development and manufacturing, Komatsu moved toward stressing international operations and dealer network development and support. Rapidly responding to external shocks and threats (oil crisis, appreciation of the yen against the dollar), Komatsu relentlessly cut costs. Program V-10 implemented in 1975 established procedures aimed at reduction of costs by 10 percent (while maintaining or improving quality); reduction of number of parts of 20 percent; redesigning products to gain economies in materials and manufacturing; and rationalization of the manufacturing system.

The Future and Frontiers program launched in 1979 redirected strategic thrust toward constant development of new products and new markets, but was also paralleled with improvements in quality and costs (EPOCHS program). Unusually bitter strikes and labor-management disputes in Caterpillar's major plants in Peoria (1979), aggravated by 1980 layoffs of 5,600 employees and financial losses in 1982–84, created an opportunity Komatsu exploited to increase its market share and expand operations in Europe, Africa, the Middle East, Asia, and Oceania.

All these strategies and procedures were tied to one, driving mission: to surpass Caterpillar as an industry leader. The implementation of subsequent strategies changed organizational procedures and aligned structure to the new challenges. It was constantly supported by a cohesive culture. Successes energized organizational members and proved that "mission impossible" was attainable.

Today Komatsu is the world's second-largest earth-moving equipment company, slowly catching up with Caterpillar in terms of market share and surpassing it in terms of profitability and return on investment. The essential component of this success was the skillful fusion of high-speed, transformational leadership, and excellent management of details. High-speed leadership ensured skillful analysis of worldwide economic and technological trends in the construction industry, common mission, development of strategies to exploit these environmental developments, creation of total commitment of organizational members, and fast implementations. Management supported transactional leadership with continuous attention to mundane operations, clear programs of action, milestones and procedures tracking progress, rewards for reinforcing desired behaviors, and constant incremental improvements of structure and procedures.

CONCLUSIONS

This chapter reviewed and explored the stream of research, current views, and exemplary cases of leadership. Four traditional perspectives that converge in the theme of transactional leader were reviewed. The paradigm of transformational leader, which gained wide recognition and acceptance in the 1980s, was reviewed. Finally, utilitizing a theory of high-speed management, the prototype of high-speed leader as an extension of transformational leader was sketched, resolving four major paradoxes associated with managing stability and change, centralization and empowerment, complexity and simplicity, and externally and internally based development of strategic capabilities. Let us now underline the major differences between these perspectives on leadership.

First, there is a transition in inward-outward orientation. Transactional leaders are primarily internally oriented because the efficiency of the organization is their major concern. Transformational leaders manage primarily organizational boundaries because effectiveness and adaptation are becoming the domain of action. High-speed leaders build organizational linkages because their responsibility is to sustain and develop organizational competitiveness.

Second, there is a transition of a leadership frame of reference. Transactional leaders manage transactions; transformational leaders develop cultural values facilitating adaptation; high-speed leaders resolve inherent contradictions of the adaptation process and development of strategic capabilities.

Third, there is a transition from stability via transformation to speed. The transactional leader fits into the framework of stable organizations. Transformational leader theory directly addresses the issue of adaptation through incremental and frame-breaking change. High-speed leadership accepts the need for adaption as clear and constant and deals with a crucial aspect of adaptation: speed.

REFERENCES

Bass, B. M. 1985. *Leadership and Performance beyond Expectations.* New York: Free Press.

Bennis, W., and B. Naums. 1985. *Leaders.* New York: Harper and Row.

Blake, R. R., and J. S. Mouton. 1964. *The Managerial Grid.* Houston: Gulf Publishing.

Burns, J. M. 1978. *Leadership.* New York: Harper and Row.

Cushman D. P. and S. S. King. 1994. *High-Speed Management: Organizational Communication in the 1990s.* Albany, N.Y.: SUNY Press.

Fiedler, F. E. 1967. *A Theory of Leadership Effectiveness.* New York: McGraw-Hill.

French, J. R. P. and B. Raven. 1959. The basis of social power. In D. Cartwright, ed., *Studies in Social Power.* Ann Arbor: Michigan Institute for Social Research.

Harvard Business School. 1988. Case Study 9-385-277, Komatsu Limited, Boston (revised version).

Hellriegel, D., and J. W. Slocum. 1989. *Management.* 5th ed. Reading Mass.: Addison-Wesley.

Kotter, J. P. 1990. What leaders really do. *Harvard Business Review* (May–June):103–111.

Kuhnert, K. W., and P. Lewis. 1987. Transactional and transformational leadership: A constructive/development analysis. *Academy of Management Review* 12:648–75.

Nadler, D., and M. L. Tushman. 1990. Beyond the charismatic leader: Leadership and organizational change. *California Management Review* 32:77–96.

Nohria, N. and C. Garcia-Pont. 1991. Global strategic linkages and industry structure. *Strategic Management Journal* 12:105–24.

Prahalad, C. L., and G. Hamel. 1990. The core competence of the corporation. *Harvard Business Review* (May–June):79–91.

Peters, T. 1987. *Thriving on Chaos.* London: Macmillan.

Rothman, M. 1990. A peek inside the black box. *California Business* (April):30–58.

Taylor, W. 1991. The logic of global business: An interview with ABB's Percy Barnevik. *Harvard Business Review* (Mar.–Apr.):91–105.

Tichy, N., and R. Charan. 1989. Speed, simplicity, self-confidence: An interview with Jack Welch. *Harvard Business Review* (Sept.–Oct.):112–20.

Tichy, N., and A. A. Devanna. 1986. The transformational leader. *Training and Development Journal* 40:27–32.

Tushman, M. L., W. H. Newman, and E. Romanelli. 1986. Convergence and upheaval: Managing the unsteady pace of organizational evolution. *California Management Review* 29:29–43.

Vroom, V. H., and P. W. Yetton. 1973. *Leadership and Decision-Making.* Pittsburgh: University of Pittsburgh Press.

Yukl, G. 1989. Managerial leadership: A review of theory and research. *Journal of Management* 15:251–89.

CHAPTER SIX

High-Speed Management and the New Corporate Culture: IBM and GE—A Study in Contrasts

Anne Maydan Nicotera

HIGH-SPEED MANAGEMENT

High-speed management (HSM) is becoming the new world order in a fast-growing global marketplace. The rapidity of new technology—manufacturing, marketing, and Management Information Systems (MIS)—combined with an emergent global economy creates a volatile business environment. To survive in this new world, corporations need to be innovative, adaptive, efficient, flexible, and—perhaps most of all—fast. They must be fast in new product development, design, manufacturing, distribution, and service to cope with a shrinking product life cycle, fast market saturation, and a growing field of competition (Fraker, 1984; Pepper, 1989). Competitive advantages in the global marketplace are unattainable without HSM and short-lived without vigilance to HSM. HSM is a set of principles and strategies that allows the organization to capitalize on rapid environmental change (see Cushman and King, Chapter 2, this volume).

An HSM response to rapid environmental change involves seven basic strategies (Fraker, 1984; also see Cushman and King,

113

Chapter 2, this volume). These strategies are as follows: (1) staying close to customers and competitors to anticipate customer needs and be the first to fulfill them; (2) constant new product R&D combined with fast financial backing to cope with short product life cycles and fast market saturation; (3) close coordination among all systems of product development—tight links among design, manufacturing, testing, marketing, delivery, and service to avoid errors and delays; (4) constant monitoring of product quality, ease of use, quality of service, and price competitiveness to remain competitive; (5) consideration of processes and costs of cannibalizing products and retrenching workers to respond quickly to short product life cycle and fast market saturation; (6) maintenance of a corporate vision that emphasizes change, allows assimilating new units with different values, and encourages learning from failure with impunity to adapt quickly to a changing marketplace and encourage future adaptation; and (7) development of a corporate strategy that constantly searches for opportunities to pool resources with other organizations to survive rapid change and competition with a technological edge, market access, market control, and rapid response (Cushman and King, Chapter 2, this volume). The last two strategies are of particular interest to this chapter.

BASICS OF THE THEORY OF HSM

At its foundation, HSM entails maintaining a balance between external economic forces and the organization's internal resources (Venkatraman and Prescott, 1990). To do so, an organization must monitor and evaluate rapid changes in the external economic environment and reorient internal resources in response. The theory of HSM offers information and communication frameworks for each of these—for the former, a theory of environmental scanning; for the latter, value chain theory (Cushman and King, Chapter 2, this volume).

Environmental scanning first tracks the competitive dynamics of the market by examining two sources: competitor's strategies, structures, and resources; and customers' tasks, preferences, and desired products. Second, environmental scanning scrutinizes the global forces—economic, technical, political, and social—which influence these competitive dynamics. Understanding these dynamics is central to reorienting the organization to survive and attain competitive advantage (Cushman and King, Chapter 2, this volume).

Value chain theory helps to identify the sources of competitive advantage and explicate the value of functional units and business processes in adding value to products. The actual value chain is the arrangement of the discrete activities involved in production into these functional unit activities and business processes. In a typical organization, the former include design, engineering, purchasing, manufacturing, distribution, sales, and service— with suppliers and customers existing outside the organizational structure at the ends of the chain. Business processes include product development, delivery, and service. Each of these activities and processes should be located where they can gain maximum competitive advantage; competitive advantages in each activity or process are added to or canceled out by performance in others. Thus, the value chain is "value-added" or "value-diminishing" (Cushman and King, Chapter 2, this volume). By using a value chain, each activity and process is examined for its ability to provide competitive advantage. Those that fail to provide advantage must be improved or replaced. Management must constantly monitor, evaluate, and modify the value chain to gain competitive advantage. (See Cushman and King, Chapter 2, this volume, for detailed explanation of these two frameworks.)

HSM proposes, then, that the key to survival in the global marketplace lies in environmental scanning and examination of the value chain. These processes allow top management to maintain control over the organization and its activities. Historically, a major source of managerial control has lain in the corporate culture (Wilkins, 1983; Wilkins and Ouchi, 1983).

CORPORATE CULTURE

Corporate culture has been a "hot topic" for theorists and practitioners alike since the 1970s. Whether taking a prescriptive or descriptive stance, organizational scholars agree that a healthy corporate culture is a vital means for insuring a company's success (Deal and Kennedy, 1982; Enz, 1986; Frost, et al., 1985; Lessem, 1990; Peters and Waterman, 1982; Schein, 1985; Schneider, 1990).

The Traditional Concept of Corporate Culture

Organizational culture is generally defined as a complex of values and beliefs that constitute the "taken-for-granteds" of organizational life (Conrad, 1990; Smircich and Calás, 1987). Traditionally, corporate culture has been seen as a strong management tool in the pursuit of excellence, the unifying force of a strong cultural value system being the primary source of its achievement (Deal and Kennedy, 1982; Enz, 1986; Frost, et al., 1985; Lessem, 1990; Peters and Waterman, 1982; Schein, 1985; Schneider, 1990). A common managerial approach to utilizing corporate culture is to provide new employees with intensive training in the corporate value system (for an example, Albert, 1987).

Organizational scholars have consistently pointed to the importance of a strong organizational value system, shared by all employees. Lessem (1990) cites several examples that trace the long history of this idea: Fayol's (1949—originally published in 1916) mention of an " 'esprit de corps' as a vital constituent of an organization's functioning"; Selznick's (1948) "homogeneity of outlook"; and Bennis' (1966) "cultural attitude." Indeed, a cherished belief among organizational theorists continues to be that "shared values are the major source of excellence. Those shared values, in turn, emerge out of a cohesive corporate culture" (Lessem, 1990, p. 6, citing Peters and Waterman, 1982). These values "are the bedrock of any corporate culture" (Deal and Kennedy, 1982, p. 21).

Deal and Kennedy (1982) argue that "the best managers . . . strive to make a mark through creating a guiding vision (and) shaping shared values" (p. 18) for and with their employees. They go on to identify IBM and GE as two of the best examples to illustrate their ideas. Guiding visions and shared values may indeed be a potent force that makes for an internally cohesive and unified corporate culture—an esprit de corps indeed. On the other hand, however strongly scholars may emphasize the unifying nature of a strong core value system, they also acknowledge that developing such a core value system is a slow process.

Under current global economic conditions, organizations need to respond quickly to rapid environmental changes. HSM allows little time for shaping values and making sure all employees are operating under a shared guiding vision. Furthermore, an important HSM technique is to quickly forge alliances for competitive advantage, seize that advantage during its fleeting window of opportunity, and then dissolve the alliance to move on to others that afford advantage (see Cushman and King, Chapter 2, this volume). According to traditional notions of corporate culture, the success of alliances should depend on shared values. Alliances that develop, perform, and dissolve quickly cannot possibly be based on shared values; yet they do succeed under HSM. Although academic treatments of corporate culture continue to focus on the importance of shared values, organizations that persist in a focus on common values are rapidly falling behind in the global marketplace. IBM is a perfect example. Although IBM may remain an exemplar of Deal and Kennedy's ideas for corporate value systems, these ideas must be modified if corporate cultures are to enhance rather than hinder quick response under HSM.

GE has succeeded in cultivating a new focus for corporate culture that allows for a strong culture to coexist with a diverse internal value system. Below, these two corporations are contrasted to illustrate the differences in form and function between the traditional concept of corporate culture and the new concept of corporate culture that must accompany HSM. First, however, we must explicate the focus of the conception of corporate culture under HSM and demonstrate its necessity.

A NEW CONCEPT OF CORPORATE CULTURE

The concept of corporate culture under HSM is simple. Diverse values are allowed to remain and are oriented to common goals under conditions of high competition and rapid environmental change. A clear corporate vision is still an important element of the culture, but the vision is focused on change and adaptation rather than a core set of values. When common goals and specific measurable performance targets become the core of the culture, any set of values can be oriented in that direction. As Weick (1979) emphasizes, coordination of action is more important than coordination of values. In addition, goals and performance targets can be altered rapidly under a corporate vision of change and adaptation. Most important, alliances for quick competitive advantage can be quickly accomplished with this new focus. Fraker (1984) specifically advocates a corporate vision emphasizing change as key in the ability to assimilate units with different values under HSM and to coalign with other organizations.

HSM AND COALIGNMENTS

Linkages under HSM

The application of value chain theory often reveals that timely response to rapid environmental change necessitates linking with groups outside as well as within the organization. The new world order of HSM is marked by the emergence of global strategic linkages (Nohira and Garcia-Pont, 1991). Linkages take several forms. Organizations engage with each other in joint ventures, acquisitions, and mergers; they create partnerships with suppliers, customers, employees, governments, and investors; and they do all of this in multinational locations. Each type of partnership can be used to improve the value chain in HSM.

Linkages between Competitors.   The new breed of joint ventures (JVs) and other collaborations between corporations involve linking with competitors (Hamel, Doz, and Prahalad, 1989; Kanter, 1989). A large percentage of intercorporation linkages fall far short of expectations (Datta and Grant, 1990; Gomes-Casseres, 1989; Kanter, 1989; Lei and Slocum, 1991; Weiss, 1987). The most prevalent obstruction in their negotiations is procedural; often, the compatible economic goals of the two parties become overshadowed by incompatible procedural expectations (Bryan and Buck, 1989). Business protocols vary based on values embedded in the cultures of the organizations; value disparities between organizations are further complicated when the organizations are based in different countries (Lei and Slocum, 1991). If corporations are to gain competitive advantage in the global market, however, they *must* link with other corporations (Datta, 1991; Datta and Grant, 1990; Gupta, 1991; Hamel, et al., 1989; Johnston and Lawrence, 1988; Kanter, 1989; Lei and Slocum, 1991; Nohira and Garcia-Pont, 1991).

In the global business environment, these linkages are complicated by disparate value systems of national cultures. The most widely researched and documented difference lies between Asian and non-Asian (particularly American) cultures: the collectivism-individualism contrast. In a study exploring whether managerial control methods of Asian corporations can be successful outside Asian cultures, Chow, Shields, and Chan (1991) found that Asians (with collectivistic values) have a higher level of performance than Americans (with individualistic values), especially when their work is interdependent with that of other workers. Further, worker interdependencies induced by Asian managerial control systems may affect American workers' performance. These results indicate that Asian managerial practices may be effective in cultures with widely different value systems. The implications for HSM are immense. In order to quickly forge mutually beneficial relationships between corporations, disparate value systems must be integrated in such a way that allows them to coexist so that the organizations can work together toward some common goal. Chow, Shields, and Chan (1991) provide some hope that this is possible.

Stakeholder Linkages.   Kanter (1989) identifies an important class of alliances that stem from preexisting interdependent relationships. In examining the business process chain, three groups of stakeholders are identified: suppliers, customers, and employee organizations. Stakeholders are generally defined as any group upon whom an organization depends to achieve its goals throughout the value chain. In linking with suppliers, organizations cut costs and improve quality. The current trend toward outsourcing is a sign that corporations are engaged in HSM. To quickly respond to environmental changes, corporations form close alliances with suppliers and redefine the vendor relationship to a partnership in the value chain.

In linking with customers, corporations capitalize on a major source of innovation. In these linkages, attention to customer service is expanded to include formal bonds such as user councils, R&D consultations, joint promotions, and joint development projects (Kanter, 1989). The recent increase in corporations creating customer alliances is another indicator that HSM is becoming common. "Timely knowledge of changing customer

requirements makes it possible to guide production more efficiently, reducing waste, inventory costs, and returns" (Kanter,
1989, p. 186). No more perfect way of "keeping customers close"
(Fraker, 1984) exists than building formal partnerships with them.
With the customer participating in the value chain, quick response to customer needs is practically guaranteed.

Kanter's (1989) description of links with employee organizations also precisely reflects HSM. "Union-management alliances
are occurring in industries undergoing rapid change, as a means
to permit innovation—to collaborate in changing work rules or
job conditions to improve competitiveness" (p. 186). Like suppliers and customers, in growing numbers, unions are being added
to the value chain. Such alliances are yet another indication of
the practice of HSM. In creating stakeholder alliances, the focus
is on joint benefits—common goals and mutual gain. In the world
of HSM such alliances need to be forged quickly. Corporations
need to find ways to succeed when made up of groups with
diverse values and to coalign with other organizations that have
disparate values.

Other groups of stakeholders can be identified. To be globally competitive, organizations also need to link with investors
and governments in multinational locations. In every alliance,
mutual benefits are the prominent motivating factors for forming a partnership. To be globally competitive, a corporation needs
to form alliances with competitors, suppliers, customers, unions,
foreign governments, and worldwide investors—and do all of
this in multinational locations.

The Problem of Diverse Values in HSM

It is with the practice of rapid coalignments that the traditional
concept of corporate culture becomes problematic. Maintaining
the assumption that a core set of shared values is the foundation
of successful organizational action is imprudent in a world where
alliances have to develop, perform, and dissolve quickly. In the
global marketplace, organizations that focus on shared values as
the core of their culture cannot keep up with rapid environmental changes. IBM is a perfect example of how corporate cultures
that focus on core values are dysfunctional in a volatile global
marketplace.

In the traditional concept of corporate culture, "culture is the process through which social action and interaction become constructed and reconstructed into an organizational reality. The symbolic constitutes what is taken for granted as organizational life. Culture and communication are vehicles through which reality is constituted in organizational contexts" (Smircich and Calás, 1987, p. 234). The foundation for such corporate culture is a strong system of shared values. Values are abstract and intangible; their transmission is accomplished through rituals and mythology (Deal and Kennedy, 1982). These symbolic forms are presumed to immerse individuals into the corporate culture, provide them with a guide by which to interpret events, give them a sense of "belongingness," build morale, and most of all provide them with a guide for actions.

The problem for HSM in adhering to this traditional notion of culture is that an organization cannot rest actions on shared values while remaining fast and agile. Values are easy to express, but difficult to transmit so that all organizational members internalize them. Diverse sets of abstract, intangible values cannot be forged into commonalities quickly enough for timely response in HSM. The notion of corporate culture under HSM must shift to a focus on common goals and measurable performance targets under an overarching corporate vision of change and adaptation.

The HSM Solution

The adaptation of focus from values to behavioral goals and targets is simple, and its basis is found in the same literature that emphasizes the traditional focus on values. As transmissions of corporate culture, rituals and mythologies necessarily focus on behavior. First, through rituals, "strong culture companies . . . communicate exactly how they want their people to behave" (Deal and Kennedy, 1982; p. 21). Theorists have emphasized rituals as the manifestations of deeply held common values (Deal and Kennedy, 1982; Enz, 1986; Lessem, 1990; Peters and Waterman, 1982; Schein, 1985). Rituals, however, are innately behavioral. The connection between rituals and values is a theoretic abstraction.

Second, through myths and stories, organizations model the way employees are expected to behave. "Stories can provide role models of desirable behavior by teaching employees about actual organizational events, managerial practices, and employee behaviors that directly support an organization's philosophy and values" (Albert, 1987, p. 71). For example, a famous IBM story tells of the newly hired security guard who blocked company founder Thomas Watson, Sr. from a secured area because he did not have his pass. The guard was commended for her adherence to the rules, and Watson sent someone to get his pass (Albert, 1987). Certainly, IBM's core values are apparent in the telling of this story. The function of this and other corporate stories, however, is to reinforce or discourage, respectively, the kinds of behaviors that are valued or devalued by the organization (Albert, 1987). As with rituals, rites, and ceremonies, theorists emphasize the underlying common values and core philosophy revealed by corporate mythology (Deal and Kennedy, 1982; Enz, 1986; Lessem, 1990; Peters and Waterman, 1982; Schein, 1985). Like rituals, however, stories are about behaviors. The link between stories and values is also a theoretic abstraction.

In practice, HSM organizations shift their focus from values to behavior in the form of common goals and performance targets. HSM corporations focus on the link between culture and behavior; culture thus becomes behaviorally defined. Under HSM, then, values (culture) are expressed as common goals and behavioral targets. The responsibility to achieve these targets is located in the individual.

Coalignment is a primary concern in HSM, and diverse values stand in the way. When values are expressed in the form of performance targets, individual values take on a self-motivating force. When the responsibility for meeting targets resides in the individual, his or her own values can be oriented toward meeting them. So, rather than train new employees into an abstract value system underlying an "organizational reality," new hires should be screened so that their own values can be oriented in the direction of concrete organizational goals and their attendant individual performance targets.

Similarly, in the case of coalignments between organizations with diverse values, an emphasis on values can block successful coalignment. GE learned this the hard way in 1988, when they took over Cie. Generale de Radiologie (CGR), a French medical equipment maker. In an attempt to boost morale among CGR managers, GE management distributed T-shirts with the GE slogan ("Go for One") to be worn to training seminars. The move backfired violently, opening "a bitter and prolonged cultural clash" (Nelson, 1990, p. A10). The clash of cultures manifested itself as a $25 million loss for CGR-GE in 1989 (Nelson, 1990).

HSM corporations must find a way to forge coalignments that allow diverse values to coexist. Diverse value sets between organizations can be oriented toward performance targets and expectations for these units. A clear set of goals for the parties becomes the keystone for successful coalignment. JVs that are successful under HSM focus on performance targets rather than shared values; this is a clear theme in the articulation of what makes for successful multinational JVs (Gomes-Casseres, 1989; Lei and Slocum, 1991).

Furthermore, within this conception of corporate culture, rituals serve the function of performance monitoring on value-added criteria. Under HSM, performance targets are primary. When performance targets are not met and the cause is out of the organization's control (as revealed by environmental scanning and value chain theory), the coalignment should be dissolved. Units can be sold; JVs and partnerships can be disbanded.

HSM rests on the ability for rapid coalignment. Under rapid coalignment, diverse values must be made to fit together. Because diverse value systems are problematic for rapidly coaligning, performance targets become the key consideration. The central concern is that performance targets are clear in the original linking agreement. If these targets are strong and the diverse value systems involved are compatible with those targets, it does not matter how those value systems compare to each other.

The key idea is that organizations are political entities composed of coalitions of people with different goals, values, and interests. Whether we discuss coalitions within a single organization or those organizations involved in alliances, these groups must link to cooperate regardless of their diverse values. Although practitioners and theorists persist in their belief that value systems are the primary source of organizational success, diverse values often stand in the way of successful coalignment. When the emphasis in corporate culture is shifted away from core value systems, performance targets can tie people together into successful coalignments.

IBM AND GE: CULTURES IN CONTRAST

IBM and GE are excellent choices to illustrate the contrast of value-focus and performance-focus in corporate cultures. Both organizations are traditional big American companies. Both were leaders early in their respective markets. (Whereas GE has a multi-industrial base; IBM is an industry-based competitor.) Both were ranked among the "ten best manufacturing companies to work for" in a survey of industry experts commissioned by the Society of Manufacturing Engineers (GE makes list, 1989). IBM has not adjusted its culture to the demands of HSM and is rapidly falling behind in the global market. GE, on the other hand, has adjusted and is a successful HSM corporation.

IBM: A Traditional Corporate Culture

Values and Socialization.   IBM's corporate culture has been traditionally guided by several basic values (IBM, 1985; this summary is also based on the detailed discussions found in Cushman and King, 1994; Cushman, King, and Smith, 1988; and Nicotera and Cushman, 1992). First, IBM's core values have included respect for the individual, with heavy emphasis on individual development, merit pay, and the maintenance of open, two-way communication with employees. Second, service to the customer has been highly valued. IBM has emphasized superior equipment maintenance and support services (although IBM often has not delivered; see Lewis, 1992). Third, the culture has been rooted in a value for the superior accomplishment of all tasks. IBM has had expectations for superior performance from all its employees; managers have been "admonished to lead in new developments, be aware of advances made by others, better them where possible, or be willing to adapt them to fit the needs of the corporation (and) produce quality products of the most advanced design at the lowest possible cost" (IBM, 1985, cited by Cushman, King, and Smith, 1988, p. 81). Fourth, effective leadership has been a core value. Managers have been required to follow certain procedures to make every employee an enthusiastic partner in IBM. Managers have been required to motivate their subordinates for superior performance, to meet frequently with them, to have the courage to question decisions and policies and the vision to see the needs of the entire company, and finally, to plan for the future with an open mind to new ideas (IBM, 1985). Fifth, heavy emphasis has been traditionally placed on obligations to stockholders, who are viewed as the providers of the capital that creates jobs at IBM. This view required IBM employees to take care of the property entrusted to the company by the stockholders, provide an attractive return on investments, and maximize opportunities for continued profit and growth (IBM, 1985). Sixth, IBM has valued a fair deal for the supplier. Suppliers have traditionally been selected according to the quality of their goods or services, their reliability, and their price competitiveness. When negotiating a contract, the legitimate interests of both the supplier and IBM have been recognized. Suppliers who become unduly dependent on IBM have been avoided (IBM, 1985). Finally, the corporate culture has emphasized that at all times, IBM should be a good corporate citizen. Competition has been recognized as imperative for protecting the public interest. However, IBM has emphasized that the competition should be vigorous in a spirit of fair play, with respect for competitors and the law, improving the quality of society, creating an environment in which people want to live and work, and making the world a better place (IBM, 1985).

IBM's culture has traditionally maintained a strong sense of unity. Fairness and respect for individuals, both within and outside the organization, have been emphasized. IBM's culture has also been based on a strong sense of community obligation. Responsibility, obligation to others, and good citizenship have been heavily emphasized. The core value at IBM may be summarized as "one for all and all for one" (Nicotera and Cushman, 1992). In addition to these general values, IBM has articulated goals for the company. For example, IBM's goals for the 1980s were as follows: (1) to grow with the industry; (2) to exhibit product leadership across the product line, excelling in technology, value, and quality; (3) to be the most efficient in everything, a low-cost producer, seller, and administrator; and (4) to sustain profitability that funds growth. In the 1980s, performance plans for various corporate levels were set up and monitored annually for meeting these goals (Cushman and King, 1994; Cushman, King, and Smith, 1988; IBM, 1985).

IBM's socialization process involves several steps designed to immerse the individual in the values of the company (Cushman and King, 1994; and Cushman, King and Smith, 1988). The socialization process is sufficiently intense as to compel the employee to embrace the corporate values. As a result, IBM's employees are strongly rooted in the corporate value system of individual respect, unity, and community responsibility.

IBM's Declining Stature.   IBM is still a giant in American industry, as of 1992 remaining each year at the top of the Fortune 500 list. As of the 1992 Fortune 500 list, IBM has remained a top company in terms of market value and stockholder equity. Although still huge, the giant is shrinking at an alarming rate. IBM's apparent success is a carryover from its past market dominance. IBM's culture has been called "dysfunctional" by some analysts (Byrne, et al., 1991). Fundamentally, IBM's slow culture cannot maintain success in a fast market; new products are obsolete or redundant by the time they reach the market—if they ever do (for example, the IBM laptop; see Byrne, et al., 1991). IBM is slow getting to market even updating its own products; in 1987 IBM promised the capacity to link all its machines. The technology still has not hit the market (Schwartz, 1991).

Technological advances in computers move at lightning speed; IBM is dead center in a market in which HSM is particularly essential. IBM, with its traditional "wait and see" attitude (Guterl, 1988), simply cannot keep up with its competitors. IBM, after setting the standard in the computer industry, is lagging behind. Its dominance over the market, established in the early years, has waned. IBM is not a player in any of today's key computer markets (laptops, medium-sized computers, and work stations), and although things have been changing, changes have been slow—in traditional IBM style. A clear sign of change at IBM is its recent alliances with Apple (McCarroll, 1991; Powell and Stone, 1991) and Wang (Markoff, 1991d); the nature of a HSM market demands such cooperation with competitors.

The Move toward Change.   John Akers, CEO of IBM until 1993, struggled with "trying to make the elephant dance" for several years (Byrne, et al., 1991; Guterl, 1988). When he became CEO in the mid-1980s, Akers started slowly restructuring IBM, recognizing that the basic values of the company were not being realized. Gradually at first, and then more rapidly, top-level executives were offered early retirement, innovative younger executives took over, and decision making became less centralized, but not nearly decentralized enough to suit the market's speed (Guterl, 1988). Working within the existing culture, Akers had some degree of success in boosting sales and profits. Indeed, from 1989 to 1990 IBM rose from fourth ($3.7 billion) to first ($6 billion) in profits. Old IBM'ers were not pleased with Akers' changes (Brown, 1992), often citing a violation of IBM's basic values. Akers himself was the target of cutbacks made by IBM's board of directors (Lohr, 1992).

These solutions were "quick-fix" measures. IBM's traditional culture simply does not allow it to compete effectively in the quick computer marketplace. Advances in sales and profit were short-term and do not reflect the overall trend. For the second quarter of 1991, earnings declined by 91.9 percent and revenues by 10.7 percent (Markoff, 1991c). For the 1980s the overall trend was downward. Operating profit margin (before depreciation) peaked in the early 1980s at just below 35 percent, steadily dropped to just over 20 percent in 1986, then dropped below 20 percent in 1991. Operating profit per employee (after depreciation, in 1982 dollars) steadily rose from 20 percent in 1981 to 26 percent in 1983, dropped to 17 percent in 1986, and climbed back to 23 percent in 1990 before dropping to 18 percent in 1991. Market share (worldwide sales of hardware, software, and services) plummeted in the 1980s. Steady at 36 percent from 1981 to 1983, it dropped every year to 23 percent by 1988, where it remained relatively steady, dropping slightly in 1991 (Byrne, et al., 1991). For 1991, IBM saw a loss of about $2 billion. Losses for 1992 total almost $5 billion (Fortune 500, 1993). IBM cannot ride on its past dominance. Change in the corporate culture is long overdue; now, pressures from IBM's economic environment are making that fact abundantly clear. The old way simply does not work anymore (Byrne, et al., 1991).

Diagnosis of the Problem.   IBM's difficulty lies in the articulation of a culture embedded in basic core values. Responsibility for meeting corporate goals is located in collective effort, which in turn, is located in the core value system. As such, any diversity of values must be worked out before action can proceed. IBM's goals are generally stated, and although performance plans are

laid out for meeting those goals the focus is *not* on specific measurable performance targets. Because of the heavy emphasis on
core values, IBM experiences goal displacement. The result is
frustration at upper management levels.

John Akers himself commented thunderously on the symp-
toms of this problem, but did not treat the cause. "The tension
level is not high enough in the business—everyone is too damn
comfortable at a time when the business is in crisis. . . . (For example,) I'm sick and tired of visiting plants to hear nothing but
great things about quality and cycle time, and then to visit customers who tell me of problems" (Akers' comments to an IBM
management seminar quoted in several sources, most notably
Markoff, 1991b; and Reibstein and Rosaldo, 1991). "I am con-
vinced that some of our people do not understand that they have
a deeply personal stake in declining market share, revenue, and
profits. A healthy level of concern and urgency, which I call
tension, is essential for everybody in IBM" (excerpt of a later
message from Akers to IBM employees, quoted from text, 1991,
p. D5).

Although pushing hard, Akers was not pursuing change in
the right direction to succeed in a HSM marketplace. Akers is
himself a product of the IBM cookie-cutter culture and in his
demand for change, he invoked the spirit of company founder,
Tom Watson, Sr. Verity and Lewis (1988) quote Akers: "The fun-
damentals that Tom Watson, Sr. built the business on: pursuit of
excellence, superior service, respect for people . . . they are as
alive and well today as ever" (p. 95). "It is just the method of
delivery (Akers) is updating," conclude Verity and Lewis (1988,
p. 95). According to our analysis, if change at IBM is to reap
sustained benefits, the focus on values must shift to a focus on
specific, measurable performance targets.

Because of the centralized structure embedded in a core
value system, IBM is sluggish. Decisions on such things as product development take too long for a HSM response. Windows of
opportunity slam shut long before IBM is ready for market. On
the other hand, new customer service programs (Lewis, 1992)
and JVs with Apple (McCarroll, 1991; Powell and Stone, 1991)
and Wang (Markoff, 1991d) are encouraging signs; IBM may yet
succeed at HSM. However, the old concept of a core value system
to tie people together must be changed if HSM is to be fully

implemented at IBM. The new idea of corporate culture is to let performance targets tie people together, while their own values let them stand alone to reach those targets. IBM could learn from GE, who does just that and is successful with HSM.

GE: A HSM Corporate Culture

Targets and Socialization. GE is a successful HSM corporation. (See Cushman and King, Chapter 2, this volume, for a detailed description of GE's success under HSM.) GE's values have been expressed in the form of specific goals and measurable performance targets (this discussion based on Cushman and King, 1993, originally drawn from GE internal publications; and on Nicotera and Cushman, 1992). First to become the most competitive corporation in the world, business units have been admonished to first or second in their respective markets. They have only invested in businesses with high-growth potential, where GE can become the first or second producer. Flexibility has been maintained by decentralization. They have strived to develop low-cost, high-quality, easily serviced products that yield high profits. Ability to meet specific productivity and financial targets has been carefully monitored. Second, to become the nation's most valuable corporation in terms of market capitalization, GE has aimed to increase earnings by 10 to 15 percent per year and productivity by 15 to 20 percent per year, to maintain stock appreciation and yield at 15 to 20 percent per year, to maintain exports as 50 percent of sales, and to maintain their managerial reputation as an entrepreneurial, agile, aggressive, knowledgeable, and effective competitor. GE's third goal has been to develop a skilled, self-actualizing, and aggressive workforce. GE has wanted its workers to be challenged by their environment; their skills should be enhanced so that they will have no difficulty finding another job if GE no longer needs them. GE has emphasized to its employees that increasing market shares is the only way to maintain job security. GE has wanted its employees to be action- and risk-oriented, to relentlessly pursue productivity and financial targets, and to be individually responsible for achieving them. Employees' skills have been developed through timely, quality education programs. High performance has been rewarded by placing more investment in the hands of those people who have succeeded in the past. Fourth, to develop open communication based on candor and trust, facts and corporation objectives have been shared with all employees. Employees have been expected to be open to discussion regarding their strengths, weaknesses, and the possibility of change. No one is misled as to expendability. Anyone no longer needed is let go.

GE's performance targets emphasize unbridled competition. The corporation and its employees are expected to be lean and mean, ready for anything and willing to take risks. Employees are expected to sufficiently enhance their skills so as to quickly find new jobs if they are no longer useful to GE. Self-reliance and self-actualization are heavily emphasized on both the individual and corporate levels. The core theme at GE may be summarized as "looking out for number one" (Nicotera and Cushman, 1992).

GE's socialization process demands that individuals continually hone their skills (Cushman and King, 1994). New managers are placed in their positions for six months before they are given any formal training. When training is implemented, these individuals are more receptive and learning is more meaningful. This delay of formal training also allows new managers to orient their own value systems to the corporation's concrete goals, rather than forcing them to adopt a core set of abstract corporate values embedded in training programs.

At GE, job security is only maintained as long as an individual remains the best person for his or her job. No matter how long a person has worked for GE, that person is expendable. If the company acquires another business—or closes down a business—which has personnel who can perform the person's job better, he or she is replaced (Cushman and King, 1994). Education is constant. At GE's Management Development Center at Crotonville, New York, managers continually experience state-of-the-art leadership development training, with a focus on problems of change (Tichy, 1989).

Self-reliance is the key to GE's success with HSM. GE has a very strong corporate culture. However, this culture is not built from employee agreement on a set of core abstract values. Instead, GE's values are articulated in the form of explicit, measurable performance targets. Unlike IBM, the responsibility for achieving goals is located in the individual. Variations in individual value systems are coordinated with the performance targets. Under these conditions, rapid coalignment is possible. GE, as contrasted with IBM, illustrates that performance targets have replaced value systems as the core of corporate cultures under HSM because of the particular dynamics and problems presented by rapid coalignment. The fundamental move is coordination. Under HSM there is a need to coordinate people so that diverse values do not stand in the way. Rigid performance targets accompanied by individual responsibility for meeting them are the answer to productivity and sustained growth.

GE's Success. The ability of a performance-based culture like GE's to succeed in HSM will now be demonstrated. GE seems to have learned from its T-shirt faux pas in France. GE's approach to Tungsram, its Hungarian light bulb company, was quite different. Late in 1989 GE acquired a 50.1 percent stake in Tungsram for $150 million (Levine, 1990). In July 1991 GE increased its stake to 75 percent, citing "confidence in the future of the business" (GE's lighting unit, 1991, p. A3). According to several sources (Greenhouse, 1990; Levine, 1990; Thurow, 1991; Tully, 1990), the acquisition of this facility was part of a strategy to gain "back door" entrance into Western Europe, where GE does not have a strong presence. Acting quickly, GE executives took advantage of the fall of communism to gain their entrance into Tungsram. In a stroke of genius, Hungarian native George Varga was put in charge of GE's Hungarian operations. Varga fled Hungary as a teenager in 1956, attended American schools, and eventually rose through the ranks to GE's top management. Putting a native at the helm in Budapest helps, as Varga put it, to perform "a cultural marriage" (Tully, 1990).

This marriage of cultures was focused on a key goal: profit. Within this goal, GE has been focused on performance targets (i.e., for projected earnings and savings) to maximize profit. An aim toward profit is not so simple as it sounds. In Eastern Europe, employees must be taught the very meaning of profit and why it is important (Tully, 1990). Eastern European "accounting" methods claim profit when shipments are sent—regardless of whether goods are actually sold. In Tungsram warehouses in Germany, GE found $3 million worth of obsolete six-watt headlights (Tully, 1990). Once Western accounting standards had been applied, Tungsram's claimed $22 million profit was reduced to $9 million (Greenhouse, 1990). The road to revamping Tungsram was not to be an easy one. Although state of the art for Eastern Europe, the facilities—physical and organizational—were woefully inadequate by Western standards.

Performance targets were employed as the basis for the emergent culture at Tungsram. Under the overarching goal of profit, several targets were put in place: raising market share by 1 percent each year; reaching earnings as 7 percent of sales (high for the industry); specific developments in high-tech, high-margin products; and specifics for cost cutting (Tully, 1990). Cost cutting took the form of computerizing the massive bureaucracy, improving efficiency in production, reducing breakage on the line (formerly in excess of 25 percent), and cutting the workforce (Levine, 1990; Tully, 1990). To improve efficiency and reduce breakage, consultants from other GE plants were brought in. Projected savings here alone totaled in excess of $500,000 a year.

Perhaps the most difficult measure involved reducing the workforce. The threat of unemployment is particularly frightening to workers in Eastern Europe, who desperately need jobs and economic development. Although they look to Western capitalists to provide the latter, they fear Western investors will impose large-scale layoffs. GE's ability to coalign the goals of diverse interdependent parties and the lesson learned in France are revealed by their actions in Budapest. Although layoffs were seen as inevitable, given Tungsram's typical Eastern European bureaucratic glut, other cost-cutting efforts were employed first. Although apprehensive, employees were eager to learn this new way of working. Their individual goals were thus oriented by GE's targets and overarching profit motivation. Recognizing that profit could be improved in other ways, Varga approached the issue of layoffs carefully and put them off as long as possible while other measures were taken (Greenhouse, 1990; Levine, 1990; Thurow, 1991; Tully, 1990). Workers have understood, however, that layoffs would be inevitable (Thurow, 1991).

Western business standards were reinforced through such things as merit pay to reward performance (Greenhouse, 1990). In addition to Western standards for performance, workers picked up Western business skills for independence in decision making and expression (Thurow, 1991). Individuals who learn these skills might indeed be affected by layoffs. If so, however, they are acquainted with Western business practices—something they would not have gained if laid off immediately. By designing and prioritizing performance targets so that employee needs for security were met, GE not only ensured cooperation in meeting those targets, but was also set up to send laid-off workers out into the world at least partially equipped for the Westernization of the Eastern European economy. Indeed, they were creating a self-actualizing workforce at Tungsram.

The Threat of Global Economic Instability. The GE-Tungsram venture did not come to its projected success. In March 1992 GE announced a ninety-day moratorium on new investments in Tungsram operations (GE-Tungsram venture, 1992). Simply put, the performance targets set up for the company were not met. GE lost more than $13 million in 1991, despite a 16 percent increase in sales. Some critics were quick to say GE's motive for entrance to European markets was apparently not worth its price. Others question the real motivation for suspending operations. An HSM analysis takes a different view, regardless of ulterior motivations for investment and suspension of investment. From an HSM analysis, GE's focus on performance targets alerted Varga to the cost/gain ratio of the Tungsram venture. In his judgment, a 30 percent inflation rate combined with rapid acceleration in the devaluation of Hungarian currency led to the inability to meet performance targets and profit goals. Under such conditions, which are beyond GE's control, the appropriate HSM response was to reevaluate the coalignment. Under HSM, linkages that do not meet performance targets and profit goals must be dissolved. From our analysis, GE simply took the time to evaluate whether this linkage still had potential to meet profit goals. If GE had found a way to adjust internal operations in response to Tungsram's rapidly changing environment, the venture might have continued. While such an evaluation takes place, investment should be suspended. The application of environmental scanning and value chain theory reveals whether a corporation can make such an alliance work. If not, it should be dissolved. At this writing, the future of Tungsram is unclear.

CONCLUSION

This chapter has provided an analysis of corporate culture under HSM. Traditional and contemporary views of corporate culture were discussed, and an explanation on HSM coalignments demonstrated the need for a new concept of corporate culture. IBM's and GE's cultures provide a contrast of corporate cultures that differ in their ability to enhance HSM. Specifically, IBM's focus on core values is inferior to GE's focus on performance targets. The successful implementation of HSM rests on a corporate culture focusing on change and adaptation, allowing for the co-orientation of diverse value systems to a common set of goals. A wide variety of coalignments can be enhanced by such a corporate culture.

REFERENCES

Albert, M. 1987. Transmitting corporate culture through case stories. *Personnel* 64(8) (Aug.):71–73.

Bennis, W. 1966. *Changing Organizations.* New York: McGraw-Hill.

Brown, W. 1992. Using psychological pressure at IBM. *New York Times,* Mar. 22, p. 13.

Bryan, R. M., and P. C. Buck. 1989. When customs collide: The pitfalls of international acquisitions. *Financial Executive* 5(3):43–46.

Byrne, J. A., et al. 1991. IBM: What's wrong? What's next? *Business Week* (June 17):24–32.

Chow, C. W., M. D. Shields, and Y. K. Chan. 1991. The effects of management controls and national culture on manufacturing performance: An experimental investigation. *Accounting, Organizations, and Society* 16:209–26.

Conrad, C. 1990. *Strategic Organizational Communication.* Fort Worth: Holt, Rinehart and Winston.

Cushman, D. P., and S. S. King. 1994. *High-Speed Management: Organizational Communication in the 1990s.* Albany, N.Y.: SUNY Press.

Cushman, D. P., S. S. King, and T. Smith. 1988. The rules perspective on organizational communication. In G. M. Goldhaber and G. A. Barnett, eds., *Handbook of Organizational Communication.* Norwood, N.J.: Ablex.

Datta, D. K. 1991. Organizational fit and acquisition performance: Effects of post-acquisition integration. *Strategic Management Journal* 12:281–97.

Datta, D. K., and J. H. Grant. 1990. Relationships between type of acquisition, the autonomy given to the acquired firm, and acquisition success: An empirical analysis. *Journal of Management* 16:29–44.

Deal, T. E., and A. A. Kennedy. 1982. *Corporate Cultures*. Reading, Mass.: Addison-Wesley.

Enz, C. 1986. *Power and Shared Values in the Corporate Culture*. Ann Arbor: UMI Research Press.

Fayol, H. 1949. *General and Industrial Management*. New York: Pitman.

The Fortune 500. 1993, *Fortune*, April 19, 1993, p. 184.

Fraker, S. 1984. High-speed management for the high tech age. *Fortune* (Feb. 13):34–60.

GE makes list of top manufacturers. 1989. *Hartford Current*, July 5, p. E2.

GE-Tungsram venture in Hungary hits snags. 1992. *New York Times*, Mar. 28, pp. B1, B29.

GE's lighting unit increased its stake in Hungary concern. 1991. *Wall Street Journal*, June 13, p. A3.

Gomes-Casseres, B. 1989. Joint ventures in the face of global competition. *Sloan Management Review* 30(3):17–26.

Greenhouse, S. 1990. Running on fast-forward in Budapest. *New York Times*, Dec. 16, pp. C1, C8.

Gupta, U. 1991. How big companies are joining forces with little ones for mutual advantage. *Wall Street Journal*, Feb. 25, pp. B1, B2.

Guterl, F. V. 1988. IBM's very tough guy. *Business Month* (Feb.):22–28.

Hamel, G., Y. L. Doz, and C. K. Prahalad. 1989. Collaborate with your competitors—and win. *Harvard Business Review* (Jan.–Feb.):133–39.

IBM. 1985. *Annual Report*. Armonk, N.Y.: Author.

Johnston, R., and P. R. Lawrence. 1988. Beyond vertical integration—The rise of the value-adding partnership. *Harvard Business Review* (July–Aug.):94–101.

Kanter, R. M. 1989. Becoming PALs: Pooling, allying, and linking across companies. *Academy of Management Executive*, 3:181–91.

Lei, D., and J. W. Slocum. 1991. Global strategic alliances: Payoffs and pitfalls. *Organizational Dynamics* 19(3):44–62.

Lessem, R. 1990. *Managing Corporate Culture.* Brookfield, Vt.: Gower.

Levine, J. 1990. GE carves a road east. *Business Week* (July 30):32–33.

Lewis, P. H. 1992. In a turnabout, IBM says, "We'll talk to anybody." *New York Times,* Mar. 22, p. C8.

Lohr, S. 1992. Pulling down the corporate clubhouse. *New York Times,* Apr. 12, pp. C1, C5.

Markoff, J. 1991a. IBM chief criticizes staff again. *New York Times,* June 19, p. D1.

————. 1991b. IBM chief gives staff tough talk. *New York Times,* May 29, pp. D1, D8.

————. 1991c. IBM net fell 91.9% in quarter. *New York Times,* July 20, pp. 17–18.

————. 1991d. Wang joins IBM in marketing alliance. *New York Times,* June 19, pp. D1, D5.

McCarroll, T. 1991. Love at first byte. *Time,* July 15, pp. 46–47.

Frost, P. J., et al., eds. 1985. *Organizational Culture.* Beverly Hills: Sage.

Nelson, M. M. 1990. GE's culture turns sour at French unit. *Wall Street Journal,* July 31, p. A10.

Nicotera, A. M., and D. P. Cushman. 1992. Organizational ethics: A within-organization view. *Journal of Applied Communication Research* 20:437–64.

Nohira, N., and C. Garcia-Pont. 1991. Global strategic linkages and industry structure. *Strategic Management Journal* 12:105–24.

Pepper, C. B. 1989. Fast forward. *Business Month* (Feb.):25–30.

Peters, T., and R. Waterman. 1982. *In Search of Excellence.* New York: Harper and Row.

Powell, B., and J. Stone. 1991. The deal of the decade. *Newsweek,* July 15, p. 40.

Reibstein, L., and L. Rosaldo. 1991. Seeing red at Big Blue. *Newsweek,* June 10, p. 40.

Schein, E. H. 1985. *Organizational Culture and Leadership.* San Francisco: Jossey-Bass.

Schneider, B., ed. 1990. *Organizational Climate and Culture.* San Francisco: Jossey-Bass.

Schwartz, E. I. 1991. 30,000 programmers later, "software gridlock." *Business Week* (July 15):134–35.

Selznick, P. 1948. Foundations of the theory of organizations. *American Sociological Review* 13:25–35.

Smircich, L., and M. B. Calas. 1987. Organizational culture: A critical assessment. In F. M. Jablin, L. L. Putnam, K. H. Roberts, and L. W. Porter, eds., *Handbook of Organizational Communication.* Newbury Park, Calif.: Sage.

Text of chairman's message to the employees at IBM. 1991. *New York Times,* June 19, p. D5.

Thurow, R. 1991. See the light. *Wall Street Journal,* Sept. 20, pp. R1, R2.

Tichy, N. M. 1989. GE's Crotonville: A staging ground for corporate revolution. *Academy of Management Executive* 3:99–106.

Tully, S. 1990. GE in Hungary: Let there be light. *Fortune* (Oct. 22):137–42.

Venkatraman, N., and J. E. Prescott. 1990. Environment-strategy coalignment: An empirical test of its performance implications. *Strategic Management Journal* 11:1–23.

Verity, J. W., and G. Lewis. 1988. The reorganization man's idea of fun. *Business Week* (Feb. 15): 95.

Weick, K. 1979. *The Social Psychology of Organizing* (2nd ed.). Reading, Mass.: Addison Wesley.

Weiss, S. E. 1987. Creating the GM-Toyota joint venture: A case in complex negotiation. *Columbia Journal of World Business* 22:23–37.

Wilkins, A. 1983. Organizational stories as symbols which control the organization. In L. R. Pondy, P. J. Frost, G. Morgan, and T. C. Dandridge, eds., *Organizational Symbolism,* vol. 1. Greenwich, Conn.: JAI.

Wilkins, A., and W. G. Ouchi. 1983. Efficient cultures: Exploring the relationship between culture and organizational performance. *Administrative Science Quarterly* 28:468–81.

CHAPTER SEVEN

Organizational Teamwork: A High-Speed Management Perspective

Yanan Ju

INTRODUCTION

High-speed management as a new theory of organizational communication is a set of principles, strategies, and tools for coming up with a steady flow of new products, making sure they are what the customer wants, designing and manufacturing them with speed and precision, getting them to the market quickly, and servicing them easily in order to make large profits and satisfy consumer needs. This new theory has at its core a new conceptualization of the role information and communication play in organizational functioning (Cushman and King, 1993; Pepper, 1989). Cushman and King (1993) identify four communication processes that are crucial for establishing and maintaining a firm's sustainable competitive advantage. Two of them are, either in a direct or extended sense, teamwork processes: a negotiated linking process and a cross-functional teamwork process. While they are by no means the only teamwork processes applied in organizational functioning, they are typical of two broad categories of organizational coalignment in a high-speed management age: interorganizational teamwork and intraorganizational teamwork.

CORE PHILOSOPHY OF EFFECTIVE ORGANIZATIONAL FUNCTIONING AND TEAMWORK IN HIGH-SPEED MANAGEMENT

Cushman and King (1993), based on the assertion that an organization's ability to continuously improve its effectiveness in managing organizational interdependencies was the critical element in successfully responding to the competitive forces of the 1990s, argue that effectiveness in managing organizational interdependencies is an organization's ability to achieve coalignment between its internal and external resources. If interdependence is the very nature of modern organizational life, then coalignment is the operationalization of interdependence, more than a mere form of it. This is to say that without coalignment between an organization's internal and external resources in various forms, the interdependencies among intraorganizational units and between the organization on the one hand and its relevant environment on the other can never be achieved. Coalignment viewed as such is then the core element of effective organizational functioning.

According to Cushman and King (1993), coalignment is a process whereby each of a firm's subunits clearly articulates its needs, concerns, and potential contributions to the organization's functioning in such a manner that management can forge an appropriate value-added configuration and linkage between units. An appropriate value-added configuration and linkage between units is one that integrates, coordinates, and controls each unit's needs, concerns, and contributions so that the outcome is mutually satisfying to the units involved and optimizing in value-added activities to the organizational functioning as a whole.

Coalignment may occur at various levels, including, for example, technologies, equipment, funds, and human resources. Simply defined, teamwork is the coalignment in which people use information and communication to manage interdependencies at all these levels for achieving organizational goals. Or simply, teamwork is another way of saying coalignment. Interorganizational teamwork is therefore just interorganizational coalignment. At the intraorganizational level, self-managed teamwork is just self-managed coalignment; cross-functional teamwork is just cross-functional coalignment; and social-technical teamwork is just social-technical coalignment. And so on down the line. Thus argued, teamwork, in the context of high-speed management, is the effort to use information and communication to forge an appropriate value-added configuration and linkage between units so that firms are able to respond to the market environment with speed and quality and maintain sustaining competitive advantage.

It would be hardly meaningful to talk about teamwork in the context of high-speed management without highlighting the word "speed." It is speed that changes the rules by which business games are played out. Speed, in the 1990s and years ahead, is the best opportunity for as well as the main killer of organizations, which have been thrown into a "rapidly altering, fast-moving, hyper-complex world that is too much for any single individual to track, understand or deal with unaided" (Barrett, 1987, p. 24). There is no better word that captures the real essence of the business and market dynamics of the 1990s and the uncertain years that lie ahead.

SPEED-TO-MARKET: A MAJOR GOAL FOR HIGH-SPEED MANAGEMENT TEAMWORK

Teamwork can never really be effective without some clearly identified and articulately defined goals in the minds of team players. One of the major goals for high-speed management teamwork in business organizations is speed-to-market. Vessey (1991, p. 23) points out that only recently has the concept of time or speed been widely accepted as a competitive advantage across all markets and product lines. Markets based on style, fashion, or fads have always been under this pressure. Today, however, producers of semiconductors, industrial vehicles and equipment, and chemicals, and others feel the same effects. Time-to-market is defined as the elapsed time between product definition and product availability (Vessey, 1991, p. 23). Competitors in the 1990s talk in terms of speed-to-market: speed in engineering, production, sales response, and customer service. Their product life cycles frequently look more like spikes than smooth-flowing curves. Vessey listed Ford Motor Company's "Team Taurus," Boeing Aerospace Corporation's Ballistic Systems Division, Unisys Corporation's Roseville manufacturing plant, and others as examples of organizations that are speed-conscious.

The desperate drive for speed-to-market has a simple reason: a mix of the fact of shrinking product life cycles and a firm's
quest for higher profits. As indicated in Vessey's Academy of
Management Executive article, a McKinsey & Co. study reported
that a product six months late to market loses as much as one-
third of the potential profit over the product's lifetime. If a company with revenues of $25 million improves time-to-market by
only one month, its annual gross profit increases by $150,000
(Vessey, 1991, p. 25). The Chrysler Corporation's development,
production, and marketing of minivans beat its competitors to
market by one year, allowing Chrysler to capture all of the market for minivans for one year, and get high-end pricing for maximum profits, and hold 51 percent of the market for the next two
years due to its time competitive advantage (Cushman and King,
1993).

Crucial to achieving speed-to-market is, among other critical factors, the effective use of information and communication
to remove all the artificial barriers that lie along the value chain
of an organization. The value chain, which involves all the essential functional units and discrete activities, may be arranged into
functional unit activities and business processes (Cushman and
King, 1993). At the functional unit level, the value chain starts
from suppliers and runs through design, engineering, purchasing, manufacturing, distribution, sales, and service, and ends at
customers. Suppliers and customers at the two ends are found
outside an organization's boundary while all other functional
activities are performed within its structure. This suggests that
the removal of barriers, through the sharing of information and
a supportive communication climate, should occur at both the
organizational and interorganizational levels. The business process of the value chain includes three stages: product development, product delivery, and customer service and management.
Each stage has some activities unique to itself and some activities
that overlap with other business processes. This demands a smooth
linkage and transition among the three business processes, im-
plying that all obstacles need to be removed a soon as they emerge.

Based on our conceptualization of teamwork as coalignment
among functional units and activities, it seems natural to claim
that the very removal of artificial barriers at both the functional
unit level and business process level of the value chain consti-

tutes teamwork. Teamwork is the use of information and communication to remove artificial barriers that lie along the value chain of an organization to achieve both organizational and interorganizational coalignment so that products may hit the market with speed and precision and gain high profits. The use of information and communication to coalign design, engineering, purchasing, manufacturing, distribution, sales, and service constitutes intraorganizational teamwork while the communicative effort to achieve coalignment between an organization and its suppliers on the one hand and its customers on the other is interorganizational teamwork. With speed-to-market as the main goal and all the challenges and stakes involved in mind, both intra- and interorganizational teamwork can be more or much more than mere talk.

TEAMWORK PATTERNS IN HIGH-SPEED MANAGEMENT

Kinlaw's Teamwork Categories

To render our discussion of teamwork patterns relevant to high-speed management, we will use Kinlaw's framework of teamwork as a conceptual basis upon which to examine four teamwork patterns from a high-speed management perspective: cross-functional teamwork, self-managed teamwork, executive-level teamwork, and social-technical teamwork. Kinlaw argues that "teamwork is a condition that may come and go. It may exist only for the time that it takes a group to perform a particular task; after the task is performed, the need for teamwork no longer exists. Group members can have teamwork one moment, then be disjunctive and at odds with each other the next. People can rally around some purpose and cooperate to achieve it, then break up and become very competitive and proprietary" (Kinlaw, 1991, pp. 1–2). He describes teamwork as consisting of both qualitative and functional characteristics. The qualitative characteristics of teamwork include quality communication climate and positive work relationships while the functional characteristics pertain to a team or an organization's functional goals that team members need to work together to achieve, such as the producing of a product or service that cannot be produced by a single person or department. Based upon these teamwork characteristics, Kinlaw distinguishes work groups from work teams and work teams from superior work teams (Kinlaw, 1991, pp. 6–7).

Work Groups. A work group is a set of two or more jobholders who make up some identifiable organizational unit that is considered to be a permanent part of an organization. Work groups are the basic building blocks of organizational performance. The tasks of individual members in groups may be performed through processes that are additive, integrative, or interactive. Various combinations of these three processes can all be effective depending on conditions. In *additive processes,* workers in the same group all use the same equipment or machine to produce the same product. The group's output is not integrated into a larger whole. Individual outputs are added together and the sum total becomes the group's output. *Integrative processes* are typically used by production-line groups where what a member does at an earlier stage is not simply added but is integrated into work that is done at later stages. All members of the group and all parts of the work are interdependent, which often follows a one-way, linear line. In *interactive processes,* the job gets done through neither a simple addition of individual outputs nor a one-way, linear integration of work parts, but through a two-way or multidirection flow of information and action among individual members of the group. Design groups, budget groups, R&D groups, and the like are typically interactive. The additive processes, integrative processes, and interactive processes are compared in Figure 7.1.

According to Kinlaw (1991), a work group that uses additive processes alone to produce a product or service may function without teamwork. Integrative and interactive processes, which obviously would require coalignment between team members, force at least minimal levels of teamwork. This is to say that groups whose tasks are integrative and/or interactive by nature must function as teams.

Work Teams. Kinlaw argues that teams differ from groups at two levels. At the qualitative level, teams tend to have a quality communication climate in which sharing information is easier, issues are aired more openly, and conflicts are resolved quickly and with positive results. At the functional level, members of a work team not only cooperate in all aspects of their task perfor-

Figure 7.1
Work Group Task Flows

Additive

$Task^1 + Task^2 + Task^3 + \ldots Task^n$ = Summary Result (Task 1 . . . N)

Integrative

$Task^1 -- Task^2 -- Task^3 \ldots Task^n$ = Integrative Result (Task 1 -- N)

Interactive

$Task^1$

$Task^n$ [_____ | _____] $Task^2$ = Interactive Result
(Task 1 --- N)

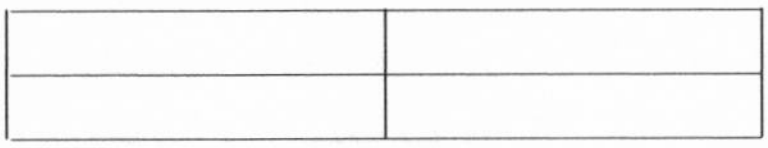

$Task^3$

Source: Kinlaw, 1991, p. 9.

mance; they also share functions and responsibilities that traditionally belong to management.

Superior Work Teams.   According to Kinlaw, superior work teams, in addition to having the same functional and qualitative characteristics as work teams, are defined by three qualities: consistency, intensity, and restless dissatisfaction. Consistency means that superior work teams are consistent in their pursuit of excellence, and "*always* make maximum use of their people; *always* achieve superior outputs against all odds; and *always* are improving every aspect of their business" (Kinlaw, 1991, p. 16). In other words, they consistently work in such a way as to maintain sustaining competitive edge. Intensity refers to the high level of energy and commitment in performing team tasks. Restless dissatisfaction reflects the belief on the part of team members that nothing is so good that it cannot be improved.

High-Speed Management Teamwork

The three qualities of consistency, intensity, and restless dissatisfaction combine to suggest that superior work teams are teams that perform high-speed management teamwork. Integrating Cushman and King's framework of high-speed management and Kinlaw's conceptualization of work groups versus work teams versus superior work teams, we view high-speed management teamwork as having the characteristics of consistency, intensity, and restless (we will change the word to "permanent" later in the chapter) dissatisfaction, and—we may add one more—speedy and effective communication, as shown in the efforts of individual members of superior work teams that perform mainly integrative and interactive tasks. Such tasks are performed along the whole value chain of an organization at both the functional unit level and business process level.

High-speed management teamwork may appear in different forms, at different hierarchical levels, and across different function units along the value chain. We now use the four qualities of consistency, intensity, permanent dissatisfaction, and speedy and effective communication as the cross-cutting themes to look at the four teamwork patterns: cross-functional teamwork, self-managed teamwork, executive-level teamwork, and social-technical teamwork.

Cross-Functional Teamwork. Increases in information and communication technological breakthroughs and in world trade in the past decade have created a volatile business climate characterized by rapidly changing technology, quick market saturation, and unexpected competition, making succeeding in business very difficult (Cushman and King, 1993). Technological change with increased competition have required companies to become more market-driven, attempting to gain competitive advantage by reaching the marketplace first with a superior product. As a result, organizations are turning to project management and relying to a greater degree on project teams and cross-functional teamwork for the development and implementation of new products and programs (Pinto and Pinto, 1990).

Cross-functional teamwork in high-speed management may be defined as a team process whereby members from different functional units work together with a team spirit of consistency, intensity, permanent dissatisfaction, and speedy and effective communication to complete some project within a certain time limit, or to achieve organizational goals without a specific time constraint. Earlier research on cross-functional teamwork tended to focus on one function's specific relationship with other functional areas, examining both the dynamics of these relationships as well as that function's specific responsibilities regarding new product implementation. These relationships could include, for example, marketing and R&D, marketing and production, marketing and engineering, and marketing and finance (Pinto and Pinto, 1990; Gupta and Wileman, 1988; Clare and Sanford, 1984; Anderson, 1981). Researchers have also inquired into various behavioral issues such as problems of personality differences between members of functional units who worked on the same project (Lucas and Bush, 1988).

What seems to be largely neglected in researchers' conceptualizations of cross-functional teamwork has been the emphasis on nonproject-oriented, general organizational goals driven interdependencies among all the functional units along the value chain of an organization. This simply means that the spirit of cross-functional teamwork should exist in the whole organization, involving all functional units on a routine, day-to-day basis. Here is introduced the principle of consistency, which, as we pointed out earlier, emphasizes "always, always, and always." It goes without saying that project-based cross-functional teamwork is of paramount importance to a high-speed management organization that needs superior products with which to hit the marketplace with speed. It is also worth emphasizing, however, that an organization that faces an uncertain and volatile business environment should be ready to act with big moves any time if need be. But this would be very difficult or simply impossible if the level of coalignment among various functional units along the value chain is not kept consistently high. The principle of consistency also applies to project-based cross-functional teamwork where a project team would need to function consistently as a superior work team at both qualitative and functional levels from the time the team is formed to the time it is dissolved.

The quality of intensity, as it is also required of cross-functional teamwork in high-speed management organizations, suggests that team members need to maintain a high level of energy and commitment. A high-level commitment on the part of members of different functional units is probably easier said than made. Commitment is more likely to come from stakeholders' true and profound understanding of the significance and importance of project-based as well as routine cross-functional teamwork for the organization. Once commitment is made, energy comes naturally.

Permanent dissatisfaction is even a higher demand of individual workers who might ask, "Why bother?" Members of work groups then need to be educated into team players using such arguments as "if we don't hang together, we'll hang separately" (Barrett, 1987, p. 24). Too easy a satisfaction with a product or service in a high-speed business environment could send you and all other organization members to dance on the rope.

Speedy and effective communication is not only a tool with which to help promote team qualities of consistency, intensity, and permanent dissatisfaction, but a necessary element of teamwork at both the qualitative and functional levels. At the qualitative level, there is the need of establishing and maintaining a quality communication climate in which different opinions are voiced in a supportive, unreserved, and timely way. At the functional level, team roles and goals need to be clarified and updated, again using speedy and effective communication, to render high-speed management cross-functional teamwork a goal-driven, value-added process, not just a managerial lip-service.

Self-Managed Teamwork. Self-managed teamwork has been a new and effective response to the high-speed management environment in which technological breakthroughs present repeated challenges to firms, the market gets saturated quickly, and competition comes from all directions, an environment that demands organizational innovation, adaptation, flexibility, efficiency, and rapid response (Cushman and King, 1993). The use of self-managed teams, to respond to such an environment, not only has gained momentum but appears to be at a record high. Self-managed teamwork appears in such team forms as quality control circles, task forces, communication teams, new venture teams, and business brand teams (Barry, 1991).

Wellins and George (1991) report that a recent nationwide study conducted jointly by Development Dimensions International (DDI), the Association for Quality and Participation (AQP), and *Industry Week* reveals that 26 percent of the 862 executives surveyed are using self-managed teamwork in at least some parts of their organizations, and that more than half of their workforces will be organized into self-managed teams within five years. It has been reported that self-managed teams, if well-managed, tend to produce good outcomes both in terms of productivity and member satisfaction (Hackman and Oldham, 1980; Hackman, et al., 1975).

Organizations that depend on the use of self-managed teamwork differ from traditional organizations in a number of ways: (1) the former are usually leaner, with fewer layers of managers and supervisors; (2) the leader is more a coach than a planner and controller; (3) the reward systems tend to be skill- or team-based, rather than seniority-based; (4) information, such as productivity data, quality data, sales figures, and profit margins, is shared readily with all employees, not just the top few; (5) employees are expected to learn all the jobs and tasks required of the team, not just a single job or task (Wellins and George, 1991). All these differences suggest that organizations dependent upon self-managed teamwork are those that follow high-speed management principles in order to respond more speedily and efficiently to a volatile business environment.

As is implied in the name, self-managed teamwork is leaderless in the traditional sense of the word "leader." This does not mean, however, that leadership is not exercised in self-managed work teams. In many ways, the opposite holds true. Barry (1991) argues that self-managed teams require even more leadership than conventional organizational units. They not only need task-based leadership on such critical issues as project definition, scheduling, and resource gathering, but also leadership around group development processes including developing group cohesiveness and establishing effective communication patterns. Barry also points out that without the presence of formal authority, power struggles and conflict around both task and group process issues become more often, adding to the overall leadership burden that must be handled by all members of the group. To explain, predict, or control leadership complexities in self-managed teams, Barry (1991) proposes a new leadership theory, called the "Distributed Leadership Model" (DLM), which he believes is uniquely suited to self-managed teamwork. DLM sees leadership as "a collection of roles and behaviors that can be split apart, shared, rotated, and used sequentially or concomitantly," and this means that "at any one time multiple leaders can exist in a team, with each leader assuming a complementary leadership role" (Barry, 1991, p. 34). Such leadership roles and behaviors as required of self-managed work teams, according to Barry, fall into four broad clusters. The first is *envisioning leadership*, a process involving "facilitating idea generation and innovation, defining and championing overall goals, finding conceptual links between systems, and fostering frame-breaking thinking" (p. 36). The second is *organizing leadership*, which "brings order to many disparate elements that exist within the group's tasks" and focuses on "details, deadlines, time, efficiency, and structure" (p. 36). *Spanning leadership* represents the third cluster. This deals with how to bridge and link the team with outside groups and individuals, involving such behaviors as "networking, presentation management, developing and maintaining a strong team image with outsiders, intelligence gathering, locating and securing critical resources, bargaining, finding and forecasting areas of outside resistance, being sensitive to power distributions, and being politically astute" (p. 37). The fourth cluster is *social leadership*. While the first three clusters of leadership pertain to task performance, social leadership is exercised in group development processes, which include "surfacing different members' needs and concerns, assuring that everyone gets his or her views heard, interpreting and paraphrasing other views, being sensitive to the team's energy levels and emotional state, injecting humor and fun into the team's work, and being able to mediate conflicts" (p. 37).

The fact that these extremely challenging leadership roles must be assumed by team members themselves suggests that the staffing and training of self-managed teams could be critical to their success. This is simply because not all workers are capable of assuming leadership roles and not all workers perform well in a team environment (Flynn, McCombs, and Elloy, 1990). To tie our discussion to the context of high-speed management, we suggest that the four qualities of high-speed management teamwork—consistency, intensity, permanent dissatisfaction, and speedy and effective communication—be used as basic criteria with which to select and train members of self-managed teams. Consistency means "always." If one is entrusted, for example, with assuming envisioning leadership in a self-managed team, he or she should "always" work hard to facilitate idea generation and innovation, help define and champion overall goals, search for conceptual links between systems, and foster frame-breaking thinking. Intensity is the high level of energy and commitment on the part of individual team members. In a self-managed team, individual commitment to team tasks and group processes, in particular, is a necessary guarantee to the effective functioning of the "leaderless" team. Permanent dissatisfaction comes from a high level of energy and commitment and demonstrates itself in the individual members' continuous effort to excel. Speedy and effective communication is probably the most important factor weighing on the success of a self-managed team with the absence of formal authority; this not only facilitates task-related information sharing, but also helps promote group development processes. A self-managed team, when it meets the criteria of consistency, intensity, permanent dissatisfaction, and speedy and effective communication, will be able to generate high-speed management teamwork.

Executive-Level Teamwork.   The emergence of teamwork at the top of an organization represents another response to the high-speed management environment characterized externally by a volatile business market and internally by the complexity of production. Ancona and Nadler (1989) argue that three factors account for the necessity of executive-level teamwork: external demands, organizational complexity, and succession. External business pressures have played a major role.

> Increasing global competition, technology-based change, and turbulence in financial markets all add to the burdens of the CEO. In addition, the need to spend more time on strategies to meet environmental instability must be balanced with a focus on short-term performance, driven by shareholder demands and concerns about takeover. As a consequence, CEOs are more often looking for strategic and operational help. (Ancona and Nadler, 1989, p. 21)

In the old CEO/COO executive structural model, the CEO is responsible for strategic issues, external relations, and overall corporate governance, while the COO takes care of internal operations. The two-person CEO/COO structure is still the dominant leadership form, but the team model is gaining acceptance and popularity.

To present an executive-level teamwork model in the context of high-speed management, we wish to add the four high-speed management teamwork qualities of consistency, intensity,

permanent dissatisfaction, and speedy and effective communication to Ancona and Nadler's model of executive team effectiveness. Table 7.1 presents the Ancona and Nadler model:

Table 7.1
A Model of Executive Team Effectiveness

Team Design	Core Processes	Team Performance
Composition	Work Management	
Structure	Relationship Management	Production of "Results"
Succession	External Boundary Management	Maintenance of Effectiveness

Source: Ancona and Nadler, 1989, p. 23.

Team Design. Team design contains elements that are determined
before core processes are set in motion. In terms of *composition*,
the selection of team members should be based on skills and
experiences and favorable personality qualities. Team *structure* is
defined by the nature of team positions (business unit heads as
opposed to functional leaders), the size of the team, the boundaries (who is in and out), the specific formal roles, the goals, and
the nature of team and individual rewards. *Succession* is the third
design element crucial for the organizational and leadership stability and continuity. To the three elements of team design as
suggested by Ancona and Nadler, we may add the quality of
intensity. The high level of energy and commitment should certainly be required of all the members of the executive team,
including the CEO. The quality of *intensity* should be used as a
major criterion with which to select team members, determine
who is in and out, and assess the succession issue.

Core Processes. The Ancona and Nadler model includes three
core processes: work management, relationship management, and
external boundary management. *Work management process* is a process where the team makes and implements decisions regarding
strategies, policy issues, and routine task operations. *Relationship
management process* involves the degree of openness between members, how conflicts are resolved, the nature of support expressed

among members, the cohesiveness of the group, and the level of trust. *External boundary management process* is one by which team members deal with factors outside the organizational boundary, such as financial markets, the media, key customers, competitors, and governments. The process could also include the managing of the boundary between the top team and the rest of the organization. For the three core management processes to qualify as high-speed management teamwork processes, we may add the quality of *speedy and effective communication*. We believe that speedy and effective communication is the only process tool that the executive-level team can use to meet the challenges from the work management, relationship management, and external boundary management in the context of high-speed management.

Team Performance.   Team performance is twofold. One is the production of results, which includes the quality of decision making, the ability to implement decisions, the outcomes of teamwork in terms of problems solved and work completed, and the quality of institutional leadership provided. The other side is the maintenance of effectiveness, which refers to the team's ability to maintain an esprit de corps and quality team climate characterized by a high level of mutual trust and support. It seems that another high-speed teamwork quality—*permanent dissatisfaction*—should fit here. When the team members feel permanently dissatisfied with team performance, sustaining of the competitive edge of the organization can then be ensured.

The remaining high-speed management teamwork quality of *consistency* should be present all through the teamwork process of an executive-level team, from team design, through core processes, to team performance. With the four high-speed management teamwork qualities of consistency, intensity, speedy and effective communication, and permanent dissatisfaction added to Ancona and Nadler's model of an executive team, we have a model that would fit the high-speed management context. The modified model is shown in Table 7.2.

Social-Technical Teamwork

It has been more than thirty years since the first article on social-technical systems was published after some field work had been done in coal mines in Great Britain (Emery and Trist, 1960). The recent enthusiasm in the sociotechnical philosophy

Table 7.2
Executive Team Effectiveness in the Context of High-Speed Management

Team Design	Consistency Core Processes	Team Performance
Composition	Work Management	
Structure	Relationship Management	Production of "Results"
Succession	External Boundary Management	Maintenance of Effectiveness
Intensity	*Speedy and Effective Communication*	*Permanent Dissatisfaction*

has been kindled by a high-speed management environment where, as Kolodny and Dresner point out when they are writing on the philosophy, "the high levels of global competitiveness, galloping technological change, and customer and client demands for increased responsiveness have made flexibility in production processes and rapid product throughout highly desirable" (Kolodny and Dresner, 1986, p. 35). Such flexibility demands both a most efficient and effective production process (technical) and an adaptive workforce (social) at the same time. Social-technical teams are designed to meet the two demands of flexibility.

Typically, the formation of social-technical teamwork is based on two kinds of analysis: technical analysis and social analysis (Taylor and Asadorian, 1985). Technical analysis is made on unit operations, key factors, and variance control while social analysis includes a functional relationships and requirements examination, focal role network, and quality of working life evaluation. The key to the success of social-technical teamwork is the organizational effort to achieve "joint optimization" of both the technical system and social system (Kolodny and Dresner, 1986; Taylor and Asadorian, 1985).

Technical Analysis. The first step of technical analysis is the identification of unit operations. A *unit operation* is defined as a meaningful transformation of an input into an output within a technical process. Technology is defined in terms of its input and product, instead of by its tools, processes, or techniques. This focus, according to Taylor and Asadorian (1985), ensures that the technical system will be analyzed separately from the jobs and work of people on the one hand, and from the supervisory and control system on the other. Identification of *key factors* represents the second step of technical analysis. This is done through three substeps. First, all the technical factors (aspects and conditions) involved in each unit operation are listed. Second, those factors with a direct or important impact on quantity, quality, or costs of the system output are singled out for detailed examination. Third, a *Key Factor Identification Chart* is drawn and probably posted on the wall so that production operators are kept aware of those factors and possible variances. *Variance control* is the step that actually forms a bridge between the technical process and the social process. Some of the crucial questions to be asked regarding variance control may include, for example, where and how the variances have originated, who controls the key variance, and how it is controlled. Variances are much better controlled by production operators—people on the front line—who keep a high level of energy and commitment, and are capable of speedy and effective communication.

Social Analysis. An organization is also a social system which, in the context of high-speed management, is "the co-ordinating and integrating buffer between the technical transformation process and the demands and constraints of a turbulent environment" (Taylor and Asadorian, 1985, p. 11). In order to survive in a turbulent environment, an organization as a social system must perform four basic functions: (1) setting and attainment of performance goals ("G"); (2) adaptation to the external environment ("A"); (3) integration of the activities of people within the system ("I"); and (4) long-term development ("L") (Taylor and Asadorian, 1985). The analysis of the four functional requirements (G, A, I, L) must be combined with the particular functional relationships (vertical, horizontal, internal, cross-boundary) which affect the satisfaction of the requirements. This combination is charted in a 4 × 4 *social system grid*. Social analysis also involves the examination of the roles and relationships within the whole work process, with a focus on the roles that are crucial in the control of key variances. This is called *focal role analysis.* The patterns of interaction (communication) can be mapped in terms of frequency and direction of contact. The third step in the social analysis is the evaluation of *quality of working life.* This is to assess how workers' individual needs, both material and psychological, are satisfied. This step is crucial in the sense that failure to ensure the quality of working life may threaten the very success of social-technical teamwork.

As we pointed out earlier, the key to the functioning of social-technical teamwork is the *joint optimization* of both the technical system and the social system. This not only suggests that the technical analysis and social analysis in the initial system design should be conducted simultaneously, but also invites the introduction of the four high-speed management teamwork qualities, namely, consistency, intensity, permanent dissatisfaction, and speedy and effective communication. When the four qualities are added to the conventional social-technical teamwork model, it will fit in a much better way in the high-speed management context. While the four qualities should apply to the overall social-technical teamwork process, it seems that the qualities of intensity and permanent dissatisfaction are more closely related to the variance control system in the technical analysis, and the quality of speedy and effective communication may have a direct bearing on the focal role networking in the social analysis. The quality of consistency, as with the other teamwork patterns, should be present throughout the social-technical process.

Having discussed the four teamwork patterns in the high-speed management context, we are now in a position to take a look at two world leaders that have been following high-speed management principles and have benefited greatly from teamwork. One is Toyota Motor Company in Japan and the other is GE in the United States. Instead of using the four patterns to examine their teamwork in a mechanical way (even though all these patterns have effectively been followed), we will try to highlight those aspects that characterize the two industrial giants' success stories of how teamwork is used to get the job done.

TEAMWORK AT TOYOTA MOTOR COMPANY

Toyota is the best carmaker in the world. And it keeps getting "better and better and better." Japan's number one automaker is so rich that now, jokingly known as the "Bank of Toyota," it sits on $22 billion in cash—enough to buy both Ford and Chrysler at current stock prices, with nearly $5 billion to spare (Taylor, 1990, pp. 68–69). Why is Toyota getting better and better and better? And why is it doing so well financially in a time when the Big Three in the United States seem to be in serious trouble? Different theories may explain the Toyota success story, but teamwork is our explanation. While the result of teamwork is certainly positive, we will focus on how it is carried out and, probably more important, why the way it is carried out is possible.

Teamwork on the Production Line

The main philosophy that underlines the whole production system is *efficiency and cost reduction.* The key to achieving efficiency and cost reduction is, understandably, the workers of the Toyota family who are required to "be contributive to the development and welfare of the country by working together, regardless of position, in faithfully fulfilling your duties; be at the vanguard of the times through endless creativity, inquisitiveness and pursuit of improvement; be practical and avoid frivolity; be kind and generous, strive to create a warm, homelike atmosphere; be reverent, and show gratitude for things great and small in thought and deed" (Toyoda, 1988, pp. 37–38). These company admonitions may all be called "teamwork principles." To translate these principles into realities, work must be started from the very beginning: to hire team-conscious people who will have lifetime employment. The company has been trying hard to enrich assembly line jobs by making the work more creative, and safer by eliminating three D's: the dangerous, dirty, and demanding aspects of factory work (Taylor, 1990).

In order to attain efficiency and cost reduction in the whole production system, Toyota uses four management concepts—just-in-time, autonomation, flexibility, and creative thinking—the realization of which depends very much on teamwork. Therefore, these four management concepts can also be called "teamwork ideas."

Just-in-time. As the name suggests, this concept emphasizes a production system that cuts back on surplus stock and keeps on hand only essential materials for a preset production tempo. Just-in-time increases efficiency and decreases capital outflow (Toyoda,

1988). To make just-in-time work, *kanban* is used. *Kanban* is an information system that transmits information to the preceding process, indicating what the current process needs. A *kanban* is a card. There are two kinds of such cards: withdrawal *kanban* and production-ordering *kanban*. A withdrawal *kanban* specifies the kind and quantity of product the subsequent process should withdraw from the preceding process. A production-ordering *kanban* specifies the kind and quantity of the product the preceding process must produce (Feschetti, 1987, pp. 50–52). Just-in-time obviously puts pressure on workers and demands teamwork that realizes coalignment between the preceding process and subsequent process. *Speedy and effective communication* is particularly important in making the kanban system work in a smooth and noninterrupting way.

Autonomation.   This refers to how man and machine cooperate to control defects. The Toyota production line is designed in such a way that whenever a defect is detected by a mechanical system or a worker, the line can be stopped. Here is introduced the idea of *kaizen*, which means "continuous improvement" in Japanese. *Kaizen* translates into "zero defect" on the production line and relates nicely to a more popular management tool called the "quality control circle," which is based on worker initiatives and their willingness to improve. *Kaizen* puts responsibility on the workers and "responsibility means freedom to control one's job" (Womack, Jones, and Roos, 1990, p. 38). Toyota workers' freedom to stop the production line, for example, demands not only that they command superior production skills that enable them to detect errors, but that they be highly responsible and committed to what they are assigned to work on. "In Toyota plants, where every worker can halt the line, yields approach 100 percent, and the line practically never stops" (Womack, Jones, and Roos, 1990, p. 38). It seems that here the high-speed management teamwork qualities of *intensity* and *permanent dissatisfaction* are particularly relevant to the success of autonomation.

Flexibility.   A flexible workforce is realized through a proper design of machinery layout, well-trained multifunction workers, and continuous evaluation and periodic revisions of the standard operations routine. At Toyota, machines are set up in a U-turn layout instead of the traditional straight line design. The U-turn layout not only helps in meeting production demands, but also encourages team spirit that is so much a part of the production system. Multifunction workers are capable of handling various machines. When one process is complete, a worker may move on to a different machine to perform an entirely different task. The U-turn machine layout helps workers switch from one machine to another in an easy and efficient way. Standard operations allow for a balance of production with minimum labor. High productivity is achieved through "strenuous work," which is defined as working efficiently without wasteful motions (Hochi, 1986, pp. 24–29). As is implied in the process, teamwork is emphasized as opposed to individual tasks orientation. Here again the teamwork qualities of *intensity* and *permanent dissatisfaction* should be present to allow for a flexible workforce.

Creative thinking. This very much refers to how to capitalize on the ideas and suggestions of the worker. Through involvement in such team activities as the quality control circle, workers are encouraged to be active participants in creating improvements in all aspects in the workplace. It seems that workers' *permanent dissatisfaction* in an increasingly tough business environment adds to the sustaining competitive advantage of the Toyota Motor Company. Table 7.3 shows a year-by-year comparison of Toyota workers' involvement in creative activities in the company.

Having discussed briefly the four teamwork-based management concepts at Toyota and having qualified each of them with one or two of the four high-speed management teamwork qualities, we wish to add that the quality of *consistency* has always been present in the whole production process, and that is why Toyota "is getting better and better and better." We also want to point out that the principle of *consistency* applies equally well in its teamwork with the relevant environment outside the boundary of the Toyota Motor Company. Our next task is now to examine how Toyota manages its interorganizational teamwork, and our focus will be on its teamwork with its suppliers and dealers/customers, the two end subsystems outside the organizational structure as shown in the organizational value chain discussed earlier in the chapter.

Table 7.3
Employee Suggestion Systems at Toyota

FY	Suggestions	% Adopted	Suggestions per Worker
1951	789	23	0.1
1955	1,087	53	0.2
1960	5,001	33	0.6
1965	15,968	39	0.7
1969	40,313	68	1.1
1970	49,414	72	1.3
1971	88,607	74	2.2
1972	168,458	75	4.1
1973	284,717	77	6.7
1974	398,091	78	9.0
1975	381,438	83	8.5
1976	463,422	84	10.4
1977	454,522	84	10.2
1978	527,861	88	11.7
1979	575,861	91	12.7
1980	859,039	94	18.6
1981	1,412,565	94	29.5
1982	1,905,642	95	32.7
1983	1,655,858	96	28.2

Source: Ancona and Nadler, 1989, p. 23.

Interorganizational Teamwork with Suppliers and Dealers/Customers

Suppliers represent the starting point of the organizational value chain. As early as the 1950s, Toyota divided its suppliers into separate tiers with different responsibilities. First-tier suppliers were each assigned a major component such as car seats or the electrical system. Second-tier suppliers would supply individual parts or subsystem components to the first-tier companies. Second-tier suppliers, in many cases, developed a third level of suppliers that supplied what the former needed. Toyota only dealt with the first-tier suppliers. These companies became an integral part of the product-development team and were well informed of a car model's performance specifications.

Teamwork between Toyota and its first-tier suppliers is possible as both expect the relationship to be a long-term and stable one. In the spirit of teamwork, Toyota is provided with the most sensitive information about the suppliers' operations, including costs and quality levels. Information sharing also occurs at meetings of first-tier and second-tier supplier associations, where advances in manufacturing techniques are discussed. As a rule, Toyota design engineers visit first-tier plants to observe and take part in the production planning for the new model. One of the most impressive aspects of the supply system is, again, just-in-time. Thanks to the cooperation between the assembler and supplier, practically all inventories are eliminated, further lowering the overall manufacturing cost of a car.

Toyota also has a close relationship with its dealers/customers. Its distribution function is divided among a number of nationwide channels, each of which sells a portion of the company's product range. One of Toyota's channels, Corolla, for example, sells its cars through 78 dealer firms. The channel owns 20 percent of the dealerships. The 30,400 employees of the channel sell about 635,000 cars and trucks a year. At each Corolla dealership, the sales staff is organized into teams of seven or eight people who are trained in all aspects of the job. Team meetings are held on a daily basis. When sales drop to the point where the factory no longer has enough orders to sustain full output, production personnel are transferred into the sales system (Womack, Jones, and Roos, 1990, p. 22). This shows that the production system of the factory and the salespeople at the dealerships are so well coaligned that they become one larger team.

Speedy and effective communication is crucial to maintain a high-level teamwork between the factory and the dealerships. Sales team members draw up a profile of every household within the geographic area around the dealership and make periodic visits to update the profile: how many cars of what age each family has; what makes of car with what features; the number of children in the household and the uses of its cars; when the family thinks it needs to replace its cars. Such information is speedily sent to the production system of the factory together with salespeople's suggestions regarding the most appropriate specifications for a new vehicle. And these suggestions are carefully studied as clues to changing customer tastes. At the factory, executives determine how different models, colors, and the like will sell; they then establish a production schedule. The objective is to get the right combination going down the line to match actual demand. The production schedule is frequently revised as the dealers gather and communicate customer feedback. Corrections and adjustments are made quickly, so the right cars go to the right customers with speed! Thanks to the close coalignment between the production system and the dealerships/customers, the whole distribution network contains an average of just three weeks' supply of finished units, compared to two months' supply in the United States (Womack, Jones, and Roos, 1990). Obviously, interorganizational teamwork is another reason why Toyota "keeps getting better and better and better."

TEAMWORK AT GE

General Electric is one of the largest and best-run companies in the world. Since the legendary Jack Welch took office in the early 1980s, 114-year-old GE, in its drive to become leaner and more competitive, has slashed over one hundred thousand jobs worldwide and kept only those businesses that rank either number one or number two worldwide or domestically. Each of its remaining thirteen businesses has annual revenues from $2.5 billion to $13 billion. In a five-year period up until 1990, GE doubled revenues and net income to $55 billion and $4 billion, respectively (Quickel, 1990, pp. 64, 62). Interestingly, although the conceptual labels that GE has been using as management tools appear to be quite different from those of Toyota's, they are, in essence, as much teamwork-oriented as the Japanese company's management concepts.

Boundarylessness

Welch's newest philosophy of management is to create a "boundaryless company." "In a boundaryless company," according to Welch, "internal functions begin to blur. Engineering doesn't design a product and then 'hand it off' to manufacturing. They form a team, along with marketing and sales, finance and the rest" (1990 Annual Report of GE). Therefore, to create a boundaryless company, arbitrary divisions between all parts of the value chain, from supplier to company to dealer/customer, are blurred or eliminated. The cross-functional teamwork, which characterizes a boundaryless organization, would allow for a faster flow of information, a more participative decision-making process, and speedy corrections and adjustments. The philosophy of boundarylessness, as it spreads in GE, reminds us of Toyota's teamwork both at the organizational and interorganizational levels.

Integrated Diversity

"Integrated diversity" is another buzz phrase that "peppers Welch's conversations these days" (Quickel, 1990, p. 66). While it could mean almost the same thing as boundarylessness, it is mainly concerned with how GE's thirteen businesses should help each other, as opposed to operating as separate fiefdoms. Welch explains: "Most diversified companies do a good job of transferring technical resources and dollars across their businesses. A few do a good job of transferring human resources effectively. We think we do the best job of transferring management practices across our businesses—the best techniques, the best systems ideas, the best generic growth and superior profitability" (Quickel, 1990, p. 66). What needs to be pointed out is the fact that GE's thirteen diversified businesses, each being an independently run, large, and complex organization, are scattered around the world. The realization of integrated diversity represents major efforts on the part of each business to manage interorganizational teamwork at the global level.

Work-Out

This is probably the best known teamwork concept that Welch created and he describes Work-Out as the ultimate boundaryless event. Welch was determined to engage the hearts and minds of GE's 291,000 worldwide employees—from the top managers of the thirteen multibillion-dollar businesses down to the factory floor. This is realized through Work-Out—a program of ongoing, companywide town meetings where employees at all levels are encouraged to chip in ideas to make GE more competitive (Quickel, 1990, p. 62). Every week throughout GE, groups of 50 to 150 employees gather in two- or three-day Work-Out sessions. These sessions are attended by employees picked from all levels, often for their expertise and involvement in the business issues stated for primary discussion. About 20,000 to 25,000 GE employees a year attend Work-Out sessions. Work-Out corresponds nicely to Toyota's practice of the quality control circle. What seems different between the two is that while the Work-Out process is more top-down and encourages employees to "speak out," quality control circle activities tend to be more on a voluntary basis. The goal is the same: *kaizen* or continuous improvement in an increasingly volatile and competitive high-speed management environment.

Best Practice Studies

The Best Practice Studies program was initiated shortly after Work-Out was introduced in GE. The program aims at discovering world benchmark processes, practices, and quality standards through a cooperative learning relationship with those companies holding the standard. Through in-depth studies of these best practices, sometimes involving personnel from an outside organization working together with GE personnel (in exchange for an opportunity to study GE's best practices), these international benchmark standards are absorbed into GE's practices and processes. About two years ago, GE completed a series of Best Practices Studies to examine the management techniques of ten world-class companies ranging from AMP and Xerox to Chaparral Steel and Japan's Honda. All ten companies accepted GE's request to study their best practices, in return for a similar detailed look inside GE's management methods. Obviously, the Best Practices Studies program relates nicely, again, to the idea of interorganizational teamwork. To be informed of the world benchmark standards seems to be crucial for each of GE's thirteen remaining businesses to stay number one or number two.

A careful reading of Welch's four management/teamwork concepts will easily lead to the conclusion that the four high-speed management teamwork criteria of consistency, intensity, permanent dissatisfaction, and speedy and effective communication appear to be best followed in the ongoing process of creating a boundaryless company—in the generation of integrated diversity, in Work-Out town meetings, and in Best Practices Studies.

A MODEL OF TEAMWORK IN THE CONTEXT
OF HIGH-SPEED MANAGEMENT

A crucial question we may ask after examining the teamwork concepts at two of the world's most successful companies is "What can we learn from Toyota and GE?" Is it that all companies need to follow suit and generate the same or similar programs? The answer is no. Organizations may well develop their own management programs and teamwork patterns since each has its own particularities to deal with. Nothing is worse than merely copying in an increasingly competitive, high-tech age. Just-in-time works well at Toyota, but not necessarily at GE. And Work-Out works beautifully at GE, but probably not at Toyota. However, we do believe, on the basis of our discussion of teamwork at Toyota and GE, that the two companies share some fundamental high-speed management teamwork philosophies, and these proven philosophies should be dealt with seriously.

First, teamwork should be a goal-driven process, and the general goal of teamwork in the context of high-speed management is speed-to-market and quality. Talking about teamwork without an articulation of some achievable goals and talking about high-speed management teamwork without having "speed-to-market" and "quality" in mind will be like talking about managerial gimmicks.

Second, the context of high-speed management presupposes the necessity of interorganizational teamwork as well as intraorganizational teamwork. Toyota's teamwork with its suppliers and dealers/customers and GE's management concept of integrated diversity and Best Practices Studies are examples of fulfilling such a necessity. The globalization of economic systems and intensification of international trade require firms and companies to manage well their inter- as well as intraorganizational interdependencies.

Third, there will be no teamwork without the commitment of team members, and highly committed team members are an ultimate guarantee of teamwork in the high-speed management context. Commitment on the part of team members generates and maintains team spirit, and high commitment leads to high team spirit. This equals the idea of "intensity," one of the four high-speed management teamwork qualities we stress in this chapter.

Fourth, teamwork in the context of high-speed management is characterized by team members' permanent dissatisfaction with products and services. Toyota's *kaizen* and quality control circle, and GE's Work-Out and Best Practices Studies are examples of such spirit.

Fifth, teamwork in the context of high-speed management follows speedy and effective communication. The essence of high-speed management is high-speed communication, high-speed sharing of information, high-speed problem solving, and ultimately high-speed to the market. Communication in high-speed management teams must be speedier and more effective not only because teams need to solve problems quickly, but also because the problems that need to be solved tend to be more complicated, and much more complicated in some cases, than in a non-high-speed environment.

Sixth, teamwork in the context of high-speed management must consistently be of high quality. As we pointed out earlier in this chapter, teamwork is a condition; it can come and go. Toyota keeps getting better and better and better, and GE is becoming increasingly competitive in the world economy, simply because they have all along been consistent in their teamwork approach.

We combine the six philosophies to form our model of teamwork in the context of high-speed management as shown in Figure 7.2.

This model consists of three clusters of elements: functional elements, structural elements, and qualitative elements. Func-

Figure 7.2
Model of Teamwork in the Context of High-Speed Management

Functional Elements
Goal
Speed-to-Market/Quality

Structural Elements

Interorganizational Teamwork	Interorganizational Teamwork (Value Chain)	Interorganizational Teamwork

Qualitative Elements

Intensity	Permanent Dissatisfaction	Speedy & Effective Communication	Consistency

tional elements include "speed-to-market" and "quality," which combine to suggest that teamwork is a goal-driven process. Structural elements belong to two main groups: intraorganizational teamwork, which occurs along all system parts of the value chain, and interorganizational teamwork, which coaligns with organizations outside the structure of an organization; they find themselves at either end of the value chain. Qualitative elements are the four qualities of intensity, permanent dissatisfaction, speedy and effective communication, and consistency. This is both a descriptive and prescriptive model, the vigor and usefulness of which are yet to be tested.

CONCLUDING REMARKS

This chapter attempts to expand on the theory of high-speed management as developed by Cushman and King (1993), and our focus is on teamwork as a major component of high-speed management. In conclusion, we wish to emphasize the paramount importance of the use of information and communication to achieve coalignment in the managing of inter- as well as intraorganizational interdependencies as the most effective response to the business environment of the 1990s and years ahead. As has proved in the success stories of the world's two most admired companies, the Toyota Motor Company in Japan and GE in the United States, teamwork will continue to be a golden key with which to open the door of success, and it belongs to all organizations that truly understand the very nature of organizational life in today's high-speed age. Toyota and GE can use it. You can, too.

REFERENCES

Ancona, D., and D. A. Nadler. 1989. Top hats and executive tales: Designing the senior team. *Sloan Management Review* 31(1):19–28.

Anderson, P. F. 1981. Marketing investment analysis. In J. N. Sheth, ed., *Research in Marketing.* Greenwich, Conn.: JAI.

Barrett, F. D. 1987. Teamwork—How to expand its power and punch. *Business Quarterly* 52(3):24–31.

Barry, D. 1991. Managing bossless teams: Lessons in distributed leadership. *Organizational Dynamics* 20(1):31–47.

Clare, D. A., and D. G. Sanford. 1984. Cooperation and conflict between industrial sales and production. *Industrial Marketing Management* 13:163–69.

Cushman, D. P., and S. S. King. 1993. Visions of Order: High-Speed Management: in the Private Sector in the Global Marketplace. In D. P. Cushman and A. Kozminski, eds., *Organizational Communication and Management: A Global Perspective.* Albany, N.Y.: SUNY Press.

Cusumano, M. A. 1985. *The Japanese Automobile Industry.* Cambridge, Mass.: Harvard University Press.

Emery, F., and E. Trist. 1960. Sociotechnical systems. In C. W. Churchman and M. Verhurst, eds., *Management Science, Models, and Techniques.* Elmsford, N.Y.: Pergamon Press.

Feschetti, M. 1987. The global automobile: Banishing the necktie. *IEEE Spectrum* 24:50–52.

Flynn, R., T. McCombs, and D. Elloy. 1990. Staffing the self-managing work team. *Leadership & Organizational Development Journal* 11(1):26–31.

Gupta, A. K., and D. Wileman. 1988. The credibility-cooperation connection at the R&D-marketing interface. *Journal of Product Innovation Management* 5:20–31.

Hackman, J. R., and G. R. Oldham. 1980. *Work Redesign.* Reading, Mass.: Addison-Wesley.

Hackman, J. R., et al. 1975. A new strategy for job enrichment. *California Management Review* 17(4):55–71.

Hochi, S. 1986. Japanese auto companies: At home in America. *Business Japan* 31:24–29.

Kinlaw, D. C. 1991. *Developing Superior Work Teams.* San Diego, Calif.: Lexington Books.

Kolodny, H. F., and B. Dresner. 1986. Linking arrangements and new work design. *Organizational Dynamics* 14(3):33–51.

Lucas, G. H., and A. J. Bush. 1988. The marketing-R&D interface: Do personality factors have an impact? *Journal of Product Innovation Management* 5:257–68.

Pepper, C. B. 1986. High-speed management for the high tech age. *Fortune* 119:34–60.

Pinto, M. B., and J. K. Pinto. 1990. Project team communication and cross-functional cooperation in new program development. *Journal of Product Innovation Management* 7:200–211.

Quickel, S. W. 1990. Welch on Welch. *Financial World* 159(7): 62–70.

Taylor, A. 1990. Why Toyota keeps getting better and better and better? *Fortune* 122:66–79.

Taylor, J. C., and R. A. Asadorian. 1985. The implementation of excellence: STS management. *Industrial Management* 27(4): 5–15.

Toyoda, J. 1988. Toyota—A history of the first 50 years. Toyota Motor Corporation.

Vessey, J. T. 1991. The new competitors: They think in terms of speed-to-market. *Academy of Management Executive* 5(2):23–33.

Wellins, R., and J. George. 1991. The key to self-directed teams. *Training & Development Journal* 45(4):26–31.

Womack, J. P., D. T. Jones, and D. Roos. 1990. How lean production can change the world. *Business World*: 21–38.

CHAPTER EIGHT

High-Speed Management and Contingency Value Chains: Time as a Competitive Advantage in the Global Marketplace

Nils Magne Larsen and Pat Joynt

In the past thirty years there has been a significant change in the focus of organization behavior—from proactive management to reactive management as well as from a national and functional focus to an international/global and multistructured organization form. With these developments, the concept of time management has emerged as one of the key criteria used by practitioners in the global competitive arena. In many respects the criterion of time, which is essentially an external factor that is easily measured and compared, is one of the few factors the organization can manage internally in an otherwise global environment where competition is the name of the game.

The emerging concepts of globalization/internationalization are central in any modern description or understanding of organization behavior, and strangely enough, these concepts have only been introduced in debate, education, and research during the past few decades. While this neglect is a theme worthy of study in its own right, it deserves some attention in the introduction of this chapter since we will be using a global perspective for the study of the management of time.

Part of the neglect may be due to the potpourri of functional fields, methodologies, descriptions, occasional theorizing, and conceptualizing, which does not yet come together into a coherent package of received wisdom. This pluralistic process in the study of the internationalization area includes elements from economic theory, financial theory, decision theory, political science, comparative psychology, and sociology as well as marketing and production theories.

The need for relevant information in terms of concepts and processes is essential today because of rapid growth in the areas of data information, development aid, international trade, globalization, and education. Closely tied to these developments is the quest for real on-line theories.

It is impossible to do justice to the large amounts of recent literature available in the areas of globalization and internationalization, since there are still differences on the very definitions of the two concepts. The concepts tend to be used with different meanings by researchers. For our purposes, we will first focus on internationalization, as the concept is taken to mean the process by which international business operations are developed—be it a firm, industry, or nation-state. Globalization, then, refers to the processes by which the firm adapts to a variety of customer needs on a global basis. While internationalization may apply to inward as well as outward activities for the firm, our emphasis is on internationalization as an outward development, bearing in mind, of course, that inward and outward movements are becoming increasingly interrelated.

A further problem in applying the internationalization and globalization concepts arises in determining exactly what it means for a firm to increase its involvement in international business operations. Simplistically, one might use a measure such as the proportion of international sales to total company sales. However, this does not capture the broad dimensions of international involvement, such as the investment aspects or the sharing of technology. In an attempt to capture the broader perspectives of internationalization and globalization, and ultimately explain the processes, it may be appropriate to consider the level of organizational commitment to international operations (resources allocated, organizational arrangements, personnel aspects), range of markets serviced, and the sales objects of international marketing operations rather than some simple performance (outcome) measure.

As noted, considerable research has already been undertaken on aspects of the internationalization process, although two areas seem to be of particular importance in understanding the process. In the first place there has been a focus on particular decisions or stages that make up part of the internationalization process, such as the initial decision to enter and then develop export operations and the initial investment decision (Buckley, 1991). While only attempting to identify the key determinants of decisions taken at a particular point, or over a limited phase, of the internationalization process, such reseach has contributed to the overall understanding of what happens and why during internationalization.

Nevertheless, the question remains of what ties the overall process together. Because of the time perspective, full analysis of a firm's internationalization process is a considerably more demanding exercise. Of course, one would expect that the observed pattern of internationalization would vary from country to country, and over time, because of environmental changes. Much recent research cautions against simplistic acceptance of the evolutionary pattern as a definitive pattern. Given the more competitive international environment in the 1990s, as reflected in the trend toward strategic alliances and global networks, it should perhaps be expected that a less cautious approach to both processes would be forthcoming. However, much research work still remains to be done in unraveling the key elements of the processes at work. It is in relation to this task that we feel this chapter offers new opportunities for understanding the internationalization process as well as globalization.

Today, researchers will look not simply to, say capital, but to a much larger interrelationship of factors such as monetary and fiscal policies, trade deficits, and savings rates. Researchers will not simply focus upon long- or short-term views of management, or upon the quality of the workforce, but on a larger sociocultural framework of factors. This approach characterizes the work of Harvard professor Michael Porter and is part of the framework for this chapter. For Porter, the ability of a firm to manage such a framework has become a key ingredient in the evolving definition of competition. This framework comprises a series of internal organizational activities, and in Porter's scheme, the aggregate of these activities are called value chains. Porter's second concept is a chain of linkages—the ones that are external to the firm, and these linkages may be even more important to the drive for competitive advantages in today's global marketplace. The elements of this external chain—suppliers, buyers, competitors, and the threat of substitutes—provide a basis for understanding the environment outside the firm.

Differential advantages and disadvantages are part of a large body of economic theory that has often formed the basis for the concepts of internationalization and globalization. We will not treat them in detail in this chapter, but it is important to keep them in mind because of the complexities of the situation at hand for most companies.

The purpose of this chapter is to focus on time as a possible source of competitive advantage in the global automobile industry. The emphasis will be on secondary information and direct information from General Motors in the United States and Europe involving activities and business processes important for the overall performance of the firm in this industry. The basis for this analysis consists of an in-depth review of relevant theories and automobile information from the area of global strategy and competition.

THE RELEVANT THEORIES

Value Chain Theory

According to the value chain model developed by Porter (1985), a typical organization can be described by focusing on nine generic activities. Porter (1989) has divided these nine generic activities into two groups: the primary activities and the secondary, or support activities.

Secondary activities are aimed at supporting the product creation process in order to secure an efficient performance of the primary activities. Each of the four support activities covers the whole product creation process, from inbound logistics to service. Porter (1989) defines the secondary activities to include firm infrastructure, human resource management (HRM), technology development, and procurement.

Firm infrastructure consists of finance, general management, organizing, accounting, legal, and stragtegic planning. Human resource management concentrates on recruiting, training, organizing, and developing personnel. Technology development consists of research and development (R&D). Procurement, which is the last of Porter's (1989) support activities, can be defined in terms of providing purchased inputs.

Primary activities concentrate on the creation of the product or service itself, and include inbound logistics, operations, outbound logistics, marketing and sales, and service (Porter, 1989).

According to Porter (1989), the individual firm creates value for customers (buyers) by performing these activities, and each activity in the value chain contributes to the value-adding process. Porter (1989) also emphasizes the interrelationship between value chain activities. He describes the value chain as a network of activities that is more than the sum of the individual activities. This interrelationship means that the performance of one activity influences the cost and efficiency of the other activities, and this requires the activities to be coordinated.

Porter (1989) emphasizes that the firm value chain is a part of a large stream of activities, which he calls the "value system." He also stresses the view that the firm's competitive advantage is dependent on its management of the whole system. Interfirm integration not only creates interdependencies, but may also represent a source of competitive advantage for a firm that optimizes and coordinates the linkages in its value system.

Competitive Advantage Theory

According to Porter (1980), a firm can gain competitive advantage by adapting one of two generic strategies: cost leadership or differentiation. Both strategies represent a competitive approach by which the firm can compete more efficiently in the industry, thereby gaining a return on investment higher than the industry average. If the firm is to achieve competitive advantage, it must make a choice (Porter, 1989). This choice of strategy is dependent on characteristics of the product, the firm, and the industry (Porter, 1980). Porter (1989) warns against pursuing both strategies simultaneously. The two strategies have their contradictions, and pursuing both of them may lead the firm into a situation in which it is stuck in the middle between the two strategies. According to Porter (1989), this will only lead to below-average performance for the firm.

The purpose of a cost leadership strategy is to achieve a competitive position in which the firm can perform the value chain activities with lower costs than competitors (Porter, 1989). In order to achieve such a competitive position, Porter (1980) emphasizes the need for establishing rational production plans, keeping tight cost controls, and avoiding the most unprofitable customers. Even if low costs are the goals in a firm's strategy, the firm cannot allow itself to ignore factors such as quality and service (Porter, 1980).

The differentiation strategy, also called niche adaptation, involves two types of approach. The first approach is a product differentiation strategy, by which the firm provides the market with a desired product or service that, from the customer's point of view, is interpreted as being unique (Porter, 1980). The second approach is a focus strategy, by which certain customers or market segments are served particularly well (Porter, 1980). The purpose of both strategies is to manage the firm into a type of monopoly situation, thereby gaining higher prices.

Time Theory

In addition to cost leadership and differentiation, *time* is looked upon as a means to gain competitive advantage. A time competitive advantage is, according to Cushman and King (1990), based on speed of response, also known as "economies of speed" (Simon, 1989). This speed of response is interpreted by Cushman and King (1990) as one key measure of the time efficiency of the firm, and it includes the speed or time it takes to develop, produce, and deliver a product to the market.

Cushman and King (1990) argue that indexes of competitive advantage based on time can be obtained by comparing the time used on the product or service, the total work hours, and the cost required by each link in the value chain of one firm with those of other firms. The three general indexes adopted by Cushman and King (1990) are overall time, overall work hours, and overall cost per product in the value chain. Since these indexes are based on an overall view of the value chain, integration and coordination of the value chain activities are seen as important in order to obtain a time competitive advantage (Cushman and King, 1990). The value chain activities must be linked and configured effectively, as well as supported by an efficient information and communication system.

According to Cushman and King (1990), it is not only the time efficiency within the value chain activities that is important in measuring time as a competitive advantage. A gained time competitive advantage in one value chain activity may be lost as a result of poor time performance in other activities; thus the authors argue that the actual performance in each activity has to be taken into consideration. Stalk (1988) emphasizes the need for reducing the use of time throughout the whole system. This means that effort should be made to make the system for closing the sale, getting the order to the factory, getting the order scheduled, and delivering the product to the customer more efficient.

According to Stalk (1988), long lead times in manufacturing, warehousing, and retailing require planning based on forecasts. As long as sales forecasts are accurate a long planning loop will not distort the system. However, if unpredicted changes take place, a planning loop with long lead times reduces the ability to respond. In order to regain a quick response ability, the firm must reduce the time delays in the flow of information and product through the system.

Simon (1989) suggests that activities should, in a larger degree, be executed simultaneously rather than in a sequence in order to improve the ability to respond to unpredicted changes in customer conditions. The value chain model developed by Rockart and Short (1989) shows this parallel execution of activities. A modified Rockart and Short (1989) value chain model is illustrated in Chapter 2. One aspect of this value chain model that makes it different from the value chain model developed by Porter (1985) is the illustration of overlapping business processes. Simon (1989) mentions premarketing as one example. The firm starts the marketing of a specific product a long time before the actual market introduction, thereby increasing the probability of as fast as possible takeoff.

Simon argues that a time-based strategy should also deal with aspects that are different from the speed of response and the consumption of time through the entire value chain, such as the right timing. The aspect of timing is important in the introduction of innovations and product developments, and suggests that the earliest as possible market introduction is not always the optimal one. According to Simon (1989), one should emphasize the importance of the right timing of a market introduction. An early as possible market introduction is not always a good strategy, such as in cases where the product market is not prepared for the launching of a new product, the product is not satisfactorily tested, or if necessary support systems, such as service and distribution systems, are missing.

Because closeness to the customer increases the possibility for an early interpretation of trends and other valuable information, the firm should keep a close watch on the customer. The firm should also observe and predict the actions of competitors in order to obtain the optimal timing (Simon, 1989).

Strategic Alliance Theory

A strategic alliance is a relatively new form of partnership between two or more multinational firms (Robock and Simmonds, 1989). According to Robock and Simmonds (1989), strategic alliances are most often formed between competitors in order to aid their serving of global markets. These authors mention increased R&D capability, cost reductions, and enlarged market access as motivations for engaging in strategic alliances. Their view is that strategic alliances enable the partners to face global competitors on more equal terms.

Corporate strategies today must emphasize the need for change, which should allow for alternative values, norms, and behaviors. Corporate strategy must also have the ability to scan the globe for alliances that will give the company a technological edge, market access, market control, and rapid response capabilities (Cushman and King, 1990). Once an organization understands the competitive dynamics of all its activities, the concept of strategic alliances begins to command attention. Value chain theory is very useful in this context, as a value chain arranges an organization's activities into functional and business processes.

Reve (1990) has adapted Porter's five elements of competition into a hybrid model that fits the context of strategic alliances much better than the original Porter models of value chain and the five elements of competition. In this chapter, we will continue to use the value chain as a concept in the different parts of the Reve model, so there is some modification here. An integrated model of strategic management thus includes the main elements in the competitive arena: suppliers, buyers, substitutes, and competitors, as well as the firm itself.

Porter (1988), Joynt (1990), and Reve (1990) identify the alliances between the "strategic core" (firm) as upstream alliances with suppliers, downstream alliances with customers, diversification alliances with substitutes and/or new areas of business, and horizontal alliances with competitors. Downstream and upstream alliances involve a positioning of the firm relative to its suppliers and customers. Horizontal alliances are usually limited to economies of scale and can be formed with potential invaders. Diversification alliances are usually limited to economies of scope and have the primary objective of taking the firm into another area.

The model in Figure 8.1 is an attempt to summarize the state of the art at this stage. Several additions have been made, including actors outside the main competitive environment such

Figure 8.1
A Strategic Alliance Framework

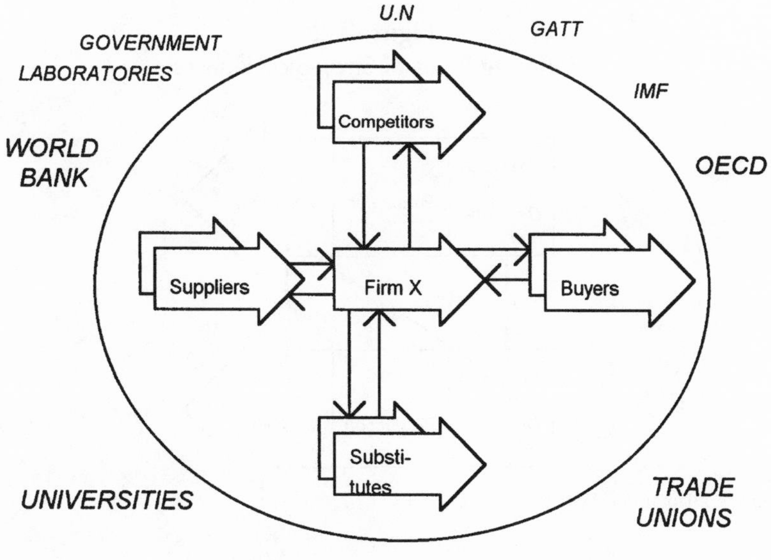

as the World Bank, IMF, GATT, trade unions, countries, and regions. Porter (1985) suggests that these bodies are part of the framework for the competitive model, and thus a new dimension has not been added to the main model, other than as a framework.

Another refinement to the model involves the aspect of choice. The newer strategic alliances are often more permanent than joint ventures (Davis, 1987) and, as such, the firm must select which suppliers, customers, competitors, and substitutes it will depend on. The model suggests that the communications links from the supplier to the firm and from the firm to the buyer are key aspects of the firms we have studied to this point (Welch and Luostarinen, 1990).

Contractor and Lorange (1988) analyzed the reasons for strategic alliances in their contribution to the Rutgers/Wharton seminar in 1986. The benefits and costs of cooperation involve risk reduction, economies of scale and/or rationalization, complementary technologies and patents, coopting or blocking competition, overcoming government-mandated investment or trade barriers, initial international expansion, and vertical (quasi) integration in a value chain. Lorange and Roos (1990) suggest that strategic alliances can be associated with some of the more traditional economic variables such as economies of scale, scope, and complementary advantage. Figure 8.2 illustrates this.

Figure 8.2
Different Types of Strategic Alliances

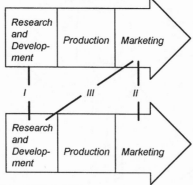

Source: Adapted from Lorange and Roos, 1990.

The first strategic alliance illustrates a linkage between two R&D departments in a highly competitive and volatile technological environment established to achieve economies of scale. The second strategic alliance illustrates two marketing departments collaborating in order to provide their customers a broad (scope) range of products. The third strategic alliance illustrates a complementary advantage between the R&D department of one firm and the marketing department of another firm.

METHODOLOGY

Secondary information is used as the main source of information to provide the necessary data for a case-oriented analysis of the entire automobile branch. The search for information was concentrated on publications of the *Wall Street Journal* and the *Economist*, but other sources were also considered. Historical change and contextual fields of information have played an important role in our analysis of a rather complex global phenomenon. Using the time variable affords us the opportunity to study some phases of time management in more detail.

One of the authors has worked as a consultant for two years in the branch studied. A detailed Career Process over a period of nine months was conducted with twenty top managers from Volvo in Gøteborg, Sweden. Much of the competitive organizational discussions involved the direct use of time as the key factor in production, marketing, service, and research. Nine of the structured interviews wer done in 1991 and eleven of the structured interviews were conducted in 1992. The question on time involved asking about the importance of time and the main functions in the business of making vehicles. Awareness of the variable has increased from the 1991 sample to the 1992 sample. In the United States, the author has also visited the General Motors plant in Janesville three times during 1991, talking with two middle managers in detail. In 1965 this author served as a power consultant for GM in Janesville for a period of two years. In addition, a middle manager from Ford was also interviewed in the United States during 1991. We have focused our attention on the assumption of qualitative research (Jick, 1979), and have used the case studies as the main vehicle for presenting the realities of the automobile branch to the reader.

ANALYSIS

Specific cases will be presented and related to the Porter value chain as well as the theoretical time framework presented earlier. Activities emphasized include research and development (R&D), tactical implementations, and manufacturing. Since the value chain as a whole may play a critical role with respect to obtaining time-based advantages, the last case (in this section) is devoted to the aspect of interdependencies.

Case 1: The Time Aspect and R&D

R&D represents both development of the existing product base and innovations including new products. In the value chain, R&D is an integrated part of the support activity of "technology" (see Figure 8.3). Our analysis in the discussion to follow will emphasize the importance of a time-based R&D; thus it is appropriate to divide the time aspect into three concepts in which the relevance of time is quite different. The three concepts are: high-speed product development, product replacement time, and timing.

Figure 8.3
Technology as an Activity in the Value Chain

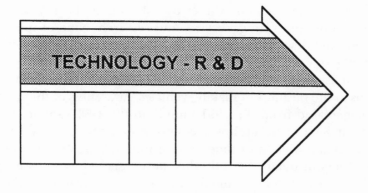

High-speed product development refers to the time it takes to develop new products (also referred to as the design time). In using a comparative approach, Cushman and King (1990) found that the design time (months per model based on 1989 figures for the U.S. market) at Toyota was forty-seven months, which is ten months lower than Ford and eighteen months lower than General Motors (GM). The ability to design a new product at a faster rate than competitors gives Toyota a better opportunity to respond to changes in consumer wants. This way, especially in an environment characterized by rapid changes in consumer wants, pays off in the short and long run (Simon, 1989).

Keeping up with changes in consumer demands is also related to the importance of product replacement time. In the automobile industry, product replacement time is the time period that elapses between the introduction of a model and the point at which this model is replaced by a new model. The difference in product replacement time between actors in this industry has, in the last decade, been rather large. This can be illustrated by using GM's Chevrolet Camaro and the Toyota Celica as examples. The Chevrolet Camaro was introduced in 1982 and will not be replaced by a new model until the beginning of the 1990s. On the other hand, the 1990 model of Toyota Celica, which is a direct competitor to the Camaro, has had three replacements within the past 10 years (WSJ, 1990a). In general, the average replacement time (years per model) at Toyota is 3.5 years compared to 9 years at GM (Cushman and King, 1990). According to Stalk (1988), the short replacement time generally obtained by Japanese manufacturers is a result of concentration on implementing incremental improvements to the product that eventually add up to superior products. Officials at the Swedish automobile manufacturer AB Volvo admit that the company's long replacement time, with model debuts of close to one per decade, has had an influence on a recent drop in sales (WSJ, 1990c). According to officials at Volvo, the company has lost market shares to rivals that have replaced approximately all their models in recent years, such as Bayerische Moteren Werke AG (BMW) and Daimler Benz AG. To regain their market position, Volvo has developed a new 900 series, and is planning to introduce at least one additional model family by 1995 (WSJ, 1990c).

The last concept in the time aspect is the importance of the right timing. Timing is crucial both with respect to product replacement and the development of a new product and its market introduction. In order to secure the right timing, effort should be put into keeping the distance to the customers as short as possible (Simon, 1989). It is of particular importance that the product designers and researchers in the company be directly tied to the customer base. Product designers of Honda spent as much as half their time talking directly to their foreign customers and dealers. They use their impressions to design new models (Ohmae, 1985).

Ford Motor Company's April–May 1990 introduction of the new Escort may represent an example of "lucky" timing. Due to rising gasoline prices caused by the 1990 Gulf crisis, the fuel-efficient Escorts have gained stronger sales arguments than otherwise would have been the case. Timing is also crucial as seen from a quality point of view. According to Hauser and Calusing (1988), quality function deployment (QFD), or the use of interfunctional teams in the design process, has led to a large reduction of cost at Toyota. The aspect of timing refers, in this case, to the timing of design changes related to a model replacement. In their work Hauser and Clausing compared the timing of design changes for a Japanese manufacturer using QFD and a U.S. manufacturer. The Japanese manufacturer had executed 90 percent of all design changes three months or more before the start of "Job no. 1" (the first car running through the assembly line). In contrast, the U.S. manufacturer reached 90 percent just before startup of "Job no. 1", and some of the design changes were often executed after the startup of assembly production. The result is higher costs and quality problems for U.S. manufacturers (Simon, 1989).

Case 2: The Time Aspect and Tactical Implementations

In the context of the following case, tactical implementation refers to both the organization's strategy with respect to technology implemented in the manufacturing of its products, and to the structuring of the production activity. As shown in Figure 8.4, tactical technology management is interpreted as an element belonging to the support activity called "technology" in the value chain, while strategies concerned with the production structure are interpreted as an element belonging to the support activity called "structure." Also illustrated is the close linkage between the manufacturing part of the organization on the one hand and tactical technology management and production structure on the other.

Figure 8.4
Internal Integration Using the Value Chain

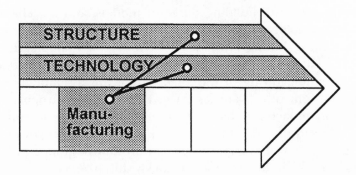

The objective of this case is not to concentrate on manufacturing, but to try to outline the possible connections among the time aspect, tactical technology implementation, and production structure. The emphasis will be placed on the flexible production systems employed by Japanese automobile manufacturers and the advantages of these systems in cases of unstable demand.

To illustrate different degrees of production flexibility, several examples will be used. In the first example, we will focus on the production of Pontiac Fiero, which GM has devoted an entire plant to (WSJ, 1990a). By using the plant exclusively for Fieros, the production run was exposed to an unstable demand. However, variation in demand can be meet by using and holding inventories (Chase and Aquilano, 1989). Use of inventories is costly, but could, for the Fiero plant, represent a means for managing more short-term fluctuations in demand around an average daily or weekly production output. With a more permanent drop in demand, the only solution seems to be to let the plant sit idle for long periods while huge fixed costs are accumulating, which was the case for GM and its Pontiac Fiero. The fact that GM has been (is) facing a structural problem, may also be illustrated by other examples. The GM Cadillac plant in Detroit has been on just one shift for several years, and GM's plant in Doraville, which is the newest and most expensive GM plant, has been running on one shift since February 1990 (WSJ, 1990d). Similar to the Fiero plant, the Doraville plant is only manufacturing one model, the Oldsmobile Cutlass Supreme (WSJ, 1990d). These examples are good illustrations of situations in which the manufacturing flexibility with respect to changing demand conditions is low.

On the contrary, assembly plants run by Japanese automobile manufacturers are building different models, and are characterized by the ability to shift production among the different models as demand is shifting (WSJ, 1990d). This is, for example, the case with the Hiroshima assembly line operated by Mazda. In addition to the manufacturing of the Miata MX-5, this assembly line also turns out four other vehicles (WSJ, 1990a). Also, European automobile manufacturers have begun adopting flexible manufacturing techniques. As an example, the German automobile manufacturer Volkswagen has a relatively newly equipped plant at Emden in which they are able to quickly shift from building Passats to Golfs without full retooling (*Economist*, Sept. 23, 1989). The advantage of such flexible manufacturing systems is the ability to respond quickly to changing demand conditions, thereby increasing the efficient use of capital tied up in high-cost plants.

From the discussion above, it is clear that the organization's choice of manufacturing technology and structural strategy affects its ability to respond to more permanent changes in demand conditions. A high-speed response is most likely to take place at an assembly line based on flexible manufacturing techniques.

Case 3: The Time Aspect and Manufacturing

To measure time-based competitive advantage, Cushman and King (1990) suggest that three general indexes be adapted: (1) overall time per product, (2) overall work hours per product, and (3) overall cost per product. As illustrated in Figure 8.5, manufacturing is only one of five primary value chain activities.

All these activities contribute to overall time, overall work hours, and overall cost per product. When focusing on only one activity, it is important to have in mind that this is only part of the overall picture.

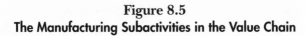

Figure 8.5
The Manufacturing Subactivities in the Value Chain

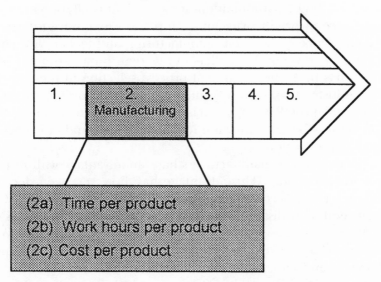

Activities (2a) and (2b) may seem identical; however, they can be separated from each other with respect to at least one important aspect: waiting time between manufacturing functions. Since a product is not accumulating value while waiting, no work time is allocted to it (Stalk, 1988). Waiting times will lead to a manufacturing time per product that differs from work hours per product in the manufacturing process.

According to Stalk (1988), the waiting time for a product in a traditional manufacturing system is so high that the product only receives value for .05 to 2.5 percent of the time it is in the factory. On the contrary, manufacturing functions in a time-based manufacturing system are more tied together, so that products can move from one manufacturing function to another with just a small delay or no delay at all.

According to Cushman and King (1990), work hours per product—that is to say, productivity—differ strongly from one automobile producer to another. By using data compiled from *Automotive News* (1989) regarding GM, Ford, and Toyota, the authors concluded that Toyota used twelve work hours per car, while the productivity at Ford and GM was seventeen and twenty hours respectively. In addition, European automobile manufacturers need an average of thirty-seven hours per car (*Economist,* Sept. 23, 1989). Without attempting to identify all sources of the difference in productivity, an example will be given to illustrate the close linkage between manufacturing and technology. Volvo makes cars on movable pallets rather than on an assembly line, which has been the traditional process selection in the automobile industry (Chase and Aquilano, 1989). According to Chase and Aquilano (1989), Volvo has a production rate lower than its competitors because they are losing the speed and efficiency of the line production.

Japanese car manufacturers have an advantage with respect to costs per model. This advantage has, however, been decreasing over time. According to a study by Arthur Andersen & Co., the overall cost disadvantage of Chrysler, Ford, and Gm is $500 to $600 per car, compared to $2,000 just one decade ago (WSJ, 1990a). The interrelationship among the variables of time, productivity, and costs must also be mentioned. Their interdependence, as characterized by Cushman and King (1990), is high, as illustrated by the following example. A high-speed manufacturing system with a high degree of automation may lead to fewer quality problems, such as defects. In 1980 a Japanese car had an average of two defects, while cars produced by Ford, GM, and Chrysler had on average 6.7, 7.4, and 8.1 defects per car, respectively (WSJ, 1990a). Defects lead to rework, which in turn means a loss in productivity and time and increased costs. According to a report from Harbor & Associates, the defect rate for U.S. automobile manufacturers is now on average 1.65 per car, compared to an average of 1.2 defects per car produced by the Japanese (WSJ, 1990a). Another example is that high productivity, given low waiting times, leads to lower fixed costs per car than what would have been the case with a low productivity and a low output.

Case 4: The Time Aspect and Interdependencies

Until now, only single value chain activities have been emphasized. It is, however, important to realize that the time aspect may also play a critical role with respect to the value chain as a whole, and with respect to the interdependence between the firm and its suppliers and customers (see Figure 8.6).

Figure 8.6
"functional units and business processes must be linked and configured effectively"
(Cushman and King, 1990, p. 14).

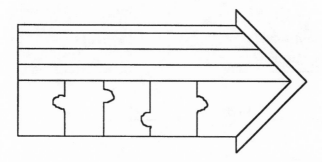

Looking back at the indexes Cushman and King (1990) suggested to use when measuring time-based competitive advantage, it seems clear that overall time per product is one of the main variables. This overall time approach requires that the entire value chain be taken into account.

The point is that a firm can gain a competitive advantage in one of the value chain activities, but it may lose it again as the result of poor performance in other activities (Cushman and King, 1990). The same argument may be used with respect to the relations among the firm, its suppliers, and its customers. Toyota's experiences with one of its suppliers provides a useful example (see Figures 8.7 and 8.8). A response time as high as fifteen days caused considerable dissatisfaction (Stalk, 1988). In cooperation and consultation with Toyota, the supplier implemented several changes, such as cutting lot sizes, reducing the number of inventory holding points, and eliminating work-in-progress inventories. According to Stalk (1988), the result of these changes was a response time of only one day, which seems more in accordance with Toyota's time-based factories. This example illustrates the importance of elements outside the firm's own value chain. The firm must also be sure that its suppliers are compatible with a time-based strategy. A manufacturing firm like Toyota, with a high-speed response ability to changing demand conditions, may easily lose out if its suppliers have a high response time.

Figure 8.7
Lead Time of Fifteen Days between Supplier and Firm

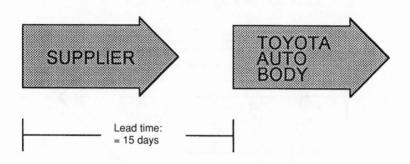

In the late 1970s, Toyota was divided into two separate firms, Toyota Motor Manufacturing and Toyota Motor Sales. At this point in time, people at Toyota Motor Manufacturing were dissatisfied with the performance at Toyota Motor Sales. According to Stalk (1988), they argued that inefficiencies in sales and distribution were frittering away a time efficiency gained in manufacturing. Compared with a two-day manufacturing time, it took Toyota Motor Sales from fifteen to twenty-six days to close the sale, get the order to the factory, get the order scheduled, and the car delivered to the customer (Stalk, 1988).

Figure 8.8
Lead Time of Fifteen–Twenty-six Days between Firm and Buyer

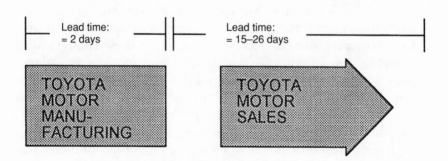

The problem was solved by merging Toyota Motor Manufacturing and Toyota Motor Sales in 1982, which resulted in implementation of actions aimed at reducing delays in sales and distribution, such as speeding the flow of information. According to Stalk (1988) Toyota had by 1987 reduced the total cycle time to eight days, including the manufacturing time.

Throughout this section different aspects of time have been emphasized, and several examples from the automobile industry have illustrated the importance of time in this highly competitive and volatile market. Even if the unit of analysis has been selected activities within the firm's value chain, it is argued that the overall picture is the most important one with respect to measuring time-based competitive advantages. Since this overall picture includes elements located outside the firm's own value chain, it was necessary to stress that these elements can affect the firm's ability to exploit time efficiencies created inside its value chain. It was also shown that a more close relationship between the firm and its external elements could represent a means of making these elements more compatible with the firm's time-based strategy. A close relationship, or a strategic alliance, with another firm may in some cases represent a way of acquiring time efficiencies.

TOWARD A SYNTHESIS

In an effort to make these results applicable and realistic for a practicing manager, some type of process orientation is necessary in order to understand today's organization. In this process orientation, technology, the environment, and networking must be understood and managed using time as a critical factor. Technology is often associated with the firm's functional activities of logistics and production management, in that technology often is defined as some type of action an individual performs on an object. The management process here is often centralized and rationalized into a "one best way" in order to gain a competitive advantage. On the other hand, the environment and networking often require a decentralized type of management process in order to get the best results, and yet each of these processes can be evaluated using the time dimension. Indeed, the Japanese have shown that a process of scanning the environment for incremental technological changes can be a competitive advantage if you get the new idea implemented and back to the customers before the competition does. Today's management philosophy involves understanding the fact that in high-speed management, centralization and decentralization go hand in hand in most organizations.

REFERENCES

Automotive News. 1989. An interview with the CEO designate of Ford Motors Co., p. E8.

Buckley, P. 1991. The state of international business theory today. Paper presented at the European International Business Association Congress, Copenhagen, Dec.

Chase, R. B., and N. J. Aquilano. 1989. *Production and Operations Management—A Life Cycle Approach.* 5th ed. Boston: Irwin.

Cushman, D. P. and S. S. King. 1990. Visions of order: High-speed management in the private sector of the global marketplace. Paper prepared for the conference. "The Global Economy and Society in the Twenty-First Century," Warsaw, Poland, June 17–22. In A. K. Kozminski and D. P. Cushman, eds. *Organizational Communication and Management,* N.Y. (Albany: SUNY Press, 1993).

Davis, S. 1987. *Future Perfect.* New York: Addison Wesley.

Dollinger, M. 1990. The evolution of collective strategies in fragmented industries. *Academy of Management Review* 15(2):266–85.

Drucker, P. 1989. From dangerous liaisons to alliances for progress. *Wall Street Journal,* Sept. 8.

Economist. 1990. Car-industry joint ventures: Spot the difference. Feb. 24, p. 74.

———. 1989. Ready, steady. . . Sept. 23, pp. 79–80.

Hauser, J. R., and D. Clausing. 1988. The house and quality. *Harvard Business Review* (May–June):52–62.

Healey, J. R. 1990. Cover story: After a slow start, Geo speeds up. *USA Today,* June 21.

Jick, T. D. 1979. Mixing qualitative and quantitative methods: Triangulation in action. *Administrative Science Quarterly* (Dec.).

Joynt, P. 1990. Organizational research involving internal networks and external strategic alliances. *Working Paper* no. 25, Norwegian School of Management, Sandvika, Norway.

Levitt, T. 1983. The globalization of markets. *Harvard Business Review* (May–June):92–102.

Lorange, P., and J. Roos. 1990. Strategiske allianser i globale strategier, Norges Eksportråd (Also Norwegian School of Management Working Paper 1989/34).

Morone, J. 1989. Strategic use of technology. *California Management Review* 31(4):91–112.

Moss-Kanter, R. 1989. Becoming PAls: Pooling, allying, and linking across companies. *Academy of Management Executive* 3(3):183–93.

Ohmae, K. 1985. *Triad Power: The Coming Shape of Global Competition.* New York: Free Press.

Oliver, C. 1990. Determinants of interorganizational relationships: Integration and future directions. *Academy of Management Review* 15(2):241–55.

Porter, M. E. 1980. *Competitive Strategy: Techniques for Analyzing Industries and Competitors.* New York: Free Press.

———. 1985. *Competitive Advantage: Creating and Sustaining Superior Performance.* New York: Free Press.

———. 1988. Changing patterns of international competition. *California Management Review* 28(2) (Winter):9–39.

———. 1989. *The Competitive Advantage of Nations.* New York: Free Press.

Reve, T. 1990. Toward a theory of strategic management. *Working paper,* Norwegian School of Economics and Business Administration.

Robock, S. H. and K. Simmonds. 1989. *International Business and Multinational Enterprises.* 4th ed. Boston: Irwin.

Rockart, J., and J. Short. 1989. IT in the 1990s: Managing organizational interdependencies. *Sloan Management Review* 30: 7–17.

Simon, H. 1989. Die Zeit als strategischer Erfolgsfaktor. *Zeitschrift fur Betriebswirtschaftlehre,* 59 Jahrgang, pp. 70–93.

Stalk, G., Jr. 1988. Time—The next source of competitive advantage. *Harvard Business Review* (July–Aug.):23–33.

Thompson, J. D. 1967. *Organizations in Action.* New York: McGraw-Hill.

Van de Ven, A. H. 1976. On the nature, formation and maintenance of relations among organizations. *Academy of Management Review* 1:24–36.

Welch, L, and R. Luostarinen. 1990. Inward-outward connections in internationalization. *Working Paper,* Institute for Management Research, Norwegian School of Management (under publication).

WSJ. 1990a. Losing control: Auto industry in U.S. is sliding relentlessly into Japanese hands. Feb. 16, pp. A1, A6.

———. 1990b. Japan cars score coup in U.S. July 6, p. B1.

———. 1990c. Volvo unveils new luxury-car series to counter Japanese rivals in Europe. Aug. 21, p. B6.

———. 1990d. Smaller giant: Auto maker takes a huge write-off to close plants, preparing for growth in the 1990s. Nov. 1, pp. A1, A13.

CHAPTER NINE

High-Speed Management and New Product Development

George Tuttle

The triangular relationship between profits, new product development (NPD) and the approval process (Food and Drug Administration, FDA) in the pharmaceutical industry goes back to 1938 with the institution of the Federal Drug and Cosmetic Act and continues today. Presently, however, the variable that threatens profitability in drug research is a turbulent environment and challenges the development of new products to control the change that results from the tumultuous marketplace. The challenge is resolved by injecting speed into the factors involved in marketing new drugs and is antithetical to a slow and often rigid government approval process.

A new management system has emerged in high-tech organizations today that facilitates NPD; it is called "high-speed management" (HSM). A logical question evolves from its tenets that asks whether or not the relationship previously mentioned can be high-speed managed. This chapter explores that question and develops six critical success factors that organizations must consider in the process of marketing new products in a turbulent environment.

THE PROFIT AND RESEARCH RELATIONSHIP

Research and development is the cornerstone of survival in pharmaceuticals. Indeed, as a whole, American companies had revenues of $57 billion in 1990 and 16.8 percent of that total was channeled back into research (*Business Week*, 1991, p. 107). According to Research Technology Management (1987) there is not a strong correlation between research and development and growth in profits. However, the drug industry in 1987 was the fourth most profitable in the U.S. economy. The positive relationship between profits and research in the drug industry has a long history, dating back to the Federal Drug and Cosmetic Act of 1938, and has allowed the industry not only to survive but to prosper. This is interesting because it adds another variable that must be considered. Harry Marks, an industry historian, identifies the variable as government regulation. He states that for over fifty years, American pharmaceutical companies have consistently generated high profits at the same time that they are highly regulated. The triple variables of science, profits, and government regulation describe the modern drug discovery environment.

When the Federal Drug and Cosmetic Act was instituted, stakeholders in the drug industry thought that research would be stifled. However, the reverse is true: research required by law stimulated medical progress. William Griggs extends this reasoning, explaining that "by making good scientific work necessary to get a drug on the market and by eliminating the undermining competition of unproven and quack products" (Marks, 1997 pp. 24–86) both the field of medicine and pharmaceutical companies were allowed to prosper. Clearly, though, drug development was heavily influenced by the interdependence of the three variables and the old method of drug discovery called the "shotgun method" (screening thousands of compounds).

In modern high-tech industries, however, including the pharmaceutical industry, the environment is characterized by rapid change, quick market saturation, and unexpected global competition, resulting in shortened product life cycles. This leads to a set of moves called "high-speed management" that are needed to harness the change so characteristic of the turbulent market.

The challenge presented to firms competing in this kind of environment is to develop a flexible process that produces high-quality products inexpensively, gaining competitive advantage with a quick response to customer needs. The translation of these generic conditions in the drug industry is as follows. R&D continues to skyrocket (the latest estimate by the *Philadelphia Inquirer* in 1990 put the average cost of bringing a drug to market at $231 million) while at the same time the product life cycle (depending on the length of time in the approval process) is usually shortened as a result of government regulation and increasingly formidable competitive products from the world market.

In addition, HMOs, PPOs, and other third party insurance providers together with the Medicare Catastrophic Act and the rise to power of the generic drug industry have severely handicapped the ability of pharmaceutical companies to be profitable. Because of the pressure to keep prices low, higher R&D costs, and tougher therapeutic targets, it is imperative for competitors in this industry to innovate as rapidly as possible. The high speed with which this is needed revolutionizes the relationship among science, profit, and regulation in pharmaceuticals.

The historical relationship among innovation, government, and profit in the drug industry is of critical importance. Furthermore, this relationship continues today but filtered through a new management style.

We will first examine the critical factors of research and marketing that any high-tech company must possess to succeed in a turbulent business world. Then we will investigate Merck Sharp & Dohme's interpretation of those factors to identify the key areas that must be exploited to develop a strategic plan that will answer the challenges of the modern market. The assumption is that Merck is without peer in its command of the factors at work here (Ballen, 1992, pp. 40–68). This will provide insight into the more important issue of how to operationalize a technological orientation that has as a barrier a governmental agency that is an advocate for consumer safety. The complicating condition is how a firm can innovate with speed when the approval process is inherently slow.

The first of the critical factors that must be addressed by an organization is that it must have an adaptable, accurate strategy. This can be accomplished by employing environmental assessment, product portfolio modeling, and unique product development based upon its resources as they align with customer needs through structured innovation. This factor is important because any one competing in an environment that is volatile must know where they are in relation to their customers to develop a steady stream of marketable products. Miles and Snow (1984, pp. 10–87) tell us that to the extent that a firm does this better than its competitors leads to an anchored fit, resulting in long-term success.

Merck obviously performs well in this regard. Not only do they have a steady stream of products that are patent-protected but they are also serving customer needs well as evidenced by outstanding sales (nineteen drugs with over $100 million in revenues). Many of their products are linked to Roy Vagelos, Merck's transformational leader, who took over as research director in 1975. One such drug is Vasotec, representing a therapeutic class of drugs that is an example of Vagelos' accurate environmental assessment. One only has to observe the magnitude of sales of Vasotec (over $1 billion in worldwide sales [Annual Report, 1990]) to understand the skill with which the company employs this important technique.

Another example of excellence in management where it concerns environmental assessment is in order. The climate should be aligned properly by linking marketing and R&D in the appropriate way to move quickly and take advantage of technological or marketing windows when they occur if environmental assessment is going to be leveraged for advantage. In 1981, when Indocin was losing its patent (Teitelman, 1987, pp. 103–6) Merck was successful in bolstering sales of the mature product by differentiating the drug using the newly acquired technology of long-acting capsules. As a result, the 1986 sales of Indocin were $200 million. This is not bad performance when one considers that sales of the drug at its zenith in 1981 were only $237 million.

One reason for Merck's demonstrated success in environmental assessment is their ability to map alternative scenarios based on technological developments. An excellent way to view this aspect of the company is to analyze their drugs in the pipeline (or drugs recently approved) relative to the changes in technology. For instance, techniques like genetic engineering and recombinant DNA have allowed scientists to study cell function in a way that allows the methods of drug discovery to be facilitated. This results in an explosive rate of information for new product development, which revolutionizes medical science. Merck has exploited the knowledge base gained from new technologies to directly influence products that it markets like Hepatitis B vaccine, which did $120 million in sales in 1987 (Annual Report, 1988). In addition, it used strategic linkages to get rights to other potentially profitable products like Repligen's AIDS vaccine. These linkages also provide additional insight to help technologies already in place that facilitate development of new drugs like Varivax for chicken pox, H-Flu vaccine for meningitis, MK-906 for prostatic cancer, and Prodiax for diabetes (*Business Month,* 1988, p. 36). These examples represent the company's ability to capitalize on new product development, which is an outgrowth of their understanding of the environment and reflects a desire to meet the changing needs of customers. These HSM issues illustrate the ability of the company to respond quickly on a technological level.

Product portfolio modeling is another aspect of the R&D and marketing interface that is critical to the nature of high-speed management and essential to a high-tech company to exploit and maintain competitive advantage (See chapter two—Cushman and King—and chapter three—Kozminski.). It is important to a firm because it represents its ability to manipulate market pull to maneuver around competitors. Within the context of quick response and adaptability this concept has come to be associated with the organization's understanding of the need to be flexible in response to changing customer needs. This is at the core of being able to dominate an industry and stay number one. Merck demonstrates its willingness to be committed to dominance by realizing that is has made successful alliances that fit its business orientation, resulting in products like Splendil and Losec (*Business Month,* 1988, p. 36).

These drugs are licensed to Merck by A. B. Astra from Sweden and are designed to take advantage of their marketing strengths in order to penetrate the calcium channel blocker drug class. This shows that Merck is maneuvering into a dominant position in the high-growth, antihypertensive drug class.

In addition, the turbulence of the market demands that companies be flexible and go quickly where opportunities exist. Merck took advantage of this when they built a $300 million research facility in Canada when that country decided to improve patent protection. This is an example of being able to move quickly to maintain flexibility and commit wherever and whenever opportunity presents itself to enhance global market position.

The final aspect of product portfolio modeling involves the firm in such a way that it must be aware of the market position of its competitors. It is interesting to point out that in regard to this, Merck was beaten to market by Squibb. The contending product was called Capoten and Merck trailed Squibb by a year in marketing their competing product. Inasmuch as Capoten is a fundamentally different drug in terms of mode of action (calcium channel blocker) than Vasotec (ace inhibitor) Merck was able to put all its strengths together and overtake Squibb in total sales. For example, it combined marketing pull by a superior sales force (Dialogue Info. Service, 1987) voted the best in the industry in 1987 along with a technological push, obtaining a new congestive heart failure indication that spurred sales in 1988 to over $900 million. The strategic use of market pull and science push is the earmark of a company that is aware of its strengths and puts them to advantage as soon as opportunities exist.

There is another communication tool in the R&D and marketing interface that high-tech firms must embrace to align themselves properly in a turbulent environment. This tool is called "structured innovation." Fundamental to this aspect of Merck's approach (*Business Week*, 1987, pp. 84–90) is their allegiance to the importance of scientific thought. Their research structure is organic and informal and divided into twelve therapeutic classes.

A champion is responsible for building a team. As more team members are added, more financial support is accumulated making the stature the product is given significantly enhanced. Underlying this is a deep appreciation for risk taking, the fuel for creative thought. Vagelos adds to this his extensive scientific background, engendering a university atmosphere that attracts the best talent in the world. In addition, the company has deep pockets and its leader keeps its thoroughbred stable insulated from business by linking his research department directly to him through Dr. Skolnick (Quickel, 1988). The only critical factor that all potential scientific candidates must have is the desire to pursue scientific inquiry "steered toward marketable products as quickly as possible."

Recent studies have supported the effectiveness of this technique. DeMeyer (1991, pp. 49–58) studied fourteen successful companies, trying to improve communication, seven of which were classified as pharmaceutical or chemical companies. The primary ingredient for an effective R&D effort is exchange of information. The idea is to have scientists feel comfortable enough to grasp the need to share information. Successful companies are able to integrate this value, ultimately establishing competitive advantage through the free flow of information. This shatters the tendency for R&D to be isolated from the rest of the company. DeMeyer suggests six broad areas in which the value can be nurtured, of which socialization and electronic communication are of primary importance. Periodic face-to-face contact is needed to develop confidence in teamwork and keep it functioning at a high level. Skolnick (Quickel, 1988) is the point man for Merck and has the necessary flexibility to effectively utilize these techniques to keep R&D and marketing coordinated enough to stay focused upon the needs of the customer.

Merck considers its passion for risk taking the underpinning for the overwhelming success of their scientific effort. Two things account for this (*Business Week*, 1987, pp. 84–90). First, Donald Hupe, a scientist for Merck, points out that underground projects are not only tolerated but encouraged. He cites the allotment of time (10–20%) given him to work with the National Cancer Institute to find potential cancer drugs. This is not within his prescribed duties but it is important to him to be able to do things without having to ask management. The point is the company knows the value of creative thought and does its utmost to create the right internal culture to sustain the growth of knowledge. Second, they keep close ties with independent thought by bestowing $50,000 grants to universities working on major breakthroughs in the field of drug discovery. Related to this, Merck supports seminars given by the most influential scientists in the world and keeps its libraries packed with the latest medical publications.

The techniques described earlier—environmental assessment, product portfolio modeling, and structured innovation—are the necessary conditions explaining why Merck enjoys a tight fit with the environment. What is important to realize is that the company has performed well for a sustained period of time. Furthermore, scholars recognize both necessary and sufficient conditions to exist when outcomes are so overwhelmingly successful. The sufficient condition to round out the performance strength of Merck is their balanced, focused strategy. The firm successfully utilizes this strategy to properly align the R&D and marketing units, integrating the values of the transformational leader with the coordination of strategic information using the above techniques. An analysis of the key moves Merck made to help employes to operationalize this strategy is in order.

In 1975, when Merck hired Roy Vagelos, a biomedical scientist from Washington University in St. Louis, he was head of the biology/chemistry department. He felt he was hired to discover marketable drugs, since at the time the firm was in the midst of an innovative drought. The board of directors did not want to diversify. Rather, they wanted to focus entirely on research, which they felt was the engine of growth. Vagelos agreed, adding (*Business Week*, 1987, p. 90), "I'm a biomedical scientist. If the Board wanted to diversify, I doubt they would have chosen me."

Because of his background, he came to the company with a bold vision to exploit new discoveries in medical science for drug research. His research was directed toward targeting biomedical reactions caused by disease. The challenge was to devise a magic bullet to intervene somewhere within the disease's chain of activity. This idea revolutionized the work in research. Formerly the "shotgun method" was widely used as the approach in discovering new drug mechanisms of action. A compound was ground up and tested to observe its activity. Once the activity was understood, it was investigated in animals to see if it had commercial applicability in humans.

The molecular targeting approach has proven to be a powerful tool when added to the culture developed by Merck to produce a consistent pattern of successful drugs. The central reason is that compounds are explored only after the disease is understood, resulting in medications that are effective in the body. This is in stark contrast to the tedious "shotgun" method, which produces thousands of compounds but no targets. The subtle difference expressed by molecular targeting is that it pursues pharmaceutical investigation from a safe orientation. This is the kind of proactive technological style that embodies high-speed management.

Research tells us that a balanced, focused strategy produces the highest percentage of sales from new products in the last five years. When you analyze Merck's performance it is significant to point out that of the nineteen drugs that are currently patent protected, and selling over $100 million, nine have been introduced since 1985. Mevacor, the blockbuster drug of the 1990s, will add to Vasotec's performance immediately and together they are predicted to account for more than $1.5 billion.

In order to develop a better appreciation for the balanced, focused strategy, attention must turn from the technological focus to the marketing orientation. John Lyon's Merck's executive vice president and marketing boss concedes that when (*Business Week*, 1987:85) "your company considers research the engine of growth a commercial division can't get in the way." Effectively, marketing is crucial but not in the traditional sense.

Merck's outlook blends the marketing department with the R&D effort in the following manner. In his statement to shareholders in 1987, Roy Vagelos (Annual Report, 1987) said, "the companies' commitment to marketing has never been more apparent." Indeed, in an article entitled "Sheer Energy" (*Business Month*, 1988, p. 36) this assessment of the leader's appreciation for marketing is supported and highlights the fact that the interface of the two departments is responsible for squeezing out every penny from today's big revenue makers to support the search for their replacements. The translation of this value is the training it gives its field staff.

Splitting salespeople into divisions according to product category training can focus on more detailed information and allow reps to have more knowledge about the medical implications of the drugs, which develops an expert image. This expert image is supplemented with lap-top computers loaded with summary articles from medical journals, allowing Merck's field staff to act as consultants about their drugs. The end result is that they are viewed as the best sales force (Value Line Information Service, 1988) in America based on technological knowledge and reputation. This credibility also facilitates more profound outcomes like postmarketing surveillance because doctors are willing to tell reps the problems they are having the field. The FDA looks at this fact favorably.

Marketing will also play a strategic role in the future (Brady, 1989, p. 16). First, Merck realizes that it has no presence in the nonprescription drug business so it formed a 50/50 venture with

Johnson and Johnson, well known for its marketing strength in sales of over-the-counter products like Tylenol and Band-Aids. This is an ideal match because it links the strengths of both companies in two important areas for future sales. To begin with, there is a more educated, self-medicating public; thus more sophisticated drugs can be pulled over the counter by a sharp sales force. Second, Merck has a bevy of mature drugs due to lose patent protection. Realizing their strength in getting drugs approved they can change the status of sales of the older pre-scription medications by applying their expertise in winning ap-proval for over-the-counter sales. This new avenue for sales can be exploited by a top flight marketer in nonprescription sales, which facilitates a competitive advantage in the fastest growing segment of the drug industry. (In 1988 over-the-counter sales accounted for $9 billion.)

The bold vision of Vagelos continues to take shape with major new prospects in the hopper waiting for approval together with a path for mature medications to continue to make major contributions in a new arena. Thus the balance of R&D and marketing is illustrated. It is important to note that in all areas of its business, research is fundamental to Merck's strategy. This is illustrated in the joint venture it developed with DuPont, which is designed to fit the strengths of both companies together in such a way that dividends will be realized in the medium to long term. The ultimate objective for the new company is an invest-ment in the future that integrates leading edge research in a broad array of therapeutic areas to attain a significant presence in the global pharmaceutical marketplace. The synergy of the strengths of the two companies is realized in the minimum in-vestment needed to start the deal, which maximizes the potential for new products in a range of therapeutic categories not pos-sible when working alone.

THE APPROVAL PROCESS

Having the skill to find the appropriate product for diseases is one thing. Getting them approved is quite another. High-speed management is based upon managing change surrounding a port-folio of products and assumes that new entrants are consistently introduced. The focus now is turned toward the obstacle that endangers the successful launch of a new pharmaceutical product: the Food and Drug Administration (FDA). This federal agency is composed of seven review divisions. The FDA first becomes instrumental in the review process when the pharmaceutical company has completed its testing in animals and is ready to begin human trials. At this time the company or sponsor applies for an Investigational New Drug (IND) application. This is considered a plan for the study in humans and is supposed to give a complete picture of the drug, including its structural formula, animal test results, and manufacturing information. The division that is to review the drug depends on the product itself and to some extent the efficiency with which the sponsor describes its action. This is an important part of the process. The review can take up to ten years and at its conclusion it is assigned a review priority based on the drug's chemical type and potential benefit.

A drug can be pigeonholed into one of six classifications under chemical type (*FDA Consumer,* 1987–88, pp. 6–10) see Fig-

Figure 9.1
New Drug Development

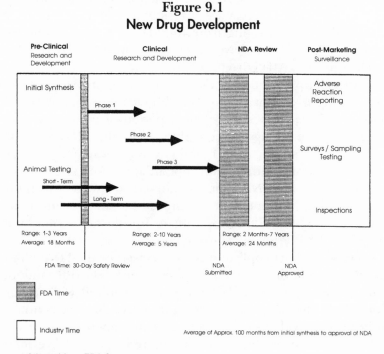

Figure 1 Adapted from FDA Consumer

ure 9.1. The first is new molecular entity, which means that an active ingredient has never been marketed before. The classifications proceed down through less important categories: new derivative, new formulation, new combination, already marketed drug, and already marketed drug by the same firm.

The classification then branches off into another category, which is called "gain." This category considers treatment or diagnosis of a disease where there are limited alternatives. This category classifies drugs by order of importance, from little or no gain, to moderate gain, to important gain. There are two other classifications called "orphan drug" and "designated orphan drug," which is a special class that applies to diseases that are rare. Drugs that are able to treat rare diseases are given special review priority.

If a drug is given the status of a new molecular entity and has never been marketed before it is given top priority. This means that all the resources of the FDA are brought to bear to speed the process of final approval. The rating of 1-A is stamped on the compound. An example of a drug that received a 1-A is Lovastatin or Mevacor, Merck's anticholesterol drug, and is symbolic of the work of every R&D facility to generate a drug that receives the highest rating from the FDA. The only rating from the FDA that would receive more attention than 1-A is a 1-AA, which is given to AIDS drugs.

An example of this is Zidovudine or Retrovir (AZT), the recently approved Burroughs Wellcome drug to treat AIDS. The first part of the process may take a period of between one and three years, the average being eighteen months. More important (Ackerman, 1987, pp. 11–15), of the two thousand chemical entities studied, two hundred show potential in early tests and only twenty may receive INDs and be allowed to proceed to human trials resulting in one product approved for the pharmacy shelf. This is reality and thus the ultimate hurdle a pharmaceutical company's R&D effort must overcome. (See Figure 9.2)

Once the IND applications are received by the FDA, Phase 1 can begin about thirty days later. This is the most costly and most time-consuming part of the review. It is involved with learning more about the safety of the drug. Initial studies are conducted on healthy individuals to determine what happens to the drug in the human body. A chief cause of failure in Phase 1 is evidence of toxicity at doses too small to produce a therapeutic effect. The initial studies are important to help determine the design of

Figure 9.2
How Experimental Drugs Are Tested in Humans

	Number of Patients	Length	Purpose	Percent of Drugs Successfully Completing*
Phase 1	20 - 100	Several months	Mainly safety	67 percent
Phase 2	Up to several hundred	Several months to 2 years	Some short-term safety, but mainly effectiveness	45 percent
Phase 3	Several hundred to several thousand	1 - 4	Safety, effectiveness, dosage	5 - 10 percent

*For example, of 20 drugs entering clinical testing, 13 or 14 will successfully complete phase 1 trials and go on to phase 2; about nine will complete phase 2 and go to phase 3; only one or two will clear phase 3 (and, on average, about one of the original 20 will ultimately be approved for marketing).

Figure 2 Adapted from FDA Consumer

later clinical trials. Information, such as how much of the drug a patient should receive or how often it should be administered as well as what precautions are necessary to ensure safety are included. If the results of Phase 1 show no safety problems, then the green light is given for Phase 2.

Human drug testing or Phase 2 proceeds to review the efficacy of the candidate in treating the disease. In addition, the studies in this segment of the process attempt to disclose short-term side effects and risks in people whose health is impaired. These trials are randomized, controlled studies, which means that there is a treatment group and a placebo group. Also, all participants, including the researchers, are "blinded" to keep the potential for human error at a minimum and to avoid researcher bias. The FDA's role is to ensure that objectivity is maintained.

The outcome of Phase 2 demonstrates the frequent side effects and adverse reactions that might commonly be observed in a short duration of use. A more complete understanding of the drug's safety along with the verification of its usefulness in treating the disease is yet to be investigated.

During Phase 3 a meeting is set up between the sponsor and the FDA to develop information that will allow the drug to be marketed and used safely. This results in trial designs structured around the conditions of medical practice. The length of time and sample size are greatly increased and the successful conclusion of this phase results in New Drug Application (NDA). This is a formal request to the FDA to allow marketing of the new drug to humans with concomitant approval for interstate commerce.

Once the NDA is filed, two things happen. First, the 180-day clock starts ticking, which is the time allowed the FDA to review the NDA. This is important in that as time elapses in the review stage, valuable marketing time is lost on the seventeen-year patent that is granted upon final approval. Frequently, the review clock takes much longer than 180 days, so the critical factor for success at this point is to ensure that the FDA will be satisfied with the results. This is a communication issue and, therefore, important to high-speed management. (The longer the time spent in this part of the process the less time allowed for patent protection—and protection is related to profit.)

The second thing that happens is that priorities are set. For example, if the drug is given a 1-A rating after IND trials the highest priority is afforded the drug so the usual formality of the order in which the NDA was received is disregarded. Correspondingly, heavy investment in the resources of time and money is given to the drug because it has been shown to be safe and effective for an illness that the FDA targets as critically important.

If the NDA is approved, then the company is allowed to market the drug and the final period of review begins. This is called "postmarketing surveillance" and is looked at quite seriously by the FDA. Often NDA approval is granted on the basis of the quality of the plan developed by the sponsor to monitor adverse reactions.

Overall, the FDA approval process boils down to two important questions: Do the results provide substantial evidence for effectiveness? Do the results show the product is safe under the conditions of use in the proposed labeling?

AN ANALYSIS OF AZT, MEVACOR, EXOSURF, AND NUROMAX

The approval process takes on average ten years to complete. The strategic framework of high-speed management attempts to significantly reduce that time through the use of communication and information tools. In order to explore the implications of high-speed management on this process and derive the critical success factors, we will briefly analyze four recently approved drugs, two of which were the fastest ever to be processed by the FDA (Ackerman, 1987, pp. 11–15): AZT, which took 107 days, and Lovastatin, which took only nine months. Once the FDA

Figure 9.3
Drug Development Timelines

ZIDOVUDINE

1964	Azidothymidine (AZT), now known as zidovudine, developed as potential cancer treatment. Shelved because of ineffectiveness.
October 1984	Preclinical tests begin for use as antiviral to treat acquired immune deficiency syndrome (AIDS).
May 1985	Investigational new drug exemption (IND) submitted.
July 1985	Phase I tests begin.
February 1986	Phase II tests begin.
September 1986	Trials terminated; phase III not conducted.*
October 1986	Treatment IND approved.**
December 1986	New drug application (NDA) submitted.
March 1987	NDA approved.

LOVASTATIN

Late 1978	Lovastatin isolated from microorganism *Aspergillus terreus.*
1979	Preclinical studies begin.
March 1984	Investigational new drug exemption (IND) submitted to FDA.
May 1984	Phase II clinical studies begin in United States.*
April 1985	Phase III studies begin.
November 1986	New drug application (NDA) submitted.
August 1987	NDA approved.

Phase I clinical studies had begun abroad in April 1980.

The study was stopped because patients on the drug clearly were living longer than those given a placebo. It was deemed unethical to continue to withhold treatment from the control group.
**Treatment protocol that allows access to the new drug before approval for marketing for patients who meet the medical criteria of the study protocol.*

Figure 3 Adapted from FDA Consumer

took over in the IND phase, both drugs came through the process in a relatively short period of time. (See Figure 9.3)

AZT and Lovastatin had a 1-AA and 1-A priority rating respectively. What is important here is what both companies did
before the process began that facilitated the high rating.

Analysis shows that Zidovudine had been a drug that the
FDA was familiar with since it was discovered by the NIH in 1964
and sold to BW Co. to market as an anticancer drug. For what-
ever reason BW Co. chose not to launch it. However, with the
spread of AIDS and the pressure on the FDA to support anything
that looked promising in treatment of AIDS patients, Zidovudine
was given a 1-AA rating as soon as it was demonstrated to be
effective. As it ran through the review the risk/benefit ratio was
found to be low (given the indication) and in view of its familiar-
ity with the drug and the communication it received from the
drug's sponsor, the FDA facilitated the process to ensure its mar-
ketability. The BW Co. and agency link was well oiled and focused upon the lowest effective does to minimize toxicity.

Merck, on the other hand, received a 1-A priority rating for
Mevacor because of its ability to effectively manage R&D (O'Reilly,
1991, pp. 48–63). From a scientific perspective they used a molecular targeting approach. Essentially, they looked at
hypercholesterolemia, understood its activity in the body, and
devised a drug to intervene. They were better able to predict the
drug's pharmacological action based on their understanding of
the disease and develop a compound specifically formulated for
intervention of the disease's chemical reactions. In their communication to the FDA they were perceived as having a command of
the drug since the outcome of their predictions on safety and
efficacy features were accurate. This was directly related to their
innovative standards on clinical testing. Most companies test compounds on 1,500 patients; Merck collected data on 5,000 patients. The issue is with an increasing sample size comes an
increasing ability to predict drug performance in the real-world.

The communication challenge for Merck is to be able to
anticipate the question and articulate the findings based on the
data clearly to the FDA. This is an integration problem and Merck
is well skilled at communicating appropriately to convey the leadership values throughout the company. Merck then looked at the
FDA as a department in their company and instituted a commu-

nication link that fed the appropriate information to convey the fit of Merck's corporate values with the prevailing values in the FDA. In this view the agency is in a supportive relationship with Merck, not in an adversarial relationship. Merck's role is to ensure that the information is unbiased and conveyed in such a manner that the FDA's confidence in the sponsor's work is maintained at a high level.

A treatment IND is an FDA procedure that allows the manufacturer to produce potentially life-saving drugs before marketing approval. Exosurf, a Burroughs Wellcome Co. product, is a good example of this kind of drug, produced from a collaboration of academic and pharmacological researchers.

The founder of Exosurf, Dr. Clements from the University of California, teamed up with a commercial researcher to test and develop the promising new drug, which helps premature babies breathe. Prior to this, of the fifty thousand premature babies born in the United States, five thousand would die. In 1985 an IND was filed to begin testing Exosurf on infants and the preliminary data at BW Co. showed a dramatic rate of success on thirty patients. To this point, BW Co. was devoting its attention to another fast-track drug called AZT but could see the potential Exosurf had. As a result, a sizable investment was made by BW Co. on behalf of Exosurf.

Many competing companies running trials in this area limited their trial size and considered the double-blind, placebo-controlled design impossible to conduct, even though the data produced were valued by the FDA as being more reliable. BW Co. developed trials to include 50 U.S. and Canadian hospitals involving double-blind tests on 4,500 patients. The results showed a 33 to 40 percent reduction in mortality of infants suffering from respiratory distress syndrome (RDS) and produced a second treatment IND drug awarded to BW Co. in 3 years. (Since June of 1987 there have only been 18 drugs granted such status.) (Shulman, 1990).

The protocol developed set the standard for clinical research for infants. It emerged from a tremendous collaboration on the part of many people within BW Co. who had a common goal to save the lives of infants born prematurely. In 1990 Exosurf was approved for marketing by the FDA, five years after its IND was filed.

Nuromax is not in the same class as a life-saving drug like AZT, Exosurf, or Mevacor. The technique used to get this drug approved by the FDA, however, deserves attention at this point. The approval of Nuromax by the FDA was facilitated by a new procedure known as NDA Day. This is designed to cut the average wait between submission and approval of an NDA by up to a year. It compresses months or even years of dialogue between the sponsor and the government review process into one intense day. The new wrinkle that Burroughs Wellcome Co. added to the process was its ability to teleconference and make the information in all BW Co. data files accessible in order to answer tough and obscure questions posed by the review committee on the spot.

Following the notice of the anticipated NDA Day, BW Co. put a task force together consisting of approximately sixty people from statistics, pharmacokinetics, pharmacology, medical, toxicology, clinical research, regulatory affairs, and communications.

The project team needed a system allowing rapid communication between corporate headquarters in Raleigh, North Carolina, manufacturing in Greenville, North Carolina, and the FDA offices in Maryland. This system would allow access to the company mainframe computer and printing along with the NDA database simultaneously displaying visual communication between participants. An avenue was discovered using corporate teleconferencing capability, linking high-speed data with visual communication through the BW Co. satellite system. The final step was to practice so that a flawless performance could be achieved.

The new system worked without a problem on NDA Day. However, while involved in deliberation an unanticipated question was asked by the advisory committee also present with the FDA review board, which required analysis by company staff in a novel way. Essentially they wanted a comparison of the data gathered on the one thousand patients involved in clinical trials of Nuromax with data for longer-acting agents. The curve ball was answered an hour later after a new program was written that linked all the critical systems needed for a thorough analysis of the inquiry and displayed the response in an understandable format. The response to this challenge was rapid and accurate. The entire review process took only ten hours and thirty minutes, considered a new NDA Day record by FDA standards. The bottom line was that final marketing approval came six weeks later, about a year ahead of schedule. This is an excellent example of the way technology should be used to facilitate a process taking place in real-time and characterized by uncertainty. The flawless operation of the system translates into a greater than 12 percent gain in gross profit with improved time-to-market performance (Versey, 1991).

Many of these advances can be credited to changes made by the former head of the FDA, Frank Young. He understood the need to get drugs out to market to help patients who need them as quickly as possible. As a result, the first of the revisions he undertook was the rewriting of the NDA itself, which allowed the data to be submitted from foreign studies where quite often drugs are released earlier than in the United States and the data that accumulate can be evaluated. He completed this in 1985. The second area that he managed to change was the treatment use of investigational new drugs, which took effect in 1987 and allows patients with serious, life-threatening diseases like AIDS to get treatment with experimental drugs that show potential benefit, provided no satisfactory approved therapy exists. This gives the promising candidate early exposure in the real-world, which is vital to its speedy approval. NDA Day is a recent procedural change at the FDA designed to make the review process more rapid. Rewards stemming from the skillful use of this procedure are self-evident.

One final note about impending changes that may affect government regulation needs to be mentioned at this point. On November 13, 1991 (*Economist*, 1991, p. 84), Vice President Dan Quayle, acting head of the White House Council on Competitiveness, announced several proposals intended to streamline the slow approval process at the FDA. The first has to do with the treatment IND. We can expect renewed commitment by the FDA to get new drugs out to patients who need them quicker, especially where there are no approved candidates. The second proposal facilitates the "staff years" needed to review data and specifically calls for privatization of fast track drugs. Outside contractors will be used to evaluate drugs in this class. The final proposal highlights the fact that the FDA should be allowed to use animal and clinical studies conducted by other national drug regulators. In other words, the work conducted by organizations to approve drugs in a foreign country will be accepted as data used for establishing the reliability of drug safety and efficacy because of the advantage of larger samples. The implications of these proposals are far-reaching and especially pertinent for those interested in high-speed management of pharmaceutical products.

THE R&D, MARKETING, AND GOVERNMENTAL INTERFACE

A successful company needs environmental assessment, product portfolio modeling, instilling a market pull, and technological push and structured innovation together with a balanced, focused strategy to guide the interface. This causes an alignment of internal processes with the external environment, producing a steady stream of products that are needed for competitive advantage. Governmental regulation also becomes instrumental in fulfilling necessary and sufficient conditions to link science with profit. How, then, does high-speed management affect the way that government regulation is traditionally understood in the pharmaceutical industry? How does it redefine the governmental process, resulting in a new set of critical success factors that facilitate quick response and flexibility?

Agency data show that NDAs judged to be complete and thorough upon initial submission are approved much faster than those not as thoroughly prepared. Also, clinical trials represent the phase of testing on which approval for marketing ultimately hinges and to ensure that they will generate the data FDA considers essential to a sound decision, sponsors of drugs being reviewed are encouraged to consult with the agency beforehand. Less than 40 percent of the companies do this. Merck is a shining example of a company that has good communication links with the FDA.

Thus the critical factors for success appear to be the following.

First, drug companies must pursue a molecular targeting approach to predict with accuracy the safety and efficacy of a drug candidate. This aligns with the predominant value of the FDA. Of particular note are the size of the clinical trials used by Merck (5,000 patients) and Burroughs Wellcome Co. (4,500 patients). This represents proactive thinking in the early stages of research that pays dividends in terms of quickening the pace of the approval process.

Second, drug companies must effectively coordinate the government regulatory agency, utilizing proactive information and communication linkages that essentially treat the FDA like a department within its influence. What must be clearly communicated is that their value system mirrors the FDA's value system. This is expressed in a constant state of readiness for any questions the FDA may ask and interpreted as being well prepared (Cominiti, 1992).

Third, drug companies must use environmental assessment, product portfolio modeling, and structured innovation tools along with a balanced, focused strategy to take advantage of FDA changes designed to streamline the approval process. The Council of Competitiveness cites three proposals that will have a considerable influence on this factor, especially regarding animal and clinical studies from foreign regulatory agencies accepted for review by the FDA. Communication master plans must be put in place to take advantage of the changes that will result from implementation of the proposals.

DeMeyer (1991) identifies six mechanisms to keep far-flung laboratories sharing information. The socialization mechanism is especially relevant, and a communication master plan must decide how to get scientists from foreign labs to meet face to face to share information with scientists from the commercial lab. This will maintain a high level of confidence in the information that must be exchanged.

Fourth, drug companies must employ effective point people who have experience in government agencies like the National Institute of Health (NIH) or the Food and Drug Administration (FDA). These people have knowledge about the mechanisms involved in the governmental process and the communication ability to exploit that knowledge for the organization's advantage. Research by Barczak (1991) notes that leaders on innovative teams make certain their members understand buyer requirements. They spend lots of time communicating about the customer and the speculation is that this is used to focus all development of the major or radically new product on market acceptance. Point people, who know how to operationalize the leader's plan, must funnel all processes of scientific investigation down to the most fundamental element: improvement of the quality of human life. If the proper focus can be maintained, then substantial synergies can be realized between marketing, R&D, and the FDA.

Fifth, drug companies must keep their R&D and marketing units understanding the benefits that sharing information has on competitive advantage. The value of this factor is observable in the fact that there is a decay in the confidence people have in information over time (DeMeyer, 1991). Therefore, the question becomes how much time is optimally allowed to pass before another face-to-face meeting is scheduled to keep the confidence in the information at a high level. Drug companies need to apply this not only to internal linkages but also to coalignment with the FDA.

Sixth, drug companies must continually upgrade communication technology to take advantage of changes in capacity to accept and review data like the FDA's NDA Day. DeMeyer (1991) points out that electronic communication is an important mechanism that successful pharmaceutical companies are using to co-ordinate the R&D effort. Specifically, the value of teleconferencing cannot be overlooked. DeMeyer concedes that nothing takes the place of a handshake.

It is important to be aware, however, that teleconferencing is in its infancy and has the potential to have a powerful influence in keeping relationships confident in highly technical scientific information. When technology is efficiently utilized, there is an immediate impact on speed-to-market parameters as evidenced by BW Co.'s experience with Nuromax on NDA Day. By bringing the product to market a year early there is a good chance to significantly enhance profits which, in the final analysis, is the ultimate judgment of performance.

REFERENCES

Ackerman, S. 1987. *Annual Report,* pp. 11–15.

Ballen, K. 1992. America's most admired company. *Fortune* (Feb. 10):40–68.

Barczak, K. 1991. Communications patterns of new product development leaders. *IEEE Transactions of Engineering Management* (May):101–9.

Brady, C. 1989. Powerful duo at counter. *Chemical Week* (Apr. 5):16.

Business Month. 1988. Merck & Company: Sheer energy. (Dec.):36.

Business Week. 1987:84–90.

Business Week. 1989. The miracle company. (Oct. 19):89–90.

———. 1991. Drugs just keep getting healthier. (Jan. 14):107.

Cominiti, S. 1992. The payoff from a good reputation. *Fortune* (Feb. 10):74–77.

DeMeyer, A. 1991. Tech talk: How managers are stimulating global R&D communication. *Sloan Management Review* (Spring):49–58.

The Economist. 1991. Radical change. (Nov. 16):84.

Farley, D. 1987–88. How the FDA approves drugs. *FDA Consumer,* pp. 7–18.

FDA Consumer. 1987–88. New drug development in the U.S., pp. 6–10.

Marks, H. 1989. The rise of university industry interactions. In *Academic Scientists and the Pharmaceutical Industry,* Baltimore, MD: John Hopkins University Press.

Miles, R. and C. Snow. 1984. Fit failure and the hall of fame. *California Management Review* (Spring):10–27.

O'Reilly, B. 1991. Drugmakers. *Fortune* (July 29):48–63.

Quickel, S. 1988. The drug culture. *Fortune* (May):85.

Shulman, S. 1990. FDA regulations provide broader access to unapproved drugs. *Journal of Clinical Pharmacology* 30:585–87.

Teitelman, R. 1987. The coming shakeout in drugs. *Fortune* (Jan. 20):103–6.

Value Line Information Service. 1988.

Versey, J. 1991. The new competitors: They think in terms of speed to market. *Academy of Management Executive* 2:23–33.

CHAPTER TEN

The Influence of High-Speed Management on Small Business

Rowland G. Baughman

The high-speed management revolution affecting the way that most large business concerns operate has also had an effect on many of the world's small businesses. The high technology of production, information, and communication processes has also made an impact on the way that many small businesses operate.

This impact is different in a number of ways from the influence imposed on larger business organizations. The concept of high-speed management is based on the requirement of fast response time in reaction and planning. A large firm's ability to gain or sustain a competitive advantage rests on its ability to sense the market's needs and respond faster than other competitors of a similar size. Thus, the advantage in this arena accrues to the firm that can best and most quickly meet the needs of the customer. For many small businesses this mandate has been the cornerstone of their successful operation. In every local market there are customers who have specialized needs. These needs can take the form of a specifically designed or configured product or for a service or product that is readily available. With their intimate knowledge of local conditions and demands, the small business organization often can respond faster and with greater applicability than a larger organization.

Thus, in a sense, small businesses have been practicing many of the basic tenets of high-speed management from their inception.

FOUNDATIONS OF HIGH-SPEED MANAGEMENT

In Chapter 2 Cushman and King proposed four basic trends that led to the emergence of high-speed management. They later listed several requirements organizations must meet to cope with a volatile business climate. These trends and concepts are the linchpin of successful high-speed management activities. On the one hand, an organization must be able to track the trends that occur. On the other hand, organizations must create an environment within their company that will allow them to be responsive to changes. The significance of the changing trends varies within each industry and each geographic area for the small business organization. Some small businesses limit their primary activity to a local area where the global dynamics will have only a peripheral influence. Such changes will, no doubt, affect certain marketing efforts and will create changes in certain competition. Such effects, however, are tangential to the vast majority of small business activities. More important is the effect of such global changes on their larger competitors and customers. These trends can have far-reaching effects on a small business' future. Therefore, it is necessary for small business managers to maintain their own environment-scanning mechanism to determine the effects of the local marketplace. Concurrently, such scanning must also include a strong awareness of their specific customer base. The major strength of most small businesses is their ability to track the needs of customers in a localized area. Responsiveness to change in a regional area is their primary strength.

WHAT IS A SMALL BUSINESS?

There has been no definitive agreement about what constitutes a small business. Much of the confusion stems from the variation of criteria exhibited by the U.S. Small Business Administration. This agency varies its standards depending on the type of business involved. In general, however, most researchers agree that a small business meets two or more of the following criteria:

1. Financing of the business is supplied by one individual or a small group.
2. The firm's operations are generally localized except for its marketing scope.
3. Compared to the biggest firms in the industry, the firm is small.
4. The number of employees in the firm is usually less than five hundred (Longnecker and Moore, 1987).

Following the above criteria, over 87 percent of all business concerns in the United States are characterized as small businesses. This large number of organizations, however, generates less than 19 percent of the total sales revenues.

Small businesses can be found under all of the various industrial and service categories. Many of these firms are very small organizations such as a neighborhood pharmacy, pizza parlor, restaurant, or grocery store, which cater to a highly localized customer base. Accordingly, little attention will be paid to this type of firm in this study.

The Evolution of the Small Firm

Almost every business got its start from small beginnings. Some, such as General Motors, gained in size through a series of mergers in their early years. Others, such as Xerox, grew large because their products were in high demand from a large customer base. Many other firms remain small, either through choice or because their particular product or service is in competition with other, larger competitors.

Those firms that remain small, however, continue to service the needs of their customers in such a way that the demand for their products continues.

A business' origin can take many forms, the reasons for starting a business are many. For some it is the desire to "be my own boss." For others, the incentive is the awareness of a market opportunity. The origin of businesses in the high-tech industry is frequently characterized by one or more personnel splitting off from a corporate giant. These people discover a gap in the products supplied by the large firms and move to fill it. The Silicon Valley and Route 128 firms often have sprung from such beginnings. Still others have embarked on an entrepreneurial track because of the desire to gain wealth. A recent survey concluded that 92 percent of employed businessmen who are millionaires are involved in their own private business.

The lure of owning one's own business is great. The media constantly are reporting about entrepreneurs who started small and built an empire. The Ray Kroc/McDonalds, Sam Walton/Walmar, Gates/Microsoft, and Jobs and Wozniak/Apple stories have proliferated in the news. Each of these stories displays a particular type of management style and business approach that enhanced the organization's success. In almost every case the basic premise followed to achieve success can be found in the concepts that are the foundations of successful high-speed management.

Benefits of the Small Firm

There are a number of characteristics and capabilities of the small firm that give it a special edge over its larger competitors:

1. They usually have a more intimate knowledge of the local community and closer ties to organizations and customers within that community.
2. They are better able to do individualized jobs.
3. They are frequent sources for new ideas.
4. They are usually more flexible in responding to change.
5. They create more innovative products than larger companies.
6. They are more willing risk-takers (Megginson, Scott, and Megginson, 1991).

Personnel in small businesses are usually called upon to perform a variety of tasks. While this requirement decreases the benefits of specialization, it enhances the degree of flexibility and response.

Disadvantages of the Small Firm

For every benefit accruing to the small firm there are an equal number of disadvantages. Following are several major factors that face most beginning small businesses:

1. Inadequate financing. The sources of most funds available to the new firm are limited to those available to the new

owner. Therefore, it is often difficult to obtain sufficient funds to weather the early period of low income and high expenses. Such limitations also inhibit the ability of the firm to respond to growth or change opportunities.

2. Limited managerial scope or talent. With few personnel available there is a need for each person to perform many functions. Often such demands exceed the available knowledge or competence. It is unlikely that an owner with a high level of technical skill will also have the requisite marketing, financial, or production skills.

3. Extreme personal commitment of the owner. The time demand of an emerging business can be great. Often new owners are called upon to invest a large portion of their time to the enterprise.

4. Government regulations. Unfortunately many reports and documents that are required of large businesses are also required of small businesses. This often necessitates large expenditures for outside assistance to fulfill all of the state, local, and federal government requirements.

5. Risk of failure. This is probably the major disadvantage to the new small business enterprise. Table 10.1 demonstrates the mortality statistics of new firms in recent years.

Thus, there is a high risk of the new business facing bankruptcy within the first three or four years of its existence. Liles (1989) estimates that only four of ten firms survive for over six years. Ricklefs (1989) lists the following factors as major causes for new small business failures: (1) lack of capital, (2)

Table 10.1
New Business Incorporations and Business Failures

Year	Business Formations	Number of Failures	Fail Rate per 10,000 Concerns
1970	264,000	10,748	43.8
1980	532,000	11,742	42.1
1985	663,000	57,078	115.1
1989	667,000	50,389	65.0

Source: Stastical Abstract of the United States, 1990, Table 184.

poor business knowledge, (3) poor management, and (4) lack of planning.

A Disadvantage That Becomes an Advantage

In spite of the great risk attendant with beginning a new business there is one heartening observation. Those firms that survive their early years stand a good chance of remaining viable. Studies have shown that the number of firms that fail after four years are few. Additionally, such resilient firms are better able to withstand changes in economic conditions, industry trends, and increased competition. In most cases, these are the firms that practice high-speed management.

High-Speed Management in Small Business

Small businesses owe much of their success to their ability to maintain awareness of their customer's needs and competitors' activities and their ability to quickly respond to changes in those activities or needs. This innate ability closely parallels the high-speed mandate to continuously scan the environment for change and opportunities. The emergence of cost-effective breakthroughs in information and communication technologies are benefiting small business as well as large organizations.

The dynamism that has resulted from use of the new technologies and the expanding globalization of markets has benefited many small businesses since they typically depend on fast response time as one of their main assets of operation. Being small, with few tiers of management and approval to contend with, small businesses can enter and leave markets with greater ease than their larger competitors. Additionally, large economies of scale are usually not a major requirement for small business operation. Since their traditional production or service function is geared to small quantities, the small business can convert or adjust to design or method change requirements easily. This fact is easily demonstrated by comparison of the return on assets (ROA) between large and small companies. In every category of industry (manufacturing, services, construction, transportation, and wholesale/retail) the firms with assets under $1 million experienced higher earning than those with higher asset bases (Longnecker and Moore, 1987).

Small businesses do not ordinarily play a large role in the global marketplace. One of their major strengths is their ability to be responsive to local demands and idiosyncrasies. Accordingly, small businesses can satisfy the needs of those portions of the market that demand specialized products or services. Such fast and specific response capabilities often elude the large conglomerates for several reasons. First, it is often impossible for large companies to gain awareness of local needs from diverse geographic areas. Second, large companies cannot afford to disrupt their production processes to cater to a small unique design or service need.

HIGH-SPEED APPLICATIONS

In order to see how small businesses are responding to the requirements of high-speed management it is important to compare their operations against the basic requirements for high-speed management success.

Stay Close to Customers and Competitors. Few large firms can boast of an ability to meet this requirement as well as the majority of small businesses. Since most small firms usually limit their marketing scope to a definite geographic area it is easier for them to maintain close contact with their customers. These customers also become more quickly aware of the activities of other firms who compete in the same marketplace and are able to respond appropriately in a shorter period of time than most large companies.

Action Equipment Company of Londonderry, New Hampshire, has come up with a way to expand and support its customer base. It established a very effective profit-sharing incentive plan that motivates all employees to find new business opportunities and to stay close to their existing customers. As a result this five-year-old firm was ranked by *Inc.* magazine as the eighteenth fastest growing company for 1985.

A similar success story is unfolding adjacent to the campus of Central Connecticut State University in New Britain, Connecticut. In 1990 Todd Szoka, a recent business school graduate, opened "The Other Bookstore." His motive was to offer a low-cost alternative to the campus bookstore. His prices for textbooks and supplies are substantially lower than the college-sanctioned Barnes and Noble outlet. He determined that his operation was better able to be responsive to the needs of the more than 12,000 CCSU students than the large book-selling chain with its nationwide pricing policy.

A technique that works well for many small businesses is to align themselves with larger organizations. A major stabilizing sales procedure for some small firms is to seek subcontract opportunities with prime contractors or producers. This technique allows these firms to assure a steady production effort. Such supplementary contracts keep the marginal firm viable during periods when their own sales efforts falter. The Detroit area has many small firms that produce specialized items for the major auto manufacturers. In Connecticut there are numerous small firms who produce specialized items on contract to major defense manufacturers such as United Technology, Sikorsky, General Electric, and Kamen. Such close associations provide the added ability for these firms to track the trends of their industry by maintaining awareness of the activities of their larger associates.

The Dynamic Metal Products Company of Manchester, Connecticut, saw an opportunity to become a guaranteed supplier to a prime government contractor. When, Howard Miller, Dynamic Metal's CEO, saw an opportunity to expand his business base he invested in a major capital improvement. Dynamic's new machinery made it possible to provide high-quality precision jet engine parts to Pratt & Whitney at a lower cost. This ability generated a guaranteed market for Dynamic's products and resulted in their being named New England Subcontractor of the year by the U.S. Small Business Administration (Moran, 1993).

Think about New Products and React Quickly. The record for this area is mixed. Many small firms are inexorably tied to a limited product line by constraints on their expertise, production facilities, or the owner's interest. Thus, they often are unable or unwilling to alter their basic product line. The classic tale of the demise of the blacksmith well illustrates this dilemma. On the other hand, many businesses practicing high-speed management are able to find new niches and develop new products, or at least adjust their product line to meet nominal changes in customer needs. This ability is the major reason why these small firms are leaders in their business.

Claudia King founded a company that specializes in managing the complex paperwork associated with bankruptcy filings. Much of the details, such as court-required notice mailings, are handled by her firm. The eight-year-old company includes such clients as the Circle K Corporation, Continental Airlines, and the Trump Taj Mahal. In 1991 the firm's revenues exceed $7 million.

Picture Tel Inc. of Peabody, Massachusetts, has taken advantage of recent developments and product cost reductions in videophone technology. It has created a patented product and entered into a joint venture with IBM to produce, market, and distribute to an emerging demand (Bulkely, 1992).

Maintain Close Coordination Within the Company. Being small has some virtues. The potential for close coordination and communication is one of them. Most small businesses have only a few tiers of management. As a consequence, the flow of information is more fluid within the company and the decision-making process is less complicated and more timely than in large corporations. The ability to disseminate information to all affected personnel is much easier and more efficient. Control systems within most small businesses are usually vested in a few people and can be adjusted easily.

The Flight Time Corporation exemplifies this concept very well. It created a computerized database of the availability, type, and prices of aircraft for charter. Its specialty is the ability for fast reaction time to make air service transportation available on short notice. In two years the firm increased its annual revenue to over $4 million (Simurda, 1987). Much of the success of this firm can be attributed to the small number of personnel needed to manage the operations. Aided by the computerized system the staff are able to quickly respond to customer inquiry and to make major decisions with little lost time.

There are numerous stories of new CEOs who have taken over failing organizations and turned them around. In most cases the formula for success has included a reduction of the levels of decision making within the organization. As organizations have grown and become increasingly successful they have tended to add tiers of management with the notion of handling the increasingly complex myriad of details. These additional levels of authority and decision making have served to complicate and impede the decision process.

The mandate to create fast, efficient decisions—which is a major requirement for high-speed management—continues to be a major strength of small businesses.

Product Quality, User Friendliness, Ease of Service, and Competitive Pricing Are Essential for Market Penetration. Since they have difficulty matching price levels with companies that can take advantage of large economies of scale small businesses must emphasize all of the other criteria to maintain the level of market share that they have. Being local to most of their customers allows small businesses to maintain a close, personal contact, which assures user friendliness and fast service response.

The pricing requirement often works to the detriment of many small businesses since it is difficult to compete with firms that operate on large volume production. This forces many businesses into specialized niches where their willingness to produce specialized products in small quantities is desired. In this area the small business pricing structure is highly competitive.

The Mozzarella Company in Dallas benefited from perfect timing when its owner offered high-quality Italian cheeses to gourmet stores and restaurants just when the demand for high-quality fresh ingredients was beginning. The variety of cheeses has been expanded over the years to respond to customer demand. Such response has resulted in a viable and profitable enterprise (Gumpert, 1990).

A Corporate Vision Must Be Developed that Emphasizes Change and Allows for New Units with Alternative Values. Again, the record is mixed for the small business enterprise. Financing, lack of R&D, and limits in the organization's level of expertise often hamper the ability to consider alternative strategies. There have been numerous cases where small businesses fail because the market has changed and the firm has been unable to cope with new technological or geographic demands. The successful exceptions are usually those companies that practice high-speed management.

Despite the fact that most "feeder railroads" are, at best, marginally successful, Jack and Marj Haley purchased the 120-mile Cedar Valley line in Osage, Iowa, in 1984. Since that time they have expanded the number of cars of cargo and added a dinner train to accommodate sightseeing visitors from around the country. Providing a unique service at a time when alternate sources were limited allowed the unlikely venture to achieve consistently high profit margins (Woodring, 1988).

The small business typically has a vision that emphasizes change in many instances. Having to be responsive to unique customer requirements enhances a firm's ability to be flexible. Thus, many businesses can adapt to dramatic changes as long as such changes do not alter their basic area of expertise.

Scan for New Areas. Perhaps this is the area where small businesses are weakest. Since most firms maintain a small number of managerial personnel, the demands of keeping track of current conditions requires the majority of the managerial resource time. This leaves little opportunity to keep current with emerging opportunities or changing conditions. Economic or political upheavals often catch many firms by surprise. Their ability to react to major changes is limited and they suffer. Attempts by government agencies to provide assistance in predicting trends affecting small businesses has not been very successful. Usually, the information, in the form of government pamphlets and newsletters, is a case of "too little, too late." Small firms simply do not have the luxury of a pool of personnel that can track the ever-changing business environment for new opportunities.

This phenomenon can be illustrated by examples from both Western Europe and the United States. Despite the potential benefits of the single EC market, small businesses in Europe are not yet moving aggressively to expand their geographic base. The twelve-nation Economic Community, headquartered in Brussels, Belgium, maintains and funds a computerized database called "BC-Net," which lists more than 14,000 companies interested in finding cross-border partners for commercial ventures. This resource is available to all firms to allow searches that could result in company alignments within countries in the EC. This service is an ideal resource for small firms seeking marketing partners across the boundaries of the economic community. To date this service has been poorly utilized, very few firms have made use of the matchmaking resource (Birney, 1990). A similar resource is also provided by the U.S. Department of Commerce and the Small Business Administration. These underutilized services have met with similar results.

It is generally agreed that small U.S.-based firms do not have a good track record in scanning the horizon for new market opportunities. A notable exception is a company in Hibbing, Minnesota, where woodlands are a natural resource. This firm currently manufactures and exports 7 million pairs of chopsticks a day to Japan, where wood is a scarce commodity (Knowles, 1988).

Clearly, the major source of small organizations that are tuned into new opportunities comes from spin-off ventures founded by former members of large organizations who have determined new fields of endeavor.

CONCLUSION

Overall, the small business community has earned high marks for its ability to cope with the dynamic business environment. Many small firms have demonstrated an ability to adjust to new trends and to find new niches to satisfy customer demands. Additionally, the small firm is an integral part of and a major reason why other larger firms are able to respond to an array of global opportunities. The small firm's ability to supply the needs of larger firms on a fast response basis has allowed such larger companies to take advantage of new emerging opportunities.

In Chapter 2 Cushman and King list the requirements for how successful organizations must employ new assumptions to practice high speed management. These new assumptions include ability to be innovative, flexible, adaptive, efficient and give rapid response. There is no doubt that such 'new' assumptions are old mandates for the small business organization.

REFERENCES

Birney, K. 1990. Small players on the big stage. *International Management* 45(3):40–42.

Bulkeley, W. 1992. The videophone era may be near, bringing new changes. *Wall Street Journal,* Mar. 10, p. A1.

Fromson, B. 1988. Where the next fortunes will be made. *Fortune* (Dec. 5):185–96.

Gumpert, D. 1990. How to stand out in a crowd. *Working Woman* (Nov):57–63.

Knowles, D. 1988. The new export entrepreneurs. *Fortune* (June 6):87–102.

Liles, B. 1989. More small businesses succeeding. *USA Today,* Dec. 5, p. 1E.

Longnecker, J., and C. Moore. 1987. *Small Business Management.* 7th ed. Cincinnati: South-Western.

Meginnson, L., C. Scott, and W. Meginnson. 1991. *Successful Small Business Management.* Homewood, Ill.: Irwin.

Moran, J. M. 1993. As a supplier, this firm is special. *Hartford Courant,* Jan. 18, p. 3.

Parker, D. 1988. Knowing when to blow the whistle, *Venture* (Apr.):10.

Ricklefs, R. 1989. Road to success less littered with failures. *Wall Street Journal,* Oct. 10, p. B2.

Robichaux, M. 1989. Fledgling honeybee learns to fly with the big guys. *Wall Street Journal,* May 12, p. D2.

Simurda, S. 1987. A 747 can be yours within hours. *Venture* (July):11.

Small Business Is Big. 1986. Washington, D.C.: Small Business Administration.

Stastical Abstract of the United States. 1990. Washington, D.C.: U.S. Government Printing Office.

Woodring, J. 1988. The little engine that could. *Venture* (Mar.):12.

CHAPTER ELEVEN

High-Speed Management and Continuous Improvement: Teamwork Applications at General Electric

Janet M. Flynn and Franca Caré

Much has been made of the concept of continuous improvement and total quality control in business circles over the last decade. A plethora of literature and applied research in companies around the world attests to the popularity of the quality movement. The attempt to achieve consistent quality and ongoing improvement of organizational process, not just in manufacturing but also throughout an organization, describes modern continuous improvement programs.

The concept of continuous improvement within a high-speed management perspective includes any organizational activity that leads to overall improvement of process and product, ensuring ongoing competitiveness on a world scale. Continuous improvement programs in high-speed management organizations cut across all divisions and sectors of a business, and place emphasis on the importance of four key communication processes: a New England town meeting process, a cross-functional teamwork process, a linking and negotiation process, and a world-class benchmarking case study process (Cushman and King, 1994).

This chapter focuses on the first two of these processes: the New England town meeting and cross-functional teamwork, through an examination of General Electric's Workout program. Workout is GE's teamwork system, conceived by James Baugham, former head of GE's Management Development Institute, and CEO Jack Welch. Workout is a vehicle for companywide cross-functional teamwork and a central tool in GE's overall program of continuous improvement. A GE Workout process model, essential tools for implementation of each stage, and proposed roles for team leaders or facilitators are discussed. Actual Workout sessions observed GE Plastics Division in Selkirk, New York, are compared against a Workout model as explicated in company literature. Comments about the potential of Workout as an effective teamwork system and analysis of key team roles and communication behaviors in Workout settings are discussed, with implications for teamwork applications in general.

Workout, operated within a format reminiscent of a New England town meeting, is one of three components of GE's plan for continuous organizational improvement. Process mapping, a detailed plotting and analysis of process from input to output, and Best Practices, discovery and application of relevant world-class benchmark standards across industries to GE's practices and processes, comprise the other two-thirds of the continuous improvement initiative at GE.

The philosophy behind continuous improvement at GE is summarized by Welch as the achievement of sufficient productivity, competitiveness, and innovation on a global scale to maintain the number one or two position in all GE businesses consistently. Welch sees this being accomplished largely through Workout, which contains the potential to unleash the key ingredients of "speed, simplicity, self-confidence" across the company (Welch, 1990): speed, to react unbound by the channels of bureaucracy; simplicity, by removing the redundancy and unnecessary complexity from processes; self-confidence, by encouraging all employees to take initiative, make decisions and participate in business improvements. The management of General Electric seeks to harness and develop these three factors through a comprehensive approach to Workout.

The need for continuous improvement at GE is reflected in this quote from company literature:

The success of GE in the 1990s and beyond will depend upon its ability to anticipate and overcome many challenges. Increasing foreign and domestic competition allows GE customers to demand faster, more reliable service and better quality for their investment. . . . By developing a sharp, responsive work force that is free to question long-standing practices and take the initiative to develop more productive and cost efficient processes, GE will be able to command industry standards for quality and customer service. Standards that no competitor could match, and no customer could ignore.

The corporate culture Welch is trying to foster is one of minimal hierarchy and total worker empowerment—a "lean, mean, machine" that can monitor change on a global scale and respond to it rapidly and adaptively. Welch believes the answer is in getting rid of needless bureaucratic layers and freeing up employees and business leaders to contribute real vision in product and process innovation.

Creating a "boundaryless company" (Welch, 1990) in which arbitrary divisions between all parts of the value chain, from supplier to company to customer, are blurred or eliminated, is part of the strategy to be best and fastest in the world. Much of the blending or elimination of boundaries occurs in cross-functional teamwork in Workout, a main component of continuous improvement. It also involves coordinated autonomy for each of the half-dozen or so businesses GE owns, a concept Welch calls "integrated diversity"—highly varied, independently run businesses that nevertheless share the best in common management practices, systems, processes, and technology through cross-functional teamwork approaches.

In a company that has as a standard being number one or number two in the world in every business, getting rid of the fat and speeding up not only manufacturing but management processes are highly important in maintaining global competitive advantage.

Continuous improvement is a primary tool for accomplishing the necessary speed and productivity of this world-class competitor. "Speed, simplicity, self-confidence" (Welch, 1990) is a framework for unleashing individual creativity and achievement throughout the company. Workout is a way to harness, direct, and enlarge individual contributions through productive teamwork on shared issues.

Although Best Practices and process mapping are thought to yield larger magnitude productivity growth for GE than Workout itself (Cushman and King, 1994; Stewart, 1991), Workout is nevertheless the key tool for spreading continuous improvement throughout the organization, because it facilitates the sharing of Best Practices and provides a locus for process-mapping activities. Additionally, Workout is the vehicle for involving wide groups of GE employees across all GE businesses in problem solving and process improvement, something Welch sees as key to long-term success in productivity. Tapping into talent at all levels in the company is his goal. Welch sees Workout as the central element in his management agenda for the 1990s as he works toward a company of integrated diversity.

WORKOUT LEVELS

The building blocks of Workout consist of five levels of the continuous improvement process. These levels have provided GE with mechanisms to launch itself as a boundaryless company.

The objective of Level 1, town meetings, is to focus on internal processes, giving individuals "voice" through the creation of a forum for dialogue. This is accomplished by encouraging bureaucracy "bashing" (removing non-value-added work), freeing up and energizing individuals, and valuing the insights of the ones closest to the work ("Management doesn't always know best") while simultaneously working within the structured event of Workout.

At the second level, Productivity Best Practices Workshops, the primary objective is to maintain an external focus. This includes performing ongoing environmental scanning by the Corporate Business Planning and Development Department, bringing the best practices of other companies to Crotonville, New York, emphasizing process over programs, and stressing "Finding a better way . . . everyday" (GE Corporate Workout Literature, 1988–91).

The major objective of the third level is to obtain integration with ongoing quality and continuous improvement efforts. At this level, the idea that "It's not about words, it's about ends" is emphasized, marking a shift from idea gathering identification of specific processes for implementing problem solutions.

The goal of the fourth level, customer/supplier Workouts, is to make it easier for external customers and suppliers to conduct business with GE. This forum allows for opportunities to develop or improve customer/supplier partnerships through intensive joint problem solving. This level emphasizes the essence of a "boundaryless relationship" within and between organizations. GE views customer/supplier relationships as one system, embracing the external stakeholders as "parents in the process" (GE Corporate Workout Literature, 1988–91). Lastly, the goal of the fifth level is to recognize emerging issues in measurements and systems, as an evolving process on the road to becoming the most competitive enterprise in world.

PROBLEM-SOLVING PROCESS: THE TOOLS OF WORKOUT

Team Start-Up

The team participants begin by developing a mission statement that expresses their collective mission as a group and the collective vision for the Workout session. A team name is sometimes chosen and a team logo and slogan can be designed to capture the spirit of the Workout. At this time, the members agree on team goals and objectives for the Workout session. Lastly, a set of operating principles are developed stating how the team wants to work together.

Problem Solving

A type of problem-solving process, utilized in whole or part in GE Workout sessions, is illustrated in Chart A. This methodology consists of a set of sequential, basic problem-solving steps, which is used to improve overall productivity, product quality, and customer satisfaction.

The facilitator informs the team that the problem-solving tools will help organize the problem, causes, and analysis in such a way that the solution to the problem is more readily addressed. An example used to demonstrate the value of such a process is the numbers exercise. This exercise emphasizes the progress that

Figure 11.1
Problem Solving Process

1. Identify Problem via Problem Statement
2. Force Field Analysis
3. Brainstorm and Storyboard
4. Gather Data
5. Cause and Effect
6. Nominal Group Technique
7. Pareto Analysis
8. Solution Impact Matrix
9. Cost Impact Analysis
10. Contingency Diagram
11. Solution via Action Plan
12. Presentation to Management with feedback and discussion

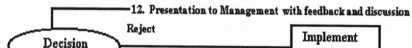

Decision — Reject — Accept — Implement Solution

the team can obtain if a systematic process is used to achieve the solution.

Problem Statement

Problem statements clearly identify the problem(s) in concrete terms. The problem statement focuses on *what* is wrong, not *who*. An example of a hypothetical problem statement is expressed in Chart B. This problem statement is sufficient because it is stated in specific terms. It expresses specifically what increase is of interest, what department has the increase, and approximately when it began.

Figure 11.2

PROBLEM STATEMENT

THERE HAS BEEN AN INCREASE IN SATELLITE BOOKING CANCELLATIONS IN THE PUBLICITY DEPARTMENT OVER THE PAST SIX MONTHS.

Figure 11.3
Force Field Analysis

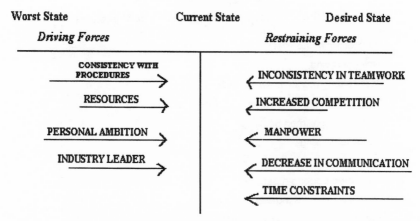

| Worst State | Current State | Desired State |

Driving Forces   *Restraining Forces*

Force Field Analysis (FFA)

This type of analysis is a creative problem-solving tool that allows the team to identify the forces impeding or aiding the desired state and provides a starting point for solving the problem. Chart C illustrates a hypothetical example of a FFA. In developing a FFA, the team begins by labeling the worst, the current, and the desired state. The team then identifies the driving forces (those forces promoting the desired state), and the restraining forces (those forces impeding the desired state). Arrows of varying length are used to illustrate the magnitude of the forces upon the states. Finally, the team develops an action plan to achieve the desired state (i.e., reduce restraining force or strengthen driving force).

Brainstorming

Brainstorming is a creative problem-solving tool used to broaden thinking to include all possibilities contributing to the problem. It helps teams produce as many ideas as possible in a short amount of time. The major brainstorming requirements are as follows: all team members are encouraged to contribute, generation of a large quantity of ideas is promoted, no criticism or discussion of ideas contributed is allowed, and team members are encouraged to use ownership knowledge. Chart D illustrates hypothetical brainstorming ideas.

Figure 11.4
Brainstorming

"What is causing the increase in satellite booking cancellations..."

Decrease in manpower

Time constraints

Poor communication between publicity and production

Poor communication between production and shipping

Insufficient confirmed bookings

Tentative bookings

Service of west coast bookings

Decreased booking supervision

Lack of timely press material to bookers

Stations receiving press material late

Shipping shortages

Insufficient tracking system

Lack of coordination between publicity, production, and shipping

Decreased teamwork in publicity

Station technical problems

Inside technical problems

Vendor technical problems

Outside production personnel not 100% competent of communications equipment

Limited training

Storyboarding

Storyboarding is a technique used to logically show ideas. This tool hones team communication and promotes consensus. Following the listing of the brainstorming ideas, they are logically clustered into general categories. Chart E illustrates the hypothetical results of a storyboard.

Gather Data

At this point of the problem-solving process, the team members gather and review the data for clarification and organizational purposes.

Figure 11.5
Storyboard

MANPOWER

Decrease in manpower
Poor communication
Decreased booking supervision
Decreased teamwork
Outside production personnel not 100% competent

PROCEDURES

Limited training
Insufficient confirming
Tentative bookings
Service of west coast bookings
Shipping's tracking system
Lack of coordination
Late press material

EQUIPMENT

Station technical problems
Inside technical problems
Vendor technical problems

RESOURCES

Shipping shortages
Time constraints

Cause and Effect Diagram

The cause and effect diagram, also called the fishbone exercise, is used to represent the relationship between the problem and its contributing causes. It allows the team to visualize the problem and emphasizes the importance of thinking in terms of process.

The effect (problem) of the causes is placed to the right of the diagram. The four major categories from the storyboard are listed to the left under causes (i.e., procedures, resources). The

Figure 11.6
Cause and Effect Diagram

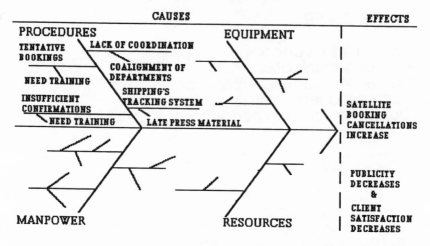

brainstorming ideas and other data are then places under their respective categories.

Chart F illustrates a partially completed cause and effect diagram. As the chart hypothetically illustrates, a contributing factor in the broad category of procedures is identified as shipping's faulty tracking system; resulting in late press material to stations, which in turn is a contributing cause to the increase in satellite booking cancellations, decreased publicity of the project, and decreased client satisfaction. The rest of the brainstorming ideas would comprise the other two-thirds of this diagram.

Nominal Group Technique

This tool requires that each team member rank the identified causes from most significant factor contributing to the problem to least significant factor contributing to the problem, combine ratings to get a prioritized list, and discuss results to obtain team consensus. Chart G hypothetically illustrates a partially completed nominal group list, in which lack of coordination is identified as being a more significant factor contributing to the problem than shipping's tracking system.

Pareto Analysis

This tool enables the team to visualize the significance of the causes and problems comparable to one another. This technique

Figure 11.7
Nominal Group Technique

PROCEDURES

NEED TRAINING	TENTATIVE BOOKINGS	3
	INSUFFICIENT CONFIRMATIONS	
LACK OF COORDINATION	COALIGNMENT OF DEPARTMENTS	2
SHIPPING'S TRACKING SYSTEM	LATE PRESS MATERIAL	7

focuses team effort in order to obtain what factor(s) have the greatest impact, emphasizing "First things first." The requirements for such an analysis include selecting a unit of measure that best expresses the problem (i.e., time, dollars), evaluating each cause affecting the problem using the nominal group technique and other collected data, and ranking the order of the causes from highest to lowest. Chart H depicts a hypothetical example of a Pareto Analysis. The bar graph lists the number of cancellations as its unit of measure (left of bar graph), indicating that shipping is the lowest rated cause, accounting for seven percent of all satellite booking cancellations.

Solution Impact Matrix

A solution impact matrix is used to display the relationship between causes of the problem and possible solutions. Moreover, it fosters team consensus on the best choice of action. Chart I illustrates this tool using hypothetical data. A–G (top of chart) are potential solutions. One through five (left of the chart) are interpreted as the causes (weighted). H(10), M(5), L(1) reflect the value of the impact relationship (high, medium, low), and the bottom numerical results equal the solution impact ratings.

Cost Impact Analysis

A cost impact analysis is used to visually compare the projected cost impact for each idea or solution. This tool helps the team reach consensus on the most effective solution(s) and prepares

Figure 11.8
Pareto Analysis
SATELLITE BOOKING CANCELATIONS

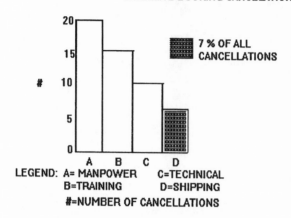

LEGEND: A= MANPOWER   C=TECHNICAL
           B=TRAINING   D=SHIPPING
         #=NUMBER OF CANCELLATIONS

Figure 11.9
Solution Impact Matrix

LEGEND:
A-G=POSSIBLE SOLUTIONS

H=10
M=5
L=1

		A	B	C	D	E	F	G
1	.30	M	L	H	—	M	H	—
2	.26	—	—	M	—	L	L	M
3	.15	L	—	M	H	—	—	—
4	.09	—	M	—	L	H	M	—
5	.06	—	M	L	—	L	—	M
		1.7	1.1	5.1	1.6	2.7	3.7	1.6

SOLUTION IMPACT RATINGS

the team for promoting the idea to management. Chart J and Chart K illustrate a cost impact analysis by comparing hypothetical solutions D, E, and F.

Contingency Diagram

This tool is used to aid the team in determining the effectiveness of the solution(s) by: identifying the negative of the problem statement (i.e., what can we do to decrease productivity?); imagining the worst case scenario; examining the Force Field

Figure 11.10
Cost Impact Analysis

PART A

Cost considerations: rated (1-5)

1 = Lowest cost
    to
5 = Highest cost

SOLUTIONS

	D VS. D	E VS. E	F F
MANPOWER	3	5	4
RESOURCES	—	5	2
TRAINING	1	5	3
TIME	2	2	3
COST RATINGS	6	17	12

Figure 11.11
Cost Impact Analysis

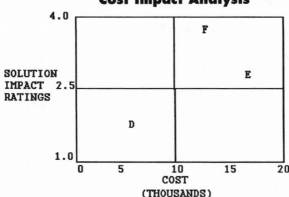

Analysis' restraining forces as possible barriers to obtaining the desired state and determining the action required to overcome these barriers; and, comparing these possible actions to the benefits of the recommended solution(s).

As Chart L illustrates, Mrs. H, an employee at A Corporation, never contributes during unit meetings. Therefore, the negative of this problem statement would be, "How can the other members of the meetings keep Mrs. H from contributing?" The

Figure 11.12
Contingency Diagram

Problem: Mrs. X, an employee at A Corporation, never
          contributes during unit meetings

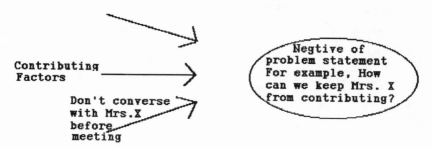

actions the members come up with to keep Mrs. H from participating (i.e., do not converse with Mrs. H before meetings) should
be similar to the factors promoting the original problem. This
allows the recommended solutions to be checked for accuracy
and effectiveness.

Action Plan

This tool specifies the goal(s) of the projected change, provides
the mechanisms inherent in achieving the change clarifies who
will be accountable to oversee enforcement of the plan, and
provides a measurement mechanism to monitor progress.

Presentation—Feedback—Decision

The closing portion of the problem-solving process begins with a
team presentation of the proposed solution(s) to management.
Before the team members present their action plan to management, the team facilitator will challenge the team on its solution
by forcing members to be as specific as possible in their recom-
mendation of a solution to the problem. If the solution(s) is accepted by management, the action plan is given the green light.

Stages of Team Development

GE recognizes a five-phase model for team development similar
to the "forming, storming, norming, and performing" group
decision-making model described by Tuckman (1965). The first
stage of team development is to cultivate a positive working envi-

ronment. This is the inclusion/forming level. This level includes becoming oriented, developing commitment, setting direction, and developing feelings of acceptance.

The second stage is labeled "storming," which deals with issues of power and control among the team members. This level includes concerns of consolidating influence, confronting dependency on the leader, expression of intragroup conflict, and low levels of task accomplishment.

The next stage of group development deals with managing conflict and establishing ground rules. This level is labeled "norming," which involves resolving control concerns and establishing group cohesion.

The fourth stage of team development, called "affection/ performing," centers around functioning as an effective group. Issues included in this stage are working productively toward shared goals, emergence of problem solutions and decision making, enhancement of open communication, trust, and conflict management.

The last stage of the team development process is labeled as "adjourning," and includes dealing with issues of group termination, such as apprehension and regression.

THE ROLE OF THE FACILITATOR IN TEAM DEVELOPMENT

GE recognizes specific facilitator duties for each level of team formation. In Stage 1, the role of the facilitator is labeled "directing," and includes climate setting, clarification of roles and expectations for team members, defining goals, and providing structure and guidance to the team-building process.

In Stages 2 and 3, the role of the facilitator is one of coaching. Here the facilitator helps bring key issues to the surface, legitimizes concerns, facilitates communication, manages conflict, invites input and feedback, and expects and accepts tension. GE offers basic and advanced facilitator training sessions that provide instruction in these coaching skills. (See Charts A and B.)

In Stage 4, the role of the facilitator is primarily one of supporting. Here, the facilitator offers his or her own ideas and resources, shares the leadership role, and is available for consultation. Finally, in the last stage of the team process, the facilitator offers support by helping the group deal with termination.

Communication Behaviors of Team Facilitators

Skillful performance of the facilitating role is critical to the success of effective teams. Many hold that facilitation is constructive communication above all else (Manz, Keating, and Donnellon, 1990; Carr, 1991; Cushman and King, 1994). At the core of good facilitating are key communication behaviors and abilities manifested by the team leader (coach, facilitator).

Carr (1991) describes the role of facilitator or team coach as that of the "unleader," advocating an emphasis on supportive rather than directive communication styles, or the use of influence rather than traditional authority to achieve organizational goals. Carr also emphasizes a focus on subtle but important coordination of team resources by the facilitator for maximum group effectiveness. Cushman and King (1994) describe this communication role of the team leader as one of "brokering," or the skilled matching of individual team contributions and abilities with team tasks in a way that produces synergistic outcomes. This is achieved through skillful assessment of both the problem components and the potential abilities and contributions of individual team members at crucial junctures in the team process.

The team coach does not tell the team what to do but rather guides team members diplomatically toward effective goal achievement. He or she must not only analyze the situation accurately and quickly, but must also know when and how to elicit the participation of the appropriate team members at various phases of the team process, and how to neutralize negative power relationships where needed. Facilitation is more than just eliciting participation; it includes preventing overparticipation (domination) by any one team member. The nullification of power roles and status hierarchies is one of the most challenging aspects of teamwork facilitation.

It is also important to make sure that team goals are verbalized and operationalized in specific ways. Targets must be measurable and the goal-setting process must be one of "candid and committed interplay" (Cushman and King, 1994). As some research indicates that the first phase of teamwork is critical (Gersick, 1988), that climate of trust and open communication must be encouraged from the very start of the teamwork process.

Facilitation and Managing in the 1990s

The importance of the facilitation role for modern businesses cannot be overemphasized. In many ways, it is the key role of managers of the 1990s. Old styles of top-down management are quickly being supplanted by a bottom-up, faster, and more productive focus on the future. Today's managers are too busy to make every decision or solve every problem; their role, instead, must be to effectively empower the employees they oversee to make good decisions and solve problems quickly and creatively in the best interests of the company. That requires a total shift in management style toward the behaviors described as facilitation or coaching behaviors. Therefore, the communication behaviors required of team coaches can be generalized to the broader setting of general management.

The key role of the facilitator in Workout illustrates how critical the new management skill of coaching is for any company using self-directed teamwork. Superior communication skills and the ability to identify and mobilize strengths of individual team members toward team goals quickly become key. Finally, the facilitator/team manager must encourage trust and candor on the team. Strong interpersonal skills and appropriate communication techniques are a necessity for managers, whose job is largely one of superior facilitation of continuous improvement.

Communication Behaviors of Team Members

The other key role in teamwork, of course, is that of team member. Although good facilitation is critical to quality teamwork, the contributions of individual team members are equally as important.

The ideal team member is someone who has knowledge or skills to contribute to the task(s) at hand. Additionally, although this is often overlooked, team members must also be able to articulate their concerns effectively in a group setting. Team members must feel motivated to contribute to the team's work and to overall organization goals. Team members must view themselves as being empowered, and must see that empowerment as positive, allowing them to have significant input in their job roles, within a framework of increased flexibility and creativity. Without these necessary attitudes and abilities, team synergy is difficult to achieve.

CONTINUOUS IMPROVEMENT AT GE: THE PRACTICE

A two-day Workout session involving three teams of GE's Plastics division at Selkirk, New York, was chosen for observation. One team of the three, the Workout team from GEP's Environmental Services department, was selected for analysis. Team members included environmental engineers involved in monitoring toxins produced in manufacturing plastics, plant foremen, a supervisor who was team champion of the idea, and chemical engineers. On the second day, a team member from Technology was added.

A facilitator from outside the department led the Workout. The team topic was the reduction of zinc in solid wastes and waste water, a need created by the anticipated tightening of EPA guidelines.

Two other Workouts were taking place simultaneously in other rooms—one in Technology (GEP's R&D), and one of employees involved in mixing and customizing functions at Selkirk. All three team presentations to plant management were observed.

Team Dynamics and Group Process

After receiving background on targeted areas from both plant management and team champions, the team, coached by the facilitator, formulated specific problem statements, listed barriers to solutions, prioritized solutions, identified key variables needed for proposed process improvements, and proposed implementation schedules. Many Workout tools were employed by this team in the problem-solving process, including brainstorming, storyboarding, Pareto analysis, cause and effect diagramming, nominal group technique, and formulation of action plans.

The Environmental Services Workout seemed to follow common stages of typical group process, in that much time was spent the first day in beginning stages such as socialization and team building and lengthy but unfocused brainstorming. The process went in fits and starts, and backtracking regularly occurred, suggesting spiral or nonlinear decision-making models like those of Poole (1981) and Scheidel and Crowell (1964). It was not until late in the first day that any tentative solutions were proposed.

Many of the team's solutions were simple and readily apparent. This may have been due to a strong leaning in the group toward convergent thinking styles rather than divergent ones

(Scheidel, 1986). The lack of apparent creativity in the solutions generated was probably due in part also to the mandate to provide immediate, no-cost solutions. A third factor might have been that only the team champion and the facilitator seemed to have enthusiasm for the Workout process.

This foreman virtually commanded the afternoon session because he knew where the errors in zinc use, storage, and disposal were occurring, and could articulate it to the group without being overbearing. He explained, for instance, that the technicians (shop floor workers) routinely dumped more zinc than needed into product mixtures in order to avoid spilling zinc on the shop floor, a situation they had been cautioned against because of the potential for increasing zinc concentration in the wastewater. Rather than risk a spill, the foreman reported that workers often added the whole bag. The chemists, having painstakingly developed the formula mixtures, were aghast at such blatant disregard for the correct formulas, not to mention issues of cost to the company.

This example illustrates not only the wide disparity in priorities, values, and concerns across functions in a company, but the potential power of Workout as a vehicle for integrating highly differentiated functions through regular cross-functional communication. Important information was communicated among departments as a result of the team process, information which would otherwise never have come to light.

The facilitator for this team was not totally effective in this setting, and group process reflected his lack of communication and analysis skills at several junctures, and in the end result of the Workout. His handling of the coaching role graphically illustrated the importance of the role in teamwork outcomes.

He had clearly been trained in supportive coaching techniques, but lacked the relational and analytical skills to push the group off center when they were stuck, to provide inspiration and motivation appropriately, or to encourage participation from players with key knowledge or ideas at different times. In short, he failed to empower the team optimally.

He was not particularly well-received by team members, and at the end of the first day, the equivalent of a Mexican standoff occurred between him and the team as he attempted to keep team members engaged in productive problem-solving. Long periods of silence were broken only by the facilitator's proddings to keep the ideas coming, which, in turn, were met with hostile glares and groans from various members of the group.

This facilitator, a supervisor who volunteered for the role and had been through the formal GE training for it, ultimately did not achieve legitimacy among team members. Part of the problem may have been that some team members knew him from years before, when he had been first a technician, and then a foreman. Workout facilitators are supposed to be neutral, unknown outsiders with no connections to the team, but this facilitator had been called in as a substitute for the orginally scheduled person.

More relevant than that, however, were the dynamics of power in the situation. The facilitator frequently exhibited a traditional, authoritarian leadership style during the two-day process. He was not effective at supporting and empowering team members toward optimal achievement. Further, at least some team members appeared to reject his guidance because they didn't see him as necessarily more "expert" than themselves, having come from amidst their ranks not very long ago.

An interesting question is raised for those who are attempting to decentralize a business and empower its total work force: Do all workers really want a key part in decision-making at all levels? Or do some, especially those who have chosen low-level, non-supervisory jobs, prefer to be led by people perceived to be more powerful/knowledgeable than themselves? What are the implications of this for the facilitator role, as well as for new styles of management, which deemphasize power and status differences? Are there inherent stresses in being empowered, which are not rewarding to all, as some of the organizational literature suggests (i.e. Conrad, 1990)? If so, how can a company sustain the genuine involvement and contribution of all workers in a process like Workout?

While GE decentralizes and eliminates management layers and tasks, a valuable management role appeared to be overlooked at GEP Selkirk: that of coaching and empowerment of Workout teams towards efficient and timely achievement of Workout results, along with coaching towards overall productivity and quality outside of the formal Workout process. This coaching role requiring communication, interpersonal, and analytic skills, is perhaps the key role of managers in the nineties.

The facilitating role during the initial two-day team meetings, executed by an outsider, is only the beginning step in a whole process of realizing Workout gains. Ongoing support, coaching, and team facilitation from within are just as critical in achieving speed and productivity in implementation stages.

The role of management in approving, rejecting, or qualifying team Workout solutions did not work like the model characterized earlier in the paper. The plant manager only listened, asked a few questions, and pointed out that the R&D team had the most powerful solution of the three teams. The assumption of workers was that the answer was yes to all solutions contained in each presentation, presumably because of the negligible cost of solution implementation, a prerequisite of these Workouts.

PROBLEMS WITH FOLLOW-UP AND MEASUREMENT AND REWARD SYSTEMS AT GEP

Team champions or other team members could conceivably be trained to conduct ongoing coaching and team support. However, there is no system support in place to encourage or facilitate this role, according to team and site committee members. Neither time nor compensation is set aside for these extra duties. That is inconsistent with other reward systems at GEP Selkirk. Whether it is a problem across GE's other plastics plants and other businesses is not known. Follow-up in Workout depends heavily on volunteer employee involvement at GEP Selkirk. Although there is a site Workout committee at GEP, theoretically with oversight responsibility for Workouts at the plant, follow-up and accountability appeared to be minimal. The facilitator, a member of GEP's Workout site committee, said that the site committee "tries to at least ask what is being done to follow up" on Workouts. But he also indicated that follow-up is a nebulous process at GEP Selkirk. Successful progress on Workout agendas is reported in the company in-house publication, *Insite*, but it seems apparent that some of Workout solutions fall through the cracks because of inadequate implementation strategies and/or manpower.

Curiously, one of the two foremen present for the Workout said very little, participating only minimally, although the comments he made were well received and helpful. On the second day, he was not even there. In conversations with him during breaks, one of the problems with GEP's Workout process became clear. The main reason he was not participating was that no direct financial incentive for Workout sessions was possible. However, creative *individual* suggestions for solutions to problems are rewarded monetarily at GEP-Selkirk, in effect creating a disincentive for Workout-generated innovation.

He reported that he had given his best ideas to Workout before, in other sessions, and he was tired of "giving for free." He was skeptical about the rewards of Workout to workers, and remained marginally involved throughout the day. His lack of participation is important for what it illustrates about potential problems with GEP's measurement and reward system.

Lack of follow-up seemd to be a growing problem with Workout sessions. As more and more people get involved in Workout teams, more and more work is generated, at least initially, in carrying out solution implementation. However, in the follow-up process, unlike the Workout process itself, no time is set aside for implementation. Solutions must be achieved on top of and during the course of other work agendas.

Although follow-up meetings are usually scheduled by team members before disbanding, follow-up was reported as sketchy. The team champion is generally responsible for implementation progress. Involvement by management in follow-up was reported to be minimal at this site. Management support was built into the three observed Workout solutions only minimally, if at all, although it was identified as important in brainstorming sessions. In all three Workout groups that made presentations, ownership of at least one solution task was assigned to people who were not even there and had not volunteered to be a part of the process.

One team member identified some of the team's solutions as having been suggested before, but never carried out. Several others in the group shared this skepticism about the power of Workout to effect critical change.

The growing workload of employees, who are often on several Workout teams simultaneously, makes them feel burdened with extra Workout duties on top of other organizational commitments. Workout participation is optional (although there is an implicit pressure on those who want to get ahead to involve themselves), so the workload of Workout is not evenly shared across the plant. Coupled with the uncertain procedures for implementation, potentially serious obstacles to Workout achievement are evident.

Because follow-up on Workout depends on essentially volunteer commitments by team champions or site committee members, because real accountability for implementation is not evident, and because there is no direct incentive provided to team champions and site managers, a potentially weak outcome might be expected from GEP Selkirk Workouts, if these characteristics are common to the experience.

DISCUSSION

Concerns

Our analysis suggests that the facilitator role is key to the success of Workout and a central component of essential new management skills required in the 1990s. Facilitating, or coaching, as it is often called, requires superior analytical and relational skills, as well as the ability to lead by suggestion and empowerment, rather than by traditional directing. In the case of the Workout sessions observed, problems in the facilitation role stemmed from ineffective relational dynamics as well as an overreliance on traditional authoritative modes of group direction. Although all facilitators of Workout are required to complete company training in communication behaviors and tools necessary to good team coaching, counterproductive communication behaviors by facilitators were observed, raising important questions for organizations using teamwork.

GE's facilitator training process is detailed and in-depth, suggesting that the problem is not with creating more or better training. Fundamental issues of intake procedures for team coaches as well as follow-up and evaluation following completion of trainings are raised. For instance, what kinds of personality and skills assessments are conducted on facilitator candidates or management personnel? Would the use of specific selection criteria that focus on relational and analytical skills improve the quality of team leaders in Workout? Has the facilitation training

process dealt with how to weed out those candidates whose communication skills are inadequate or who cannot fully accept and
articulate the transitions from traditional authoritative leadership styles into the empowerment model of contemporary teamwork? Are feedback and performance evaluations of team
facilitators vital measurements in continuous improvement programs utilizing teamwork?

Related to these critical facilitating skills is the role of managers in coaching effective teamwork throughout the organization. This management coaching role continues to be needed
long after the two-day Workout session is over. Designated, skilled
team coaches are needed throughout follow-up and implementation stages of Workout. Any teamwork setting requires this facilitating function to be successful.

At least in the limited context of this observation, it appears
that management at GE could play a more pivotal role in relation to the coaching of Workout and overall continuous improvement. Team members from more than one GE business expressed
the belief that management should take increased responsibility
in evaluating proposed action plans during presentation and play
a larger role in the implementation process. Although some of
those comments may reflect an uneasiness with empowered decision making on the part of employees, we concur that management has a role in teamwork follow-up that is not being
maximized. In particular, capital and other resources needed for
solution implementation require increased involvement by management to be realized. Also, the important coordinating role
performed by the team facilitator during actual Workout sessions
continues to be needed after Workout is over, but appears to be
too loosely structured in some cases to be effective. Team champions are often assigned primary responsibility for implementation and monitoring of team progress in achieving agreed-upon
changes. The Workout site committee, comprised of GE staff
members across a division, is also charged with overseeing solution implementations. Accountability for completion of action
commitments, however, is decentralized to the point that it is not
clear where final accountability rests. GE's mechanisms for insuring execution of action plans are ambiguous and rely on the
volunteer commitment of team champions and site committees

who are often involved in multiple Workout projects in addition to constantly increasing workloads as GE streamlines its workforce.

In short, the considerable investment of both time and money by GE in preparation for and conducting of Workout sessions seems diluted by a lack of direction and support in the last and very crucial stage of the Workout process, that of solution implementation.

A second major consideration in achieving team synergy is the ability to maintain a dynamic atmosphere conducive to open interaction between team members, with mutual commitment to achievement of team goals. Workout is repeated daily across GE sites, and since its inception several years ago, many employees have participated in numerous Workouts. Repetition of the process within the fixed structure of Workout seems to lead to boredom with team process and resistance to full participation in some cases. Employee "burnout" with the Workout process, especially in light of larger workloads on top of multiple Workout commitments, could be a real problem as Workout matures in the company. Instead of the empowerment Welch wishes to achieve, Workout could be viewed by tired employees as one more management encumbrance.

The detailed and sequential problem-solving stages followed in Workout have the danger of being too rigid for repeated use. For Workout to be sustained long term with creative and productive outcomes, it may be necessary to customize and make the process as flexible as warranted by the requirements of each GE division. Other common problems of team process, such as overly convergent thinking patterns (i.e., "group think") may be exacerbated by the inflexibility and repetition of the Workout structure.

A third major issue in assessing the effectiveness of Workout is the connection between Workout and GE's measurement and reward system. In this case study, the reward and evaluation system seemed loosely tied to Workout achievements. Conflicts with other company reward systems for individual efforts was evident. Reward and measurement need to be correlated with team achievements, in addition to traditional pay programs which focus on individual performance.

GE businesses are actively working to revise reward systems to reflect new emphases on team efforts, but complex issues dealing with union agreements, equity, and appropriate measurement of team outcomes are obstacles that must be addressed in meeting this challenge.

Strengths

In spite of the concerns mentioned above, Workout has already achieved some significant gains for the company. There are many accounts of major productivity increases and process innovations resulting from Workout sessions across GE businesses. Just one substantive cost-saving or process innovation outcome from a Workout session potentially offsets the investment in less productive Workouts.

Additionally, the value of cross-functional education in company processes should not be overlooked as an important positive outcome of Workout. A more thorough understanding of any GE division or business is an almost certain outcome of Workout sessions, because of the cross-functional composition of Workout teams. Process mapping is facilitated by the Workout approach, which leads to improved integration and coordination. The specific results of the environmental services Workout at Ge plastics, for example, might readily have been gained outside a teamwork approach, as they are of the category of "low hanging fruit" (Welch, 1988). However, the indirect benefits mentioned above may justify the team process.

SUMMARY

In summary, three principal recommendations, based on this analysis of GE's Workout, are made for any organization employing teamwork:

1. Careful attention to the role of facilitator is key, and should include attention to selection and monitoring criteria for facilitators, especially as they relate to communication skills and analytical abilities.
2. The importance of maintaining flexibility and fluidity to the teamwork process structure is critical to preserving a dynamic and productive team climate. This is especially important in organizations that use teamwork widely throughout all levels of the organization.

3. Organizational reward systems must be connected to team-work efforts throughout a company, and must be consistent with other reward programs already in place.

More important than any of the above considerations taken individually, however, is the necessity for coalignment of all these factors in promoting productive teamwork. If any one of these components is missing or flawed, the resulting teamwork will reflect that weakness. The optimum teamwork setting must some-how harness and coordinate these three elements, as well as other critical success factors.

REFERENCES

Bossidy, L. 1990. New ways of working together. *GE Executive Speech Reprint.*

Carr, B. 1991. The unleader. *Training and Development Journal,* September: 36–42.

Conrad, C. 1990. *Strategic Communication: An Integrated Perspective.* Chaps. 5–9. Holt, Rhinehart, and Winston, Inc.

Cushman, D. P., and S. King. 1994. *High Speed Management: A Revolution in Organizational Communication for the 1990s.* Albany, N.Y.: SUNY Press.

General Electric Corporate Workout Literature. 1988–91.

Gersick, C. J. G. 1988. Time and transition in work teams: To-ward a new model of group development. *Academy of Management Journal* 31(1):9–41.

Manz, C., D. Keating, and A. Donnellon. 1990. Preparing for organizational change to employee self-management: The managerial transition. *Organizational Dynamics.* 19(2):15–26.

Poole, M. S. 1981. Decision development in small groups I: A comparison of two models. *Communication Monographs* 48: 1–24.

Scheidel, T. M. 1986. Divergent and convergent thinking in group decision-making. In *Communication and Group Decision Making.* Beverly Hills: Sage.

Scheidel, T. M., and L. Crowell. 1964. Idea development in small discussion groups. *Quarterly Journal of Speech* 50:140–45.

Scherkenback, W. W. 1986. *The Deming Route to Quality and Pro-ductivity.* Washington, D.C.: CEEPress Books.

Stewart, T. A. 1991. GE keeps those ideas coming. *Fortune* (Aug. 12):41–49.

Tuckman, B. W. 1965. Developmental sequence in small groups. *Psychological Bulletin*: 63, 384–399.

Welch, J. F. 1988. Managing for the nineties. *GE Executive Speech Reprint.*

————. 1990. A boundaryless company in a decade of change. *Executive Speeches* 3(12):19–23.

CHAPTER TWELVE

High-Speed Management at the Toyota and General Electric Companies

Scott R. Olson

A Ford worker stands in front of a Toyota plant holding a sign that says, "Japan said your (*sic*) lazy/no to Japanese imports" (Fighting words, 1992, p. E1). This hostility toward Toyota exists because of its considerable success in manufacturing and marketing automobiles, a success driven by high-speed management strategies and techniques incubated and matured there. Ford struggles to adopt many of these techniques and transform itself into a high-speed manufacturer; other U.S. firms such as General Electric have not only made widespread use of it, they have added some management innovations of their own. Toyota and General Electric are solidly positioned for the 1990s; Ford looks increasingly like a relic of the industrial era. The issue of whether or not a Camry or Tercel manufactured in a U.S. plant is an "import" aside, the Ford worker might consider the extent to which his own job will more and more look like jobs at General Electric and Toyota.

Toyota certainly deserves to be considered a high-speed management pioneer, although many of its tools have been borrowed from American theorists and manufacturers. Its original strategy to become a global competitor was to use decreased production costs to target high-volume segments of the low-end automobile marketplace (Porter, 1980); this resulted in subcompacts like the original Tercel. More recently, Toyota abandoned the low end of the market, concentrating more on the development of upscale automobiles in response to lower cost exports from Korea (Hyundai) and Yugoslavia (Yugo) that have a comparative advantage in labor costs. As the Tercel has come to look more like a sedan, it has yielded a bigger profit per unit (A. Taylor, 1991).

The shape of management at Toyota can be primarily attributed to former Toyota vice president Taiichi Ohno. Ohno implemented many of the techniques that have come to associate his company with efficiency, responsiveness, productivity, and—perhaps most important of all—quality. Ohno took a company that was manufacturing almost exclusively for its home market and, from the end of World War II to the late 1970s, transformed it into one of the most powerful manufacturers in the world.

General Electric evolved out of the Edison Light Company and has by and large maintained the level of commitment to experimentation and innovation of Edison himself. Historically, GE was known for its enormous size, broad product line, vertical and horizontal integration, and extensive advertising (Porter, 1980). It has always been on the cutting edge of American management theory and practice; according to Stewart (1991), it originated the concepts of strategic planning, decentralization (Greenwood, 1974), and market research. While its airplane engines have had a seminal impact on that industry, its less glamorous appliance division has been its real workhorse (Magaziner and Patinkin, 1989b).

Since the beginning of Jack Welch's tenure as CEO in the early 1980s, GE has not been satisfied to remain in any industry in which it is not a leader (J. Taylor, 1991), so Welch brought the company through a painful reorganization that eliminated 100,000 jobs, shed $9 billion in assets, collapsed the management hierarchy, and compressed 350 product lines into 13 businesses (Stewart, 1991). A good case study of GE's management philosophy can be found in its uneasy relationship with NBC. Since it was acquired by GE in the 1980s, NBC has been losing market share and profitability, and GE has never wanted to participate in an industry in which it was not the leader. In addition, the corporate culture of GE, based on efficiency and know-how, is incompatible with the charismatic and relationship-oriented culture of the entertainment industry (J. Taylor, 1991). The friction is evidenced in *Late Night with David Letterman*'s flagrant and public contempt for GE and Welch; Letterman is broadcast on NBC.[1] Welch himself sees the change in GE's corporate culture as a difficult, decade-long process, but one which, when completed, will cause "lines to blur" (Stewart, 1991, p. 49), hierarchies to collapse.

This chapter will examine the evolving use of information technology, the impact of increased world trade, the effect of the volatile business climate, and the new approach to management found at Toyota and General Electric. These issues are closely interrelated; it is difficult to talk about the use of information technology in a Toyota plant, for example, without discussing the flexible, rapid response management style such a system requires. It will be shown that these two companies are not merely reacting to the demands of high-speed management. In many ways, they have helped create and define it. But as pioneers, they have also encountered the limits of high-speed management.

EVOLVING USE OF INFORMATION TECHNOLOGY

The centrality of information and communication to the manufacturing process in the 1990s can hardly be overstated, and embodies perhaps the most tangible aspect of high-speed management. The use of information and communication has always been the work of management, but its significance seems to be spreading throughout the corporation. Arno Penzias, vice president of research at AT&T Bell Labs, says that most workers already engage in "information work" (1989)—decision making based on the accumulation and interpretation of signs, codes, and signals. This decentralization of communication requires a significant redesign of communication flow and speed, usually requiring such new technologies as computer-aided design (CAD), computer-aided manufacturing (CAM), flexible manufacturing systems (FMS), computer-integrated manufacturing (CIM), and automation (e.g., robots) (Hayes and Jaikumar, 1988). By bringing information to workers in a quick and accessible manner, these technologies make high-speed management possible. They manifest themselves in new manufacturing techniques, new marketing strategies, and new management styles.

New Manufacturing

The most touted arena in which new technology has revolutionized work is in the plant, where it is called the "factory of the future." Such a factory increases the efficiency of production while empowering worker through teams. They are also more ideal than reality—the greatest challenge to factories in the 1990s is to undergo the radical transformation from being a place that produces mass quantities of a single thing to one that produces small quantities to meet customer needs at low prices (Cusumano, 1988). In order to achieve this shift, new manufacturing must integrate computer and telecommunication systems into engineering and production (Cushman and King, 1993). This has the effect of speeding up the process while lowering unit cost. General Electric and Toyota have in many ways been leaders in the implementation of new manufacturing procedures, and their plants have already been transformed through flexible manufacturing systems. They serve as models for factories of the future.

The designer of the Toyota production system, Taiichi Ohno, designed it to make small quantities of many different products using a single efficient manufacturing process (Stalk, 1988), fulfilling Cusumano's (1988) ideal. This system, which has served as the basis for most factory redesigns, is based on three objectives: control over quantity, assurance of quality, and respect for stakeholders. Quantity control is the ability to adapt production day-to-day to meet changing demand; conventional factories, on the other hand, are compelled by both hardware and software to meet rigid daily expectations, leading to over- and underproduction. Quality assurance requires that each product be of good quality before moving down the line; it was assumed, even tolerated, that traditional factories would produce a high proportion of inferior quality products, what is often called the "scrap and rework" mentality. Respect for stakeholders means that the needs of humanity must be weighed against matters of cost (Monden, 1983); while this does not mean that humanitarian concerns will necessarily outweigh other factors, it does mean that at least they will be considered.

Quantity, quality, and respect are achieved in a number of ways. One way, innovated at Toyota but now widely emulated, is "just-in-time" production, which requires standardized production procedures and a supplier-management system (Mizuno, 1988) as well as fast change and set-up times for the machines (Cusumano, 1988). Another is "autonomation," which prevents defective products from proceeding; this limits the need for rework, increasing efficiency. A third is employing a flexible workforce, allowing Toyota to vary the number of employees working on a product based on market demand; if consumer interest in a particular product increases, more workers are set to the task of manufacturing it with a minimum of retraining. A final element of these objectives is *soikufu*, the solicitation and use of worker suggestions (Monden, 1983). This has the effect not only of encouraging employee pride and responsibility, but also of hearing about a product from the people who know it best. The success of soikufu speaks for itself: in the 1980s, about 95 percent of employee suggestions were implemented (Peters, 1987), ensuring that quantity, quality, and respect were nurtured.

High-speed management technology is not limited to the factory floor, however. Communication technology links the factory scheduling system to Toyota dealerships, so the plant knows instantly what products are in demand. Because of the sophistication of the factory, it is able to act on these reports immediately, beginning production on car orders without delay—a mix of models is produced daily to flexible production cells. The dealership and car buyer are notified immediately of the production status of the requested product. Since the plants are designed to allow for "high uptime" (i.e., continuous operation) and "high yield" (i.e., output that maximizes use of input), the production cycle operates at fast speed (Bower and Hout, 1988).

General Electric has followed Toyota's lead and built one of the most sophisticated and automated factories in the world, often called the "first of its kind" and "its own prototype" and noted for its low tolerance of imperfections (Magaziner and Patinkin, 1989b)—an American autonomation. Although it makes unglamorous rotary compressors for refrigerators instead of state-of-the-art airplane engines, the transformation of the plant has been spectacular. Major Appliance Business Group Building 4 was still using 1950s technology and even older techniques to make refrigerators during the early 1980s, but since foreign competition was only beginning to enter the U.S. market, widespread inefficiency was tolerated. Increasing competition from Japanese compressor manufacturers quickly compelled GE to fight back on both cost and quality. The factory they built was designed in tandem with the design of the new compressors, so that the two were perfectly suited for each other; this represented a significant departure from ordinary procedure in which the product is designed, then a factory made to build it. As a matter of principle and a statement of capability, every piece of equipment in the plant was made in the United States. New sensing technology and gauging systems had to be designed to ensure the factory was meeting specifications that exceeded any mass-producing plant in the world.

As important as these technological innovations were, however, GE realized that a twenty-first-century plant with a twentieth-century workforce would be no investment in the future. It embarked on a $2 million extensive retraining program that resulted in one of the most skilled factory workforces in the United States. Workers were closely integrated into setting up the factory and writing the training manuals in teams with the engineers.[2] Consequently, the plant has never needed managers or supervisors to keep it running, making it incredibly efficient (Magaziner and Patinkin, 1989b). The work that is being done is a marriage between the "information work" Penzias (1989) described and the high-speed management philosophy: workers at plants such as Building 4 are as likely to be standing in front of computer terminals as drilling, stamping, or assembling (Magaziner and Patinkin, 1989a).

Sophisticated manufacturing that uses new information technology has shown itself to be the future of factory design. It was often assumed by managers that speeding up manufacturing would be enough—that it would solve their productivity problems. Once the wrapping was off all the new equipment in the factory of the future, however, it became clear that this was not enough. In fact, it became apparent to many managers that the real bottleneck had never been so much in the production as in the delivery. New marketing techniques would be needed to get information and products to consumers as quickly and efficiently as possible.

Marketing

The stakes in marketing are high, since it is here that the most value is added to the product (Ohmae, 1990), and conventional techniques cannot withstand a high-speed onslaught. According to Cushman and King (1993), new marketing techniques entail the use of computers and telecommunication to scan, test, and track merchandising. This allows for quick, even immediate, response to shifts in consumer taste and needs. Perhaps the biggest shift in marketing caused by the new technology is that it allows products to be tailor-made for specific customer tastes so that the era of the "mass market" is being replaced by the "micromajority" (McKenna, 1988), requiring "total customer responsiveness" on the part of the corporation (Peters, 1987). The key to high-speed marketing is staying close to the customer, which requires sophisticated communication technology and old-fashioned interpersonal competence.

At Toyota, top priority was given to making the marketing system run as smoothly as the production system. It was discovered that while Toyota Manufacturing could make a car in two days, it took the sales division up to twenty-six days to make a sale and deliver the car. Toyota management came to see the manufacturing/sales dichotomy as an artificial, nineteenth-century way of thinking about doing business, so it merged the sales division into the manufacturing division and designed a computerized sales system that cut through many levels of management and allowed sales to go in small batches. This cut the sales time in half (Stalk, 1988). By staying close to the customer and by responding quickly and specifically to customer demand, Toyota was able to gain market share and lay down a high-speed challenge to its competitors (Bower and Hout, 1988). This marketing base allowed Toyota to venture into new marketing challenges, such as targeting its Lexus at the "German Segment" (which would normally buy Mercedes) through a new image and distribution system (Ohmae, 1990).

General Electric has also relied on customer-oriented marketing, and is known as a company that widens customer choice as much as possible. In order to do this effectively, from its turbine engine production (Porter, 1980) to home appliances, GE has relied on extensive customer research in product development in addition to its effective marketing. For example, responding to customer complaints that it was not listening to their concerns, GE created the "GE Answer Center," a toll free phone service to deal with consumer concerns. All GE consumer products are covered by the Answer Center, whose operators use computers to retrieve detailed information about 8,500 products. This has had the desired effect of creating an image of GE as a consumer-responsive corporation: purchasers of GE products using the Answer Center report 94 percent satisfaction (Benjamin, et al., 1984).

Although GE and Toyota have been pioneers in the effective use of new communication and information technology in marketing their products and staying close to their customers, the future holds more challenge. Communication technology allows an unprecedented level of customer programmability, pushing the boundaries of consumer choice as far as they will go. McKenna (1991) has called this radical transformation the beginning of "unlimited choice"; because consumers have access to the information they want and need, and because such information will not stay proprietary for long, manufacturers must be even more aggressive in their use of it (Ohmae, 1990).[3] Unlimited choice is the ideal marketing milieu for which GE and Toyota strive.

Of course, merely manufacturing and marketing products is not enough. The sophisticated hardware and software required to enable these systems necessitates equally sophisticated design and execution. High-speed manufacturing and marketing mandates high-technology management.

Management

Computers, interactive media, CAD/CAM systems, and other new technology have changed the nature of managerial work. One major implication of these technologies is the decentralization of information and power at the office or factory. Rather than hold information and decision making close, the manger uses new technology to spread it around. Such new management techniques make use of computer and telecommunication systems to support decision making and facilitate team coordination (Cushman and King, 1993). This increases the effectiveness of management through tighter integration between management vision and worker implementation. Both General Electric and Toyota have been shown to be innovators in these new management techniques.

The traditional management philosophy at GE through much of the twentieth century was based on four tenets:

- General Electric will continue a planned growth and development, fulfilling—in the national interest—its new industrial and social responsibilities.
- Professional managers hold stewardship responsibilities to the shareowners, to customers, to employees, to vendors, and to the public generally.
- An intelligent and creative approach in the discharge of managerial responsibilities will help fashion an environment where new opportunities for human happiness are abundant.
- Managing is a discipline as well as a profession, and the development of the highest quality of professional leadership is the best insurance of future industrial growth and progress (General Electric Company, 1953).

While these tenets reflect a commitment to managerial excellence, they do not embody the high-speed competitive spirit needed for GE to survive contemporary competition. This management philosophy has been replaced with Welch's more simple credo for the 1990s, the words themselves an embodiment of their own commandments: "speed, simplicity, self-confidence" (Stewart, 1991, p. 41).

This new management philosophy has been as effective in practice as on paper. Peters (1987) has observed that GE excels at communication management, for example, citing their development of aircraft engines. Widely circulated status reports, daily meetings, and computer-integrated manufacturing were used to make sure that communication was being used effectively. Another example is found at GE plastics which, in an attempt to get as close as possible to its customers, gave an MRP system (Material Requirements Planning—a computer terminal and electronic linkage to GE) to its distributors, making it easier than ever to convey requests, queries, invoices, and payments (Peters, 1987). The relationship among GE, its customers, and its suppliers has been sped up, simplified, and made more confident in compliance with Welch's admonition.

Toyota's management innovations have been marked by less radical shifts than those at GE, in part because high-speed management has been built into its structure bit-by-bit for some time, and in part because Toyota represents a logical evolution in management style from the days of Henry Ford, a situation in which

> the Japanese translation of the Fordist system. . .was simple. Toyota was the great innovator here, taking the minds + hands philosophy of the craftsman (*sic*) era, merging it with the work standardization and assembly line of the Fordist system, and adding the glue of teamwork for good measure. Management did not think of workers as replaceable cogs in a great production machine; each worker was trained for a variety of jobs and skills. (Krafcik, 1988, p. 43)

Adding teams to the production process was a management strategy that built upon existing strengths in automobile manufacturing techniques—something Ohno and Toyota regarded as a logical progression in improving the manufacture of automobiles, not a radical reinvention of the manufacturing process. Such teams lead to other benefits, which reflect themselves in the management strategy. One such benefit is commitment to quality. Teams working under the quality philosophy at Toyota plants have lowered costs by as much as 60 percent (Hauser and Clausing, 1988). Teams do not exist in a vacuum, however. High-speed management is required to connect high-speed manufacturing to high-speed marketing through advanced communication systems.

Of course, sophisticated information technology is not a panacea. It can be a costly mistake to rush into complex computer systems without due consideration of the value they will add to the product; nevertheless, some companies have done just that. The potential problems with introducing new technologies are many. Not least of these is that workers will often be intimidated by it, so companies need to proceed at a manageable pace. GE in fact introduced "toy shops" where workers could acclimate themselves to new technologies in a fun, low-pressure atmosphere (Peters and Waterman, 1982); this greatly reduced the stress associated with strange and intimidating hardware and software.

Extensive technology changes may not even be necessary for high-speed management, whose technology does not need to be particularly sophisticated to be effective. Many have been struck by the "absurd simplicity" of the communication system at the Toyota-GM plant: an amalgam of paper flip charts and simple status lights (Peters, 1987). The primary technology of the *kanban* system, discussed below, is nothing more than paper cards.

Whether its technology of communication is paper cards or a Cray 9000 supercomputer, it is clear that high-speed manufacturing, marketing, and management are needed for a company to remain competitive. The need for this increased competitiveness comes in part from the increased interconnectedness of the world economy, where no product, process, or nation is an island for long.

INCREASED WORLD TRADE

Because the world economy has become increasingly integrated, manufacturers have had to change their assumptions about what it means to be competitive. Its integration has not been uniform or consistent, however, leading to the dominance of regional markets, what Ohmae (1990) calls the "Triad." This Triad—the Japanese/Pac Rim market, the European market, and the North American market—dominates world trade and sets the tastes and standards that the rest of the world follows; it is difficult for countries outside the Triad to either persuade it to make products conform to their tastes or to market their own products. When giants like General Electric and Toyota become Triad players (as they have), the clashes of culture and whims of regional taste can dwarf the problems of international technical standards or language barriers. GE and Toyota have become a part of the global economy and major players in its three core markets.

All companies do not enter the global economy at the same time or with the same foresight and vision. Toyota has been a part of this economy since World War II almost by necessity, whereas for many years GE did not see foreign competition as a threat. In fact, so long as productivity at a GE plant increased from year to year, what the competition was doing was considered irrelevant by its management (Magaziner and Patinkin, 1989b). A "global economy" was not perceived; the U.S. market was thought to be the only mitigating factor. Increased competition forced GE to rethink this position, however; for example, when GE's own Canadian refrigerator plant began buying compressors from Singapore in the 1980s (Magaziner and Patinkin, 1989a, 1989b), GE knew it had become a global competitor by default.

Since that time, GE has steadily moved into the global economy. Everything from marketing down to research and development has gone global. For example, in the late 1980s General Electric joined forces with Toshiba, Hitachi, ASEA, AMU, and Siemens to improve the performance of nuclear reactors. While the R&D that this consortium developed was available to all members, they kept their distribution markets distinct, so that each profited in the home market from the work they did together (Ohmae, 1990).

This approach to the global economy—using world-level thinking to develop local market products—is perhaps the most effective way to participate. Such "global localization" (Ohmae, 1990) also allows corporations to make their products available in markets other than their "home" market through minor modifications in color and style,[4] a process at which Toyota has been quite successful through both its U.S. plants and its joint venture plant with General Motors, "NUMMI," which create products to suit American tastes.[5] Localization alone does not account for Toyota's success, however; it can also be attributed to being seen as irrelevant for too long by U.S. automakers (Schwartz, 1991), giving Toyota a valuable window of opportunity to exploit.[6] Its globalization strategy had been to coordinate global production of small cars (Porter, 1985), which provided its first entree to the U.S. market. This global base allowed Toyota to learn more quickly about trends and tastes, so that it made substantial gains in many markets (Porter, 1980).

Because each of the Triad's three markets has its own tastes and needs, each of them designs products to suit themselves and the others. Occasionally, the appeal of these products travels easily across national borders; a good example of this is Coca-Cola. More likely, however, each market will have preferences in the design of the product—small or large—that distinguish it from the others. Automobile owners in Japan and the United Kingdom, for example, are required by law to drive from a different side of the car than owners in Germany or the United States; washing machines are usually expected to open on top in the United States but from the front in England. Toyota is somewhat inhibited in the European market due to import duties; it has a relatively free market available to it in the United States, although voluntary import quotas have been a factor. GE has a more varied position in the Triad due to the diversity of its product line. Both are attempting to work across the Triad to survive in a highly competitive climate.

VOLATILE BUSINESS CLIMATE

It is not quite correct to say that the volatile business climate of the 1980s pushed Toyota and General Electric in new directions; more precisely, it was the new directions of Toyota and General Electric which, combined with other corporate and environmental factors, led to the volatile business climate. Peters (1987) cites GE as an example of the company of the 1990s: flat; a coalition of autonomous units; differentiating; quality- and service-oriented; responsive; innovative; and flexible. This structure has led to rapidly changing technology, quick market saturation, and unexpected competition, which in turn have formed the volatile climate that GE and its competitors share.

In anticipation of this sort of intense market pressure. Welch cut over one hundred thousand jobs at GE and engaged in a flurry of businesses acquisitions and sales in an attempt to stay ahead of the competition (Peters, 1987). GE's most effective way of staving of unexpected competition, however, was its use of "total customer responsiveness," a close alliance among suppliers, distributors, and customers. The GE plastics division, for example, attached its distributors to a centralized computer system, making their job easier but also feeding important purchasing data back to GE, which allowed it to carefully monitor developments in purchasing. It also hired an aggressive, ambitious, but personable staff who were designed to be advocates for the customer. These factors helped give GE a competitive edge. Toyota has also recognized that competition requires quick saturation, which in turn requires a well-trained, highly motivated salesforce. Consequently, Toyota regularly sends its line workers out to sell cars (Peters, 1987), bringing sales expertise back to the plant.

While this volatile business climate leads to intense competition, competition itself cannot and must not be the driving force behind high-speed management. Competition implies a reaction to external forces, whereas the high-speed manager must either proact by creating a new way of doing business or "preproact" by manipulating the environmental factors so that they favor a particular long-term strategy. Neither of these is easy to do. As Ohmae (1990) has demonstrated, however, real strategy always emanates from a careful consideration of what the customer wants and needs. To do this, the company must be willing to go back to the starting line, or what he calls "the zero base," in every decision. Merely watching the competition only leads to reaction.

NEW APPROACH TO MANAGEMENT

In order to hold together the manufacturing, marketing, and management technology and a global perspective while remaining proactively competitive, a new philosophy of management has had to emerge. It requires management to put its priority on five principles above all others: innovation, adaptation, flexibility, efficiency, and rapid response. Such a philosophy has been pioneered at Toyota and General Electric. When articulated as a corporate management style, these maxims are, at their best, a mix of contemporary Eastern and Western philosophy. Such a mix is revealed in the values of the NUMMI joint venture between Toyota and General Motors: (1) *kaizen*, the never-ending quest for perfection; (2) the development of full human potential; (3) *jidoka*, the pursuit of superior quality; (4) build mutual trust; (5) develop team performance; (6) every employee a manager; (7) provide a stable livelihood for all employees (Peters, 1987, p. 283). New approaches to management such as this have led to increased market share and profitability.

Innovation

High-speed innovation requires a continuous quest for improvement through new products and processes. This is often interpreted to mean a company should "do more better," but as Ohmae (1990) has shown, this is not enough. "Doing more better" results in competition rather than innovation—that is, satisfaction in doing what is already being done in more or less the same manner but at a faster pace or with greater efficiency rather than questioning the process itself or looking for a new thing to do.

Innovation means going beyond doing more better. As Kanter (1984) has argued, "innovation may be the only hope for the times ahead" (p. 55) and it needs to be conducted at a fast pace (Peters, 1987).

Innovation has always been an important part of Toyota's corporate culture, and its belief that improvement is a continual process rather than an occasional one is in large measure responsible for its success. Ohno embodied this strive for constant innovation in the production process, during his tenure from 1948 to 1978, implementing most of the processes and techniques that guide Toyota today. These innovations include the "pull" system, whereby shop workers, assemblers, and even marketers go back to the previous station on the line to retrieve work-in-progress (in contrast to the "push" system, whereby items push their way forward on the line from worker to worker); the *kanban* system (discussed below) and the just-in-time delivery it allows; assembly synchronization; process difficulty indicator lights; worker and machine flexibility; reduced set-up times; and other innovations (Cusumano, 1988). Innovation at Toyota is not limited to the production process, however. Changes in procedure are evolution, not revolution, so the manager must create an environment in which research and development—where milestone innovation really occurs—is strongly supported. This often means providing sufficient backing to the R&D team and allowing them to take risks and make mistakes.

Allowing risks and making mistakes has not been something historically a part of GE's corporate culture (Magaziner and Patinkin, 1989b) but that is changing. Innovation at GE has traditionally been a product of "bootlegging": entrepreneurs within GE were obliged to gather in bits and pieces enough capital and personnel to experiment with a new process or product (Peters and Waterman, 1982). While this piecemeal approach resulted in a number of important breakthroughs, it was insufficient for the high-speed marketplace of the 1980s; in order for innovation to be effective, it needs to be an institution, not an aberration. To institutionalize it, GE developed a technique called "Workout" that brings management and workers together into a confrontation on the manufacturing process. After outlining a plan of attack, usually streamlining some process, the manager leaves the meeting. The remaining workers divide into teams to address different aspects of the problem, develop ideas, and prepare a presentation to steer management toward the appropriate remedy. The manager returns two days later to listen to the diagnosis and prescription. On the spot, the manager must either agree to take the prescribed action, say no, or establish a development team to seek more information about it (Stewart, 1991). By compelling such a rapid response, the Workout encourages innovation that actually bears fruit; there is no time for developing sophisticated rhetorical defenses about why a process "will never work." Welch's dictum of "speed, simplicity, self-confidence" is put into practice. At the very least, Workout gives an opportunity for workers to vent frustrations; at most, it results in significant changes in the manufacturing process.

Innovation may be a cornerstone of the new management, but ideas that are not put into practice change nothing. Implementing a new vision is where the second and third aspects of high-speed philosophy come into play.

Adaptation

Adaptation is the ability to adjust products and processes to changing environmental factors. As with biological adaptation, companies do not want to find themselves in an environmental niche that dooms them to extinction. Also similar to biological adaptation, the fittest survive because they are able to learn how to move from niche to niche. An organization must develop a learning plan to make sure that it is learning what it needs to about the environment. The most important avenue to learning is through education, so a high-speed organization must commit itself to continually reeducating its workers. In this model, education is not something attained prior to the work, but a part of the work itself.

Education has always been a feature of GE's strategy. In fact, its influence on corporate education has been so profound that the top executives of no fewer than fourteen major U.S. corporations received their training at GE under Welch (Reese, 1991) before moving on to other challenges. One of the sites at which they were trained, GE's Management Development Institute, borrows faculty from the best business schools in the United States: Harvard, MIT, Standford, and Northwestern (Stewart, 1991). Its courses and workshops are aimed at a higher-level audience; its applications are pragmatic rather than theoretical. Almost one hundred thousand managers have gone through retraining in strategic planning and technology management (Peters, 1987). GE has also invested extensively in training for its blue-collar workforce, a program that received an overwhelming response. When GE offered training in new skills, such as computer operation, it emphasized to the employees that these would be on their own time, without pay. Nevertheless, workers were anxious to participate (Magaziner and Patinkin, 1989a). Since those who undergo education like to have some recognition of their accomplishment, General Electric corporate training facilities display the names of those who have completed retraining courses on plaques in the main lobby (Kouzes and Posner, 1990).

In order to successfully execute an adaptation, an organization needs to be able to see the future with sufficient clarity to adapt before major social changes send shock waves through it. On the one hand, this means demographically and culturally shaping the organization now for the way its industry will look in the middle-term future. To do so, the company must carefully analyze trends. Both General Electric and Toyota have had some success at shaping themselves for the direction of industrial evolution. In anticipation of the changing demographics of the workforce of the future, for example, the workforce at the Toyota plant at Georgetown, Kentucky, is 15 percent minority while the surrounding community is only 3 percent minority (Kenney and Florida, 1991). By taking a proactive stance to projected shifts in population growth, Toyota will be able to regenerate its culture while other organizations can only react. So, on the one hand, adaptation means anticipation. On the other hand, it means being flexible.

Flexibility

Flexibility is also needed to manage in a high-speed environment; if adaptability means being able to learn how to survive in different niches, flexibility means being able to move easily from niche to niche. The considerable flexibility of the Toyota manufacturing system has already been discussed, but only from the point of view of the flexibility of its manufacturing technology; even more important to its survival is its certainty that its workforce is flexible. After all, a flexible worker can learn a new machine, but a flexible machine cannot produce without a worker.

There are several ways that GE and Toyota have promoted flexibility. One is to have loosely defined (or no) job descriptions—worker are expected not only to be able to perform a number of different tasks, but to be able to learn new ones readily, so that their job in a few years may be totally different than their job now. The Toyota-General Motors joint venture NUMMI plant has made use of more simple and flexible job descriptions, iconic representations of how to do each job, and careful hiring (Whitney, 1988). It has also put peer group leaders on the production floor (Kenney and Florida, 1991), helping to make it one of the most flexible plants in America. Implementing a system in which job descriptions are this irrelevant can be threatening to many workers, but it is in fact a way of empowering them—it creates a situation in which they are listened to and heard, where their work is in teams that involve them in a wide variety of decisions, where their incentive pay is increased, and where the corporate bureaucracy's power begins to disseminate (Peters, 1987). Since human beings are valued for their flexibility, they are valued for their minds. Perhaps because workers feel the company values them, unions have not been able to make substantial inroads into U.S. Toyota plants (Kenney and Florida, 1991).

This flexible job philosophy finds its way into GE as well: its research and development divisions push engineers to understand how design relates to cost, speed, and customer satisfaction (Peters, 1987). Further, GE has a successful personnel rotation program that moves employees between business units. This helps create a unity of culture and procedure as it educates managers about the opportunities of interrelationships. This has a number of other benefits, including the inculcation of a belief in corporate themes, the entrepreneurial development of new intracompanies, and increased flexibility (Porter, 1985).

Flexibility has been increased at Toyota through "deintegration," a process that removed levels of management while increasing horizontal networks (Cusumano, 1988). Fewer levels clearly lead to more flexibility since decision making is quicker and more direct; since this speeds development and production, it also lowers costs and increases profits. Deintegration has had a profound effect on Toyota, making it look quite different from its competition: it has five levels of management while U.S. automakers average seventeen (Peters and Waterman, 1982).

Flexibility also requires a management style that solves problems and uses communication in new, less predictable ways. General Electric CEO Jack Welch embodies the sort of communication flexibility a high-speed organization requires. He installed a special phone line in his office whose number was only available to GE purchasing agents. Whenever they made a good buy, they were asked to call and give the good news to Welch directly. Regardless of what sort of meeting he was in, Welch would always take the call, congratulating the agent for a job well done (Kouzes and Posner, 1990), providing direct recognition. This displays a sophisticated awareness of the importance of interpersonal communication in motivating employees, an ability to be flexible in the structuring of one's own time, and a recognition of the primacy of competitive advantage through cost-effective purchasing.

Welch has also tried to increase flexibility through the elimination of the concept of "the boss" (Stewart, 1991). Part of this plan is increasing flexibility through encouraging teams to think for themselves and to get managers and workers out of a rigid interpretation of their job description and into a process-based, cross-functional matrix. By increasing flexibility, GE and Toyota are able to increase their efficiency.

Efficiency

Efficiency is another important factor in high-speed management. It entails creating the greatest output with the least input and is closely related to the other concepts of high-speed management. Historically, many industries were content to produce airplane engines or automobiles inefficiently, with a large volume of defective products coming off the line. This practice could be tolerated when industries had no effective competition and with high-end pricing—what difference did efficiency make when profits were huge anyway? The fierce global business climate of the 1980s and 1990s put an end to such bloat, however; with too much scrap-and-rework, manufacturing ceases to move at high speed, outputs are minimized, and waste overwhelms the process. Toyota and General Electric have managed to increase their efficiency and are surprisingly lithe for companies of their size.

Toyota is perhaps the most efficient automobile manufacturer in the world (Cusumano, 1988), in part because it uses a "lean" production system (Krafcik, 1988).[7] This means that its processes provide the inputs necessary for the desired output and little more. Such efficiency does not happen through management fiat, of course; Toyota has instituted devices so that workers have control over the manufacturing process. Because they see the process as it actually is, they see where the inefficiencies lie. At the Fremont, California Toyota/General Motors NUMMI joint venture plant, line workers have been provided an overhead cord pull. If a worker feels that a defective part is proceeding or that he or she is overwhelmed by the pace of the work, he or she can pull the cord (like a passenger on a bus indicating a stop). The line slows down or stops, allowing for time to insure that the product is still being built to quality specifications. Interestingly, it is not even necessary for the cord to be pulled for it to have the desired effect; the mere fact that workers have the ability to pull it increases performance by prioritizing quality. Because of this cord-pull technique, the number of defects at the plant fell from five to ten per car to one in ten cars (Kouzes and Posner, 1990), as much as a 1,000 percent improvement. Worker control means efficiency. Because it implements 95 percent of the quality improvement suggestions of its employees, for example, Toyota No. 9 Kamigo engine plant has become the most efficient in the world (Peters, 1987).

General Electric has also been concerned with efficiency as a way to lower costs and increase competitiveness. Its plants have gone from 30 percent scrap and rework rates in factories that looked like old auto garages to near zero tolerance in factories of the future (Magaziner and Patinkin, 1989b). Its efficiency drive has meant that during the 1980s its productivity increase climbed to nearly 6 percent annually while the average for other U.S. industry declined to −1 percent (Stewart, 1991). Much of this success is due to Welch's systematic turning over of power and decision making to "process champions" who make things run more efficiently rather than to traditional middle managers (who have historically added to the inefficiency). These champions are those who excel at diagnosing where inefficiencies lie in the production process and correcting the deficiencies. They use a technique called "process mapping," which entails the creation of a flow chart showing each and every step that goes into the creation and production of a product. This map represents what actually happens in the process and is compared to a map of what managers and workers believe happens (Stewart, 1991). When laid out in such a graphic form, the inefficiencies manifest themselves, leading to a streamlining of the process. This allows the implementation of a final high-speed technique: rapid response.

Rapid Response

To compete effectively in the world marketplace, companies must respond rapidly to changes in supply and demand—a combination of innovation, adaptability, flexibility, and efficiency. They must become what Bower and Hout (1988) call a "fast-cycle" organization, one that makes a strategic move before its competitor can, one that sees itself as a continuous system in which each part tries to speed the process of the whole. Toyota and General Electric have been able to move into a fast cycle and use rapid response as a competitive weapon.

In fact, Bower and Hout (1988) use Toyota as an example of a "classic" fast-cycle organization. Although it has designed its system so that information needed by managers and workers moves as quickly as possible through development, ordering, scheduling, production, and delivery, these different stages in the process are seen as interrelated parts of a whole, not discrete activities. Teams assist in speeding response time, and because of their proximity to suppliers and customers, they further help to speed up the product life cycle.

Another way Toyota increases its speed of response is to track closely the use of time throughout the production process (Bower and Hout, 1988). One method of doing this is the *kanban* system, a Toyota innovation comprised of six processes: production smoothing (allowing subassemblies to occur at a constant speed); reduction in the time it takes to set up a particular piece of equipment; logical and flowing machine and layout design; job standardization (creating a multifunctional worker); activity improvement; and autonomation, which has been discussed above (Monden, 1983). This just-in-time system speeds up the manufacturing process considerably. Some (see Schmenner, 1988; Krafcik, 1988; Zipkin, 1991) see it as the single most important tool for improving productivity.

Toyota's plant in Georgetown, Kentucky, is an embodiment of this sort of strategic rapid response. It has developed links to local suppliers such as Johnson Controls, a maker of auto seats, to deliver their product just-in-time—no small feat of coordination. This has helped Johnson and other suppliers in the area to coevolve with Toyota and share in its prosperity. To maintain and enhance its sphere of coevolution, Toyota has set up the Blue-grass Automotive Manufacturing Association, which promotes the interests of these local suppliers to its plant (Kenney and Florida, 1991).

General Electric's rapid response strategies are largely modeled on Toyota's (Zipkin, 1991). It uses teams that cross and interlink functions in a system called "Quick Response." The goal of Quick Response is to make fundamental efficiency changes in the manufacturing and distribution process to allow GE to respond as quickly as possible to changes in customer demand. Often, the inability to respond rapidly does not reside in the actual manufacturing of the product; while it takes only a few hours to build a dishwasher, for example, it takes sixteen weeks for the plant to respond to changes in consumer taste (Stewart, 1991). Quick Response at GE relies on two important principles: that consumer demand cannot be adequately predicted, so that turnaround time must be kept to a minimum and that no path once ventured down cannot be quickly and easily abandoned; and that inventory costs go down when suppliers deliver their products just-in-time. Response time is cut further when several models in a product line make use of the same components, which can be stored adjacent to the cell in the plant where they are needed (Stewart, 1991).

The ultimate goal is for spontaneous response—products made to order instantaneously. Such a goal would have seemed ridiculous in the mass culture of a decade ago, but high-speed communication, new technology, and radical approaches to management point to a day when a consumer calls a factory and electronically inputs specifications for a custom made product which goes into immediate production on the line and arrives the next day at his or her door via Federal Express.

Using these five new approaches to management has enabled Toyota and General Electric to push the boundaries of enterprise. Because they are so sophisticated in their management, and because they have moved ahead faster than their competition, Toyota and General Electric now confront another problem: high-speed management's successes sow the seeds of its own limitations.

THE LIMITS OF HIGH-SPEED MANAGEMENT

High-speed management has brought Toyota and General Electric to the cutting edge of industry. It is not only lonely at the top, however; it is dangerous. Employees, suppliers, and even nation-states are threatened by this success, and can exert pressure against a high-speed company. A high-speed manager needs to recognize the limitations of the technique.

One limitation is the political and social pressure brought to bear on a successful company, particularly in the global marketplace. Because Toyota and General Electric are so good at what they do, indigenous industry often pressures governments to limit access to labor, capital, resources, and markets. This forces a high-speed company to make concessions, inhibiting their strategy. The concessions can be both "hard" (financial) or "soft" (public relations), and are best seen in the relationship between Toyota and the United States. Examples of hard concessions occurred after threats of American import quotas forced Toyota to agree to slow down production (Levin, 1991), resell U.S. cars in the Japanese market (Maynard, 1991), buy more American-made automobile parts (Firm unveils, 1992), and form alliances with competitors (Spot the difference, 1990). Although implementing these is all within the realm of possibility, they are not always within the realm of desirability; from a psychological standpoint, it may be difficult to slow down a company as successful as Toyota. Soft responses are aimed at public sentiment rather than specific legislative proposals and attempt to proact against hostility. For example, Toyota created good will by running an advertising campaign touting its contributions to schools, local sports, and other civic events (Foltz, 1990). Such actions, necessitated by political reality, would not be otherwise part of Toyota strategy.

Another limitation to high-speed management is the lag between theory and implementation. Management theory makes it very clear what sort of leader and worker produce the best results, but real people find these roles difficult to fill, especially when they are accustomed to other styles of management. Too much democracy and too many teams can lead to chaos; management that moves too fast to implement change is perceived by employees and stockholders to be intimidating. Jack Welch, for example, while usually considered to be quite intimidating, has asked that GE begin to value self-confidence and self-empowerment (Holusha, 1992). So, both Toyota and GE are attempting to recraft themselves as "kinder and gentler" companies (Levin, 1991; Holusha, 1992), not so much as a high-speed strategy, but as a public relations defense against detractors. Related to this is the inevitable culture clash between managers from the nation that owns the company and workers from the country where it is housed; Toyota has found this clash particularly challenging in England, but the United States has produced its share of problems, too (Lean, mean, 1991).

A further limitation occurs as a product of the speed itself. Since state-of-the-art management moves very quickly, allegiances and alliances come and go. Corporations link together for temporary, mutually beneficial projects, then go their separate ways. Combining forces at NUMMI, Toyota and General Motors found that working together would be difficult. Ironically, they are still competitors, in spite of the fact that they have formed an alliance. To use a military metaphor, a competitor might be something to beat, to join, or to flank, depending on the project at hand. As in World War II, today's ally might be tomorrow's mortal foe. To manage at high speeds, a company must be willing to form links, but this is to risk giving away ideas and approaches to a competitor.

There is another limit to high-speed management, but of a different sort. There is little question that high-speed management enhances the quality of life of investors, but more research and analysis need be done about the effect it has on the quality of life of employees, communities, and nations. This management style has contributed to an acceleration of everyday life, and it can be seen as a phenomenon related to cellular telephones, fax machines, home computers with modems, 100-channel cable television systems, and other artifacts of life at the end of the millennium. There is certainly more information available, and it is moving faster, but the extent to which everyday life has been enhanced is unclear. Do people have more leisure time? Is there work more fulfilling? More prosaically, does a faster world make them happier? These issues are seldom considered in management theory, but perhaps they ought to be; in information and media theory, there is a growing consensus that less may be more (Ronell, 1989 on telecommunications; Winston, 1986, Meyrowitz, 1985, and McKibben, 1992 on media; and Yurick, 1985 and Baudrillard, 1983 on culture and capitalism, to name a few). There is a body of literature, perpetuated by the management journals, which is uncritically and unanalytically enthusiastic about high-speed management, but ignores these concerns; it examines process, not outcomes.

In spite of these limitations, high-speed management serves as the model for well-managed companies in the 1990s. Political and social pressure, the gap between expectations and abilities, the uncertainty of who is friend or foe, and the desirability of a faster world notwithstanding, high-speed management will set the pace for change in global business.

CONCLUSION

For many industries, the implementation of high-speed management can no longer be a matter of preference. Toyota and General Electric have laid down the gauntlet, and their competitors have no choice but to implement factories of the future, high-technology marketing, and computer-assisted management; to operate in a global economy by competing in the Triad; to be thrust into an ever more volatile business climate; and to implement a management philosophy based on innovation, adaptation, flexibility, efficiency, and rapid response. As more and more companies adopt high-speed management techniques, the question for Toyota and General Electric becomes: where to next?

One answer is to transform the organization yet again, from something that changes its shape every so often to one that has no shape to begin with—a protean matrix that adapts immediately and efficiently to its environment. There is only one way to enact such a transformation: a company needs to become what Singe (1990) called a "learning organization"—an organization that recognizes that

1) today's problems come from yesterday's "solutions"...
2) the harder you push, the harder the system pushes
back... 3) behavior grows better before it grows worse...
4) the easy way out usually leads back in... 5) the cure can
be worse than the disease... 6) faster is slower... 7) cause
and effect are not closely related in time and space... 8)
small changes can produce big results... 9) you can have
your cake and eat it too, but not at once... 10) dividing an
elephant in half does not produce two small elephants...
11) there is no blame. (pp. 57–67)

Both organizations seem to be moving in the direction Singe
indicates. In order to become a first magnitude learning organization, GE sent its best researchers to successful companies
in other industries to ask them to what they attribute the se-
cret of their success. This project, known as "Best Practices,"
revealed that successful companies focus on processes rather
than functions—how the company integrated as a whole rather
than how specific units performed. This meant that these successful companies developed new products more quickly and
efficiently, stayed close to suppliers and customers by treating
them as partners, and closely controlled inventory to keep
capital working rather than tied up in storage. From this GE
learned that how something is done is as important as what is
being done, that GE has much to learn from other companies,
that processes must be continually improved, and that processes need someone willing and able to implement change
(Stewart, 1991).

The only future to management in many industries is high
speed. The Ford auto worker with the sign critical of Japan is
really protesting a shift from nineteenth-century management
hierarchies to twenty-first-century flexible matrices. Hierarchies
can be comforting; one knows one's place in them. A protean
matrix, on the other hand, means stress and uncertainty. It is in a
state of perpetual chaos. In saying "no to Japan," the worker is
saying no to the frightening apparition of high-speed management. In the world of high-speed management, where Toyotas
are made in Kentucky and General Motors cars in Mexico, this
no seems like a leaf against the wind.

NOTES

1. *Letterman* head writer Steve O'Donnell has said of Welch's management changes at GE, "I've seen more boneheaded cost cutting than innovative management" (Stewart, 1991, p. 49).

2. This, of course, yielded manuals written from the perspective of the user rather than the maker, making them much easier to use and consequently increasing their use. This saved time and increased quality, since operators knew what they were doing.

3. It is not enough just to do extensive surveys either. Ohmae (1990) argued that it is more useful to spend two hours with three customers than to spend days poring over extensive data. The data are shaped by the kinds of questions that are asked, but the real design breakthroughs come in ways that the designer of the questionnaire has not conceived.

4. It is questionable, however, that there is such a thing as a "home market." Manufacturing has become such a global enterprise, that in some ways a Honda is a more "American" car than a Ford, GM, or Chrysler, since more of its components are manufactured and assembled in the United States (cf. Reich, 1990, 1991).

5. This plant is called the New United Motor Manufacturing plant, or NUMMI.

6. While GE perceived the Singapore competition to its compressors in time enough to proact against it, U.S. automakers perhaps dismissed foreign competition for too long, forcing themselves to play catch-up. Interestingly, the auto worker with the "Japan says your (*sic*) lazy" sign seems to see the problem as a betrayal by the American car buyer or a foreign power rather than as poor management by U.S. automakers.

7. Krafcik (1988) contrasts Toyota's "lean" production system with the U.S. automobile industry's "buffered" system. The latter is characterized by high inventory levels, constant rates of production, an enormous and inflexible workforce, and high levels of scrap and rework. The "lean" system (just-in-time inventory, variable production, a smaller and more flexible workforce, and an emphasis on "quality," which is doing it right the first time) contains higher risk, but yields higher returns.

REFERENCES

Baudrillard, J. 1983. *Simulations.* New York: Semitotext(e).

Benjamin, R., et al. 1984. Information technology: A strategic opportunity. *Sloan Management Review* 25(3):27–34.

Bower, J. and T. Hout. 1988. Fast-cycle capability for competitive power. *Harvard Business Review* 66(6):110–18.

Cushman, D., and S. King. 1994. *High-Speed Management: A Revolution in Organizational Communication in the 1990s.* Albany, N.Y.: SUNY Press.

Cusumano, M. 1988. Manufacturing innovation: Lessons from the Japanese auto industry. *Sloan Management Review* 30(1):29–40.

Fighting words. 1992. *New York Times,* Jan. 26, p. E1.

Firm unveils plan to boost purchases of U.S. supplies. 1992. *Wall Street Journal,* Oct. 10, p. A4.

Foltz, K. 1990. Toyota effort seeks to show how it cares about the U.S. *New York Times,* Oct. 2, p. D24.

General Electric Company. 1953. *Professional Management in General Electric.* New York: General Electric Company.

Greenwood, R. 1974. *Managerial Decentralization: A Study of the General Electric philosophy.* Lexington, Mass.: Lexington Books.

Hauser, J., and D. Clausing. 1988. The house of quality. *Harvard Business Review* 66(3):63–73.

Hayes, R., and R. Jaikuman. 1988. Manufacturing's crisis: New technologies, obsolete organizations. *Harvard Business Review* 66(5):77–85.

Holusha, J. 1992. A call for kinder managers at G.E. *New York Times,* Mar. 4, pp. D1, D6.

Kanter, R. 1984. MSR Forum: Innovation—the only hope for times ahead? *Sloan Management Review* 25(4):51–55.

Kenney, M., and R. Florida. 1991. How Japanese industry is rebuilding the rust belt. *Technology Review* 94(2):24–33.

Kouzes, J., and B. Posner. 1990. *The Leadership Challenge: How to Get Extraordinary Things Done in Organizations.* San Francisco, Calif.: Jossey-Bass.

Krafcik, J. 1988. Triumph of the lean production system. *Sloan Management Review* 30(1):41–52.

Lean, mean, and through your windscreen. 1991. *Economist* (Feb. 23):68–70.

Levin, D. 1991. Too American for its own good. *New York Times,* Oct. 27, pp. 3-1, 3-6.

Magaziner, I., and M. Patinkin. 1989a. Cold competition: GE wages the refrigerator war. *Harvard Business Review* 67(2):114–24.

————. 1989b. *The Silent War: Inside the Global Business Battles Shaping America's Future*. New York: Random House.

Maynard, M. 1991. Toyota offers to sell U.S. cars in Japan. *USA Today*, May 23, p. B1.

McKenna, R. 1988. Marketing in the age of diversity. *Harvard Business Review* 66(5):88–95.

————. 1991. Marketing is everything. *Harvard Business Review* 69(1):65–79.

McKibben, B. 1992. Reflections: What's on? *New Yorker* (Mar. 9)40–80.

Meyrowitz, J. 1985. *No Sense of Place*. New York: Oxford University Press.

Mizuno, S. 1988. *Management for Quality Improvement: The Seven New OC Tools*. Cambridge, Mass.: Productivity Press.

Monden, Y. 1983. *Toyota Production System: Practical Approach to Production Management*. Norcross, Ga.: Industrial Engineering and Management Press.

Ohmae, K. 1990. *The Borderless World: Power and Strategy in the Interlinked Economy*. New York: Harper Business.

Penzias, A. 1989. *Ideas and Information: Managing in a High-Tech World*. New York: Norton.

Peters, T. 1987. *Thriving on Chaos: Handbook for a Management Revolution*. New York: Knopf.

Peters, T., and R. Waterman. 1982. *In Search of Excellence: Lessons from America's Best-run Companies*. New York: Harper and Row.

Porter, M. 1980. *Competitive Strategy: Techniques for Analyzing Industries and Competitors*. New York: Free Press.

————. 1985. *Competitive Advantage: Creating and Sustaining Superior Performance*. New York: Free Press.

Reese, J. 1991. General Electric as CEO boot camp. *Fortune* 123(7):12.

Reich, R. 1990. Who is us? *Harvard Business Review* 68(1):53–64.

————. 1991. Who is them? *Harvard Business Review* 69(2):77–89.

Ronell, A. 1989. *The Telephone Book: Technology, Schizophrenia, Electric Speech*. Lincoln: University of Nebraska Press.

Schmenner, R. 1988. The merit of making things fast. *Sloan Management Review* 30(1):11–18.

Schwartz, P. 1991. *The Art of the Long View: Planning for the Future in an Uncertain World*. New York: Doubleday Currency.

Singe, P. 1990. *The Fifth Discipline: The Art and Practice of the Learning Organization.* New York: Doubleday.

Spot the differences. 1990. *Economist* (Feb. 24):74.

Stalk, G. 1988. Time—the next source of competitive advantage. *Harvard Business Review* 66(4):41–51.

Stewart, J. 1991. GE keeps those ideas coming. *Fortune* 124(4):40–49.

Taylor, A. 1991. Getting a first look at Japan's new cars. *Fortune* 124(13):113–20.

Taylor, J. 1991. Wither NBC's peacock? *Forbes* 147(5):40–41.

Whitney, D. 1988. Manufacturing by design. *Harvard Business Review* 66(4):83–91.

Winston, B. 1986. *Misunderstanding Media.* Cambridge, Mass.: Harvard University Press.

Yurick, S. 1985. *Metatron.* New York: Semiotext(e).

Zipkin, P. 1991. Does manufacturing need a JIT revolution? *Harvard Business Review* 69(1):40–50.

CHAPTER THIRTEEN

Communication and Management in the Global Economy

Sarah Sanderson King and Donald Peter Cushman

"Rapidly changing technology, quick market saturation, unexpected global competition—these all make succeeding in business . . . harder than ever today" (Fraker, 1984:34). These volatile economic forces, when combined with regional core market recessions and sector economic recessions such as automotive and real estate, are placing considerable stress upon organizations participating in the global economy. The fallout in the form of bankruptcies, consolidation, rationalization, and precipitous drops in income, profits, and stockholder values have been significant.

However, several so-called well-managed global corporations such as General Electric, Asea Brown and Boveri, and Toyota have not only avoided this stress, but have watched their sales and profits increase and have flourished. As indicated in our previous chapter, we believe that high-speed management played an important role in the adjustment of these successful global corporations to environmental change. More specifically, we argued that the fundamental problem confronting organizations that participate in the global economy is one of carefully monitoring in real-time the major economic forces, market forces,

291

and competitor plans throughout the globe, and the rapidly reorienting of an organization's value chain in such a manner as to obtain value-added competitive advantage relative to one's competitors throughout the world.

Such environmental scanning and organizational adaptation processes confront what many management experts have come to see as management paradoxes. An organization to be successful at this adaptation process must be at the same time global and local, big and small, centralized and decentralized, fast and slow, achieve economies of scale and produce highly specialized products. Caught in this swamp of seemingly paradoxical environment demands, the management systems of most organizations have become disjointed, sluggish, fat, and unresponsive.

However, once again for a very small set of globally successful organizations, the opposite has been true. They have met these seemingly paradoxical demands with an organizational management system that manifests a slimmed down administrative system characterized by tight and efficient integration, coordination and control of environmental scanning, and organizational adaptation processes. It will be the central claim of this chapter that what characterizes the management systems in those successful, as opposed to the unsuccessful, global corporations is a new understanding and implementation of the unique communication component in effective management systems. In order to justify this claim we shall (1) explore the attributes of successful organizational global management systems that exist today and how they are evolving to meet tomorrow's volatile economic environments; (2) analyze in detail the unique management and communication components involved in those systems; (3) demonstrate that it is the unique communication component in this process that is generating successful environmental scanning and organizational adaptation; and (4) reflect on what this implies for the further development of communication and management within the global economy.

Prior to entering into the main body of our analysis, it may be worthwhile to define what is meant by global organizations, management, and communication. A *global organization* for our purposes is most effectively conceptualized as an organization that looks at the world as having a single economy with regional core markets and thus scans the globe for the most effective use

of the factors of production while still treating marketing, distribution, sales, and service as regional or localized problems. In so
doing, a global organization seeks to leverage comparative advantage gained in one part of the world in order to obtain competitive advantage in other parts of the world (Main, 1989; Agthe,
1990; Stewart, 1991).

The task of *management* remains as it has always been "to
make people capable of joint performance by giving them common goals, common values, the right structure, and the ongoing
training and development they need to perform and respond to
change" (Drucker, 1988:65). However, this traditional role for
management becomes complicated in a global organization by
creating the need to rise above merely local differences in management style to develop a global management perspective and
style. This involves the selection of a common language, goals,
values, structures, and training that is at once neutral to national
differences and adaptive to local issues.

Communication in such a context has been traditionally viewed
as the successful transfer of symbolic information (Berlo, 1960).
In its organizational context, communication may be viewed as
the successful transfer of information necessary for the production and sales of products. However, communication in its global
context creates a new set of demands. Cultural diversity requires
that communication be capable in its global context of allowing
for the explanation and understanding of diverse cultural interests, concerns, and contributions to the production process and
then the fair, open, and consensual molding of those diverse
interests, concerns, and contributions into a common and effective course of action. It is in this process of joint action that the
organizational concern for integration, coordination, and control meet and that communication and management become
interdependent.

ATTRIBUTES OF A SUCCESSFUL GLOBAL ORGANIZATION

While it is clear from our previous chapter that a successful global
competitor carefully monitors changes in global economic forces
and regional and local markets and then quickly reorients an
organization's value chain to meet those changes in ways that create value-added activities and thus competitive advantage, it is far

from clear what specific organizational processes are involved in such an outcome. Fortunately, several well-documented studies have explained this problem in detail with convergent results (Rockart and Short, 1989; Porter, 1986; Cvar, 1986; Smith, et al., 1989).

The Center for Information Systems Research at MIT Sloan School of Management in 1989 summarized these convergent studies when they stated that an organization's ability to continuously improve its effectiveness in managing organizational interdependencies was the critical element in successfully responding to the competitive forces of the 1990s. Effectiveness in managing organizational interdependencies refers to an organization's ability to achieve coalignment among its internal and external resources in responding to environmental change.

Coalignment is a unique form of organizational interdependence in which each of a firm's subunits clearly articulates its needs, concerns, and potential contributions to the organization's functioning in such a manner that management can forge an appropriate value-added configuration and linkage between units. An appropriate value-added configuration and linkage between units is one that integrates, coordinates, and controls each unit's needs, concerns, and contributions so that the outcome is mutually satisfying to the units involved and optimizing in value-added activities to the organizational functioning as a whole.

The critical communication and management processes involved in organizational coalignment are an organization's integration, coordination, and control processes. Organizational integration is achieved by three overlapping subprocesses: leadership, corporate climate, and teamwork. Each has its unique function. Organizational leadership creates a focused set of goals for an organization. An appropriate corporate climate is achieved when an organization's various stakeholders—workers, investors, customers, suppliers, and governments—work together in such a manner as to make these goals achievable. Teamwork functions effectively when separate units, individuals within units, and systems across tasks, are coaligned for goal attainment.

Organizational coordination is achieved through the sharing of information in such a manner as to optimize the value-added activities of each of an organization's subunits and environment. This normally involves linking customers, regulators, R&D, marketing, manufacturing, distribution, sales, and service in such a manner that the issues, concerns, and contributions of each link in the value chain can be optimized.

Organizational control involves the planning, including the setting of targets for sales, productivity, and quality; monitoring progress toward those targets in real-time; and the assessment after the fact of improvements that can be made in performance. These planning, monitoring, and assessment functions, if they are to be realistic, also involve coalignment processes between environmental demands and the value chain, which normally takes the form of specific targets or goals and the review of individual and group progress toward these goals, which then forms the basis for the organization's recognition and reward system.

The coalignment of each of these processes is the essential feature in organizational competitive advantage in the global economy.

THE FUNDAMENTAL MANAGEMENT PROCESSES FOR COALIGNMENT

The paradigm management tools for successful coalignments in the global economy are undergoing change today. Therefore it is necessary to explore what we are changing from and what we are changing to. (See Table 13.1)

Table 13.1
Fundamental Management Tools

Organizational Management Processes	Current Organizational Tools	New Organizational Tools
Integration Process	Transformational Leadership	Global Warrior Leadership
	Matrix Management	Global matrix Management
Coordination Process	MIS Network	Telecommunication
	Teamwork	Continuous Improvement
Control Process	Goals, Semi- and Annual Reviews	Stretch Goals and Targets Weekly Review

The coalignment of organizational management processes in the global economy are currently rooted in several rather specific management tools. Organizational integration processes are shifting from an emphasis on transformational leadership and matrix management to an emphasis on global warrior leadership and global matrix management. Whereas transformational leaders employ their anticipatory, visioning, value congruence, empowerment, and self-understanding skills to present and implement successive visions for changing a corporation in response to environmental change, a global warrior develops and implements a single innovative, adaptive, flexible, efficient, and rapid response organizational framework that allows the organization to rationalize its response to change in a manner coherent to workers, investors, suppliers, customers, and regulators.

Whereas matrix management takes the various units in an organization's value chain and subjects them to the supervision of multiple managers with multiple interests—normally a product division manager and a market location manager—global matrix management changes the management team to a local market manager, a product team manager, and an international synergy manager.

Organizational coordination processes are also in the process of change. Centralized and decentralized MIS systems and the extensive use of teamwork systems are giving way to interactive telecommunication and continuous improvement systems. Whereas centralized and decentralized MIS systems require fixed-entry, rigid frameworks for rapid information exchange, interactive telecommunication allows for multiple-entry, flexible memory frameworks that can more adequately meet the need to coordinate individual differences as well as commonalities.

Whereas cross-functional, self-managed, and social-technical teamwork was instrumental in increasing quality, productivity, and profits, more permanent continuous improvement systems allow for individual as well as team responsibility in constantly improving these processes.

Organizational control processes are also involved in a radical change process. Whereas organizations used to set yearly performance targets or goals and conduct semiannual or annual reviews of individuals and unit contributions to those goals, responding to a volatile environment has forced organizations to employ stretch goals, namely, those adjusted to quarterly fluctuations and weekly performance reviews in an effort to more rapidly adjust to increases and decreases in environmental change.

Each of these changes is an attempt to achieve more rapid, accurate, and continuous adjustment of organizational co-alignment aimed at optimizing the value-added activity of each organizational unit. All of these changes have moved the global corporation deeper and deeper into high-speed management systems.

COMMUNICATION AS THE UNIQUE AND PIVOTAL COMPONENT IN MANAGEMENT CHANGES

What, then, are the unique contributions of communication to each of these shifts in a global organization's integration, coordination, and control processes? Do we have clear examples of how each shift works in a global context?

The shift from transformational leadership and matrix management to global warrior leadership and global matrix management involves two changes. First, the global warrior as leader seeks to develop a single organizational framework of goals and values that allows for the successful rationalization of organizational change in regard to workers, investors, customers, and regulators. This can be done only when the organizational framework consists of goals and values each stakeholder in the organization can buy into and considers each group's interests, concerns, and contributions to organizational effectiveness. When such a framework is constructed appropriately, a successful rationalization of organizational activity can be made through an appropriate appeal to these interests, concerns, and contributions. This process of constructing such an integrative framework and utilization of the rationalization of organizational activities is uniquely and primarily a coalignment communication activity.

A prime example of such a global warrior framework is the articulation of the four goals for General Electric by Jack Welsh, the CEO of the General Electric Corporation.

The first goal is to become the most competitive corporation in the world. This goal is currently operationalized to mean invest only in business with high-growth potential where GE can become number one or two in market shares; divest low-growth businesses; decentralize power and responsibility to become more rapid and flexible in response to market forces; develop low-cost, high-quality, easily serviced products; monitor carefully the ability of each business to meet productivity, quality, and financial targets; and intervene when necessary to make each business a "win-aholic."

The second goal is to become the nation's most valuable corporation. This goal is currently operationalized to mean the most valuable in terms of market capitalization. To do this GE, now worth $58.4 billion, would have to leapfrog IBM with $74 billion, Exxon Corporation worth $68 billion, and Philip Morris worth $62 billion. This goal is operationalized to mean keep sales and profits rising at 10 to 15 percent per year and stock appreciation at 15 percent, shift earning mix to high-growth areas, keep production rising at 10 percent, keep exports at 50 percent, and maintain management's reputation as entrepreneurial, agile, knowledgeable, aggressive, and effective as competitors.

The third goal is to develop a skilled, self-actualizing, productive, and aggressive workforce. This goal is currently operationalized to mean GE wants to create an environment that will be a challenging place to work and will significantly enhance workers' skills so that they can find another job if the company no longer needs them—a place where employees are ready to go but eager to stay, to develop employees' awareness that the only road to job security is increasing market shares, to hold employees responsible for meeting productivity, quality, and fixed goals while upgrading their own skills.

The fourth goal is to develop open communication based on candor and trust. This goal is operationalized to mean sharing corporation objectives, facts, and vision with all employees; opening each employee up to discussion regarding his or her strengths, weaknesses, and the possibility for change; and to motivate employees to become happier, more self-confident, energized workers.

This organizational framework allowed Welsh to rationalize the selling of over $11 billion in businesses, to acquire over $9 billion in other businesses, to cut 130,500 employees, undertake a $1 billion stock buyback program, invest billions in modernizations, close 73 plants, and reduce 100 businesses to 13. Over a five-year period, revenues increased 27 percent, earnings 42 percent, stockholder equity 43 percent, with an average annual growth in earnings at 10 percent per share. GE's market value went from $12 billion (eleventh in the nation) to $58 billion (second in the nation).

The shift from matrix management to global matrix management subjected units in an organizational value chain to three manager/supervisors rather than two. This can be effectively implemented only when each manager is aware of each of the other manager's demands upon those units and integrates his of her demands accordingly. When such a structure is created, it only works when the interests, concerns, and contributions of each manager are integrated in such a manner as to yield consistent action. This process is uniquely and primarily a coalignment communication activity.

A prime example of the effective use of global matrix management is Asea Brown Boveri. The organizing logic of ABB's global matrix is as follows. At the bottom, ABB consists of some 1,100 local businesses averaging 200 employees in size. The manager of each local unit is responsible to the leaders of some 50 business areas worldwide and to a country manager. The 50 business managers and over 80 country managers are grouped into 8 business areas and 4 geographic regions responsible to the 13-member executive committee and the CEO. The business areas are global in focus and make product strategy and performance decisions irrespective of national or regional and local issues in product design and mix. The local managers focus on the running of their local units. All managers interact at the management level in English and at the local level in their appropriate local language.

Last year ABB had sales of $21 billion, profits of $589 million with 85,000 employees who, due to the organizational integration processes of global matrix management, were able to think globally and act locally, to be big and small, to be centralized and decentralized, and to be fast and slow through communication.

The shift from MIS networks and teamwork to telecommunication networks and continuous change involves two significant changes. First, the shift from MIS networks to telecommunication networks involves a shift from pure information systems, which are rigid and focused on the consensual use of data, to telecommunication networks, which are flexible, multichannel, and allow for both system commonalities and individual differences in perspective and messages. This encourages the coalignment of both similarities and differences through human interaction.

An excellent example of this telecommunication networking is the Ford Motor Company. Ford platforms R&D and manufacturing from four specialization centers throughout the world: one located in Europe, one in the United States, one in Latin America, and one in Australia. The products from each of these centers are then shipped to and combined with products from the other centers at the point of distribution and sales. In order to coordinate this effort, Ford has a telecommunication capability in each office and factory around the world. Audio, visual, and data interaction are possible among all units. This coordination effort has allowed the coalignment of commonalities and diversities globally.

Teamwork has given way to continuous improvement processes around the world. Continuous improvement processes may involve either individuals, groups, or teams and allow for short- or long-term focus. Several recent studies have demonstrated that teamwork is not the only way to get organizational improvement and not necessarily the best way for most problems (Lefton and Buzzota, 1987). What separates continuous improvement processes from teamwork is the communicative coalignment of worker and task whether it be by individuals, groups, or teams.

One example of such a continuous improvement process is GE's Workout program. Each week the managers of various units meet with workers to discuss problems within the organization. Then workers and managers decide upon the best structure for solving the problems, be they individual training, group, or teamwork processes. Responsibility is delegated for solving the problems and a timeframe established. Each week this process is repeated. Over the first two years of its operation at GE plastics, it is estimated that over $3 million in savings occurred from this Workout process (Paul, 1991).

The shift from long-term goals and annual and semiannual reviews to quarterly stretch goals and weekly reviews involves two changes: (1) recognition that in a volatile economic climate, long-term goals and annual reviews are necessarily vague and shifting; and (2) recognition that short-term goals and weekly monitoring allow the adjustment of both goals and performance to change in a predictable manner. The communication of changes in stretch goals and weekly performance evaluation is another instance of organizational coalignment in setting and meeting realistic targets.

One example of the effective use of such a control process is the Cypress Corporation and its CEO T. J. Rodgers' implementation of four overlapping software programs aimed at channeling interaction and work within tightly specified boundaries in order to minimize errors (Rodgers, 1990). Cypress is a semiconductor manufacturer within the volatile computer chip market. Rodgers believes that effective organizational management can be broken down into four subprocesses: hiring, setting and meeting goals, resource allocation, and performance appraisal. For each of these processes, his firm has an interactive computer program that monitors each system carefully and gives instant feedback. For example, in the case of manufacturing, its "killer software" shuts down the system if any critical rules and procedures of the system are violated.

Let us explore in detail one of these software processes. Each week, each manager is encouraged to set challenging organizational goals and stipulate a timeframe, preferably a week or less, for meeting these goals. These decisions are entered into a database. By Tuesday morning, each manager's manager reviews these goals for possible conflicts, challenges, and time problems, and talks with the individuals involved. By Friday, each manager is expected to complete the goal or indicate the problem and new timeframe. For individuals, it is expected that they will complete 75 percent of their goals within a week, for groups 70 percent. Managers can track subordinates and groups of subordinates on a weekly basis, and take corrective action when necessary. Once a week each VP checks each division under him or her and takes corrective action if necessary.

The result is that goals are met 75 percent of the time and the organizational targets can be accurately adjusted on a quarterly basis. At Cypress, completed goal reports trigger a mini-performance review, which is used to update performance evaluations more easily and make setting achievable stretch goals equally. Early diagnosis of goal or performance problems leads to rapid response in correcting problems. Setting manageable goals leads to the better allocation of individual and group resources and the more predictable coalignment of organizational activities.

At the center of each of these changes in organizational coalignment is the need for interactive communication in an open and frank manner and, equally significant, the appropriate inclusion of individual interests, concerns, and contributions into the organizational outcomes. When organizational integration, coordination, and control processes function in this manner, value-added activities and organizational adaptations achieved at one point in the value chain add to those obtained in other parts of the value chain in such a way as to create a sustainable competitive advantage.

SUMMARY AND CONCLUSIONS

What, then, has our rather long inquiry into communication and management within the global economy taught us about communication and management processes in the latter half of the twentieth century?

First, let us consider management. Here Drucker's definition of the process remains constant. However, the strategies and tools involved in order to respond to a new larger and more volatile environment have changed. A new form of leadership has emerged—global warriors, leaders with a global perspective who will scan the globe for needed resources, who will establish portions of the value chain for their organization wherever they can generate value-added activities, and who monitor diverse markets for product opportunities while providing an organizational framework of goals and values capable of rationalizing innovative, flexible, efficient, and rapid responses to customers and competitor activities. Such leaders employ global matrix management, telecommunication networks, and continuous improvement programs, setting short-term, achievable stretch goals that can be monitored accurately on a weekly basis in order to reorient the value chain rapidly to environmental change.

Second, let us consider communication. Here again, our definition of the process remains constant. Effective communication follows a strategy of coalignment of diverse interests, concerns, and contributions through the use of an open, flexible communication system that allows for the coalignment of both similarities and differences into an innovative, flexible, efficient, and rapid response system. Coalignment is made more complex by including within a single organizational structure, culturally and linguistically diverse people who want and demand a recognition of their differences as a prerequisite to the formations of communities that allow for the effective integration, coordination, and control of organizational activities.

It is clear from our analysis, that communication and management are interdependent.

REFERENCES

Agthe, K. E. 1990. Managing the mixed marriage. *Business Horizons* 33 (Jan.–Feb.):37–43.

Berlo, D. 1960. *The Process of Communication.* New York: Holt, Rinehart and Winston.

Cvar, M. 1986. Case studies in global competition patterns of success and failure. In M. Porter, ed., *Competition in Global Industry.* Boston, Mass.: Harvard Business School Press.

Drucker, P. F. 1988. Management and the world's work. *Harvard Business Review* 66 (Sept.–Oct.):65–76.

Fraker, S. 1989. High-speed management for the high tech age. *Fortune* 119 (Feb. 13):34–60.

Lefton, R. E., and V. R. Buzzota. 1987. Teams and teamwork: A study of executive level teams. *National Productivity Review* 7 (Winter):7–19.

Main, J. 1989. How to go global and why. *Fortune* 119 (Aug. 28):70–76.

Paul, T. 1991. Human relations management at GE Plastics: A high-speed management analysis. M.A. theses, SUNY-Albany.

Porter, M. J. 1986. Changing patterns of international competition. *California Management Review* 27 (Winter):9–39.

Rockart, J., and J. Short. 1989. IT in the 1990s: Managing organizational interdependencies. *Sloan Management Review* 30 (Winter):7–17.

Rodgers, T. J. 1990. No excuses management. *Harvard Business Review* 19 (July–Aug.):84–98.

Smith, K., et al. 1989. Predictors of response time to competitive strategic action: Preliminary theory and evidence. *Journal of Business Research*: 245–58.

Stewart, T. A. 1991. Brainpower. *Fortune* 123 (June 3):44–62.

Taylor, W. 1991. The logic of global business: An interview with ABB's Percy Barnevik. *Harvard Business Review* 69 (Mar.–Apr.):91–105.

Contributors

Rowland G. Baughman is professor of management and former associate dean in the School of Business at Central Connecticut State University. He received his doctorate in Business Administration from George Washington University. He has written mostly in the areas of organizational communications and labor relations. Recently he has emphasized international and global management issues with special attention given to the emerging economy in Poland.

Franca Caré is Director of Operations for Translink Communications, Inc., based in New York City. She received a BA in Speech Communication from Iona College and holds a master's degree in organizational communication from The State University of New York at Albany.

Donald P. Cushman is professor of communication at the State University of New York at Albany and holds a Ph.D. in Communication from the University of Wisconsin. He has served as a consultant for governments and private corporations in Australia, Bolivia, Canada, Germany, Great Britain, Japan, Korea, Mexico, and Yugoslavia. Cushman has written over sixty articles in journals and five books including *Message-Attitude-Behavior Relationships* with R. McPhee (Academic Press, 1980); *Communication in Interpersonal Relationships* with L. Cahn (State University of New York Press, 1985); and *High-Speed Management: Organizational Communication in the 1990s* with S. King (1994).

305

Janet M. Flynn is a communication consultant for the College of Business at the University of Colorado at Boulder, where she works with individual clients on a variety of management communication issues. She also teaches undergraduate business classes and conducts frequent workshops and trainings dealing with personal and organizational effectiveness. Flynn holds a Master's degree in organizational communication from the University at Albany (SUNY system).

Pat Joynt is chair of Management Development at Henley Management College, England. He was professor of organization behavior at the Norwegian School of Management and visiting professor in management at the University of Wisconsin, Madison. He received his doctorate from Brunel University in London and sits on the board of governors at Henley Management College in the United Kingdom. Prior to that, Joynt had some fifteen years of practice in various management positions. He presently sits on the board of directors in four international firms and is also active as a career and firm strategy consultant. He is the author of twelve books and over fifty articles dealing with international management, career management, and business strategy.

Yanan Ju is professor of communication at Central Connecticut State University. He received his Ph.D. in Political Science from the University of Belgrade, Yugoslavia. He has written five books in Chinese and one in English and is the author of over fifty articles. Ju's most recent books include *The Handbook of Public Relations*, coedited (Shanghai Culture Publishing House, 1990); and *The Great Wall in Ruins: Communication and Cultural Change in China* with Godwin C. Chu (SUNY Press, 1993).

Sarah Sanderson King is professor of communication at Central Connecticut State University. She was chair of the Division of Communication Arts at Marist College, Central Connecticut and chair of the Department of Communication at Central Connecticut State University. She has been the recipient of $350,000 in grants from such agencies as NEH, NIMH, University of Hawaii, East-West Center, and the State of Connecticut. She was the former chair of the Department of Communication at the University of Hawaii and has served as fellow or research associate at the

University of Chicago, Ohio State University, Harvard University, and the East-West Center in Honolulu. She was a Fulbright scholar to Yugoslavia. Her publications include *Political Communication: Engineering Visions of Order in the Socialist World* (co-edited with Don Cushman), *Human Communication as a Field of Study; Effective Communication Skills; An Interactional Approach*; and *Effective Communication; Theory into Action.*

Branislav Kovacic is an assistant professor at the University of Hartford and received his Ph.D. in Communication and Sociology from SUNY–Albany. He was a former journalist and magazine editor in Yugoslavia. He is currently editing a book on organizational communication to be published by SUNY Press.

Andrzej K. Kozminski, Ph.D., is professor and chair of the Management and Organization Department in the School of Management of Warsaw University. He is also director of the Postgraduate International Management Center at Warsaw University and president of a private management education and consulting firm, International Business School. In recent years, he has served as government and parliamentary expert in Poland and taught regularly as a visiting professor at Anderson Graduate School of Management at UCLA and the University of Orleans in France. He has also taught at George Washington University and Central Connecticut State University in the United States and the Technical University of Lisbon in Portugal. He wrote over two hundred scientific articles and books in Polish, English, French, Italian, Czech, Russian, Hungarian (among them fifteen books). His latest books published in English are: Organizational Communication and Management: "A Global Perspective" coedited with D. Cushman (1993) and Catching Up? Case Studies of Organizational and Management Change in the Former Socialist Bloc" (1993).

Nils Magne Larsen is Assistant Professor in International Marketing and Strategy at the College of Harstad, Norway. He holds a Master of Science Degree in Business from the Bodø Graduate School of Business, Norway, a Lic.rer.pol Degree in International Relations from the University of Mannheim, West-Germany, and an MBA in International Business from the University of Wisconsin-Madison, USA. Larsen has been the recipient of a number of scholarships, most notably a Fulbright Scholarship from the Board of Foreign Scholarships, United States of America, a Ruhrgas Scholarship from the Norwegian Research Council for Science and Humanities (West-German/Norwegian Scholarship Scheme in Economics), a scholarship grant from the Board of Higher Education in Troms, Norway, and a research scholarship from The Export Council of Norway.

Krzysztof Obloj is associate professor of management, School of Management, University of Warsaw, and director of the MBA program at International Business School, Warsaw. He has been doing research in the fields of strategic and international management, and lectured at universities in the United States, France, Israel, Norway, and Denmark. He serves as consultant to Polish companies and foreign corporations investing in Poland. He is an author and coauthor of over sixty articles published in scholarly journals and four books, including *Management: A Practical Approach, Strategic Management, An Outline of Theory of Organizational Equilibrium* (in Polish), and *Managing in Different Cultures* (in English). His last coauthored book on management systems in global environment will be published by Kent Publishers.

Scott R. Olson is an associate professor in the Department of Communication at Central Connecticut State University. He is the author of articles published in *Critical Studies in Mass Communication,* the *Journal of Communication,* and other communication journals as well as chapters in several collections. He has been coprincipal director of grants from the Department of Human Relations, Connecticut Humanities Council, Hartford *Courant Foundation,* and others. He received his Ph.D. in 1985 from Northwestern University.

George Tuttle is a Senior Professional Representative for the Burroughs Wellcome Company. He has worked for BW Co. for over sixteen years and in that time has served in different capacities in the marketing department of the pharmaceutical company. Currently, he is working as a specialist in the sales and promotion of antivirals. He received his MBA from Central Connecticut State University in 1989 and is an adjunct instructor in the communication department at the school.

Index